ALL
MEN
ARE
JERKS

15th ANNIVERSARY EDITION

ALL MEN ARE JERKS

Take Charge of How Men Treat You!

*until proven otherwise

DAYLLE DEANNA SCHWARTZ

adamsmedia

Avon, Massachusetts

Published by
Adams Media, a division of F+W Media, Inc.
57 Littlefield Street, Avon, MA 02322. U.S.A.
www.adamsmedia.com

ISBN 10: 1-4405-6278-4
ISBN 13: 978-1-4405-6278-5
eISBN 10: 1-4405-6279-2
eISBN 13: 978-1-4405-6279-2

Printed in the United States of America.

10   9   8   7   6   5   4   3   2   1

This publication is designed to provide accurate and authoritative information with regard to the subject matter covered. It is sold with the understanding that the publisher is not engaged in rendering legal, accounting, or other professional advice. If legal advice or other expert assistance is required, the services of a competent professional person should be sought.
—From a *Declaration of Principles* jointly adopted by a Committee of the American Bar Association and a Committee of Publishers and Associations

Many of the designations used by manufacturers and sellers to distinguish their product are claimed as trademarks. Where those designations appear in this book and F+W Media was aware of a trademark claim, the designations have been printed with initial capital letters.

This book is available at quantity discounts for bulk purchases.
For information, please call 1-800-289-0963.

Dedication

This book is dedicated to my daughter, Tami Schwartz, for growing into a lovely young woman who makes me prouder every day, for proving that a girl can develop a strong sense of self and autonomy at a young age, for giving me the most wonderful love and support possible, and for adding the most special blessing to my life.

Acknowledgments

I must begin by thanking God and the Universe for all of my blessings. Without my strong belief in a higher power, I wouldn't be where I am today.

I'd like to heartily thank all the people who supported my efforts in writing this book. Thanks to the people in my groups and classes who encouraged me to write it. Thanks a million times to all of you who shared experiences, opinions, and growth with my readers. Your input has enhanced the book tenfold!

A very special thank you to my agent, Linda Konner, for believing in my concept and my ability to write it, for working so hard and quickly on my behalf, and for giving me great representation on all levels. Thanks to Florence Isaacs for encouraging me to get the book out and for sending me to Linda. Thanks to my first editor, Ed Walters, for your faith in my book, for being open-minded about what women need, and for being a thorough pleasure to work with. And BIG thanks to my current editor, Brendan O'Neill, for spearheading this fifteenth-anniversary edition of *All Men Are Jerks—Until Proven Otherwise* and for being a pleasure to work with as well.

Thanks to my friends for providing insight into men and putting up with me as I sorted through my own slew of jerks. A special thanks to Ellen Penchansky, my best friend for most of my life, for giving me love and encouragement during the days I thought I'd die without a man, for being there as I tormented myself over one jerk after another, and for cheering me on as I found myself. Thank you again Eva Rex-Vogel for helping me find my way. A special thanks to my parents, Ruth and Bob Herman, and my sister Carla Herman and brother-in-law Doug Landy, for providing me with an incredible support system of love and encouragement.

Contents

PART THREE:
Survival Tactics 165

Introduction to This Edition

As a shy and insecure college girl, I found *All Men Are Jerks—Until Proven Otherwise* on my sister's bookshelf eight years ago. Unfortunately, I tended to cling to relationships to give me a sense of security. This book made me realize that the supposed security I felt wasn't real, and the only security I needed was something I must create within myself. Once those words really sank in, I was able to take control of my life. Over the past three years, I have made it a point to stay single to love and nurture myself. As a result, I know and love myself in ways I never imagined. My new inner strength enabled me to move away from home and excel in a new career and make many new friends. I have created life on my own terms. I have a career that I love, a sweet little puppy who relies on me, and wonderful friends who truly care about me. I am ever grateful for that fateful day that led me to that bookshelf, where I found that curious book that changed my life. —Shauna Marie H.

In the fifteen years since I wrote this book, I've heard from thousands whose lives changed after reading it like Shauna's did. What might surprise you is how many women said it helped save their current relationships. That's because this book taught them to love themselves and their own lives first, then re-evaluate their relationship with their significant other. It also taught them to have more reasonable expectations of what they should get from their man.

My mantra, "If you want a man, get a life," was a big factor for improving these readers' relationships. Often, women make their worlds revolve around men instead of creating happiness that isn't dependent on having one. (Even if you're married, you should have your own interests and friends!) Once women realized they could and should create their own happiness, they were more secure with themselves and were therefore happier in their romantic relationships too. As it turns out, many of those potential jerks *were* proved otherwise when women took care of themselves first! They knew if they didn't shape up, she'd move on.

I actually heard from someone living in Iran who was hired to translate the book into Farsi. She thought the problems I write about were limited to women in countries like hers and was shocked that Western women let jerks control them. She now refuses to settle for a man and is happy. And surprise: *All Men Are Jerks—Until Proven Otherwise* was banned in Iran!

This book differs from most other relationship books because it doesn't teach how to find and keep a man. I want you to find and keep *yourself.* When you do, you can control what you need from men, and your responses to them. I want to help you recognize your power, which attracts more men than playing games, flirting, or dressing in a provocative way can. Whether you meet a guy in a bar, online, or through a friend, it's so important to objectively see all of his behavior, not just the aspects that you like, and set boundaries on what you don't like, or move on.

I've even gotten thanks from men who were ready to hate this book because of the title but loved the content. Why? They appreciated that I implore women to accept men as they are instead of trying to mold them into the Prince Charming of their dreams. And, men hate when women become dependent on them, which limits their time for "guy activities" because she wants him with her constantly. They love that I encourage women to develop autonomy. Owning your power to choose a man instead of chasing him can be very attractive to most men. Several male readers actually wanted to date me! The jerk who motivated me to write this book called after he read it to say he was honored to have inspired such good wisdom! (He wanted a second chance, but soon proved he's still a jerk. I said, "see ya" fast.)

The book actually helped me personally when I did a media tour to talk about the book's lessons on TV and radio, and in bookstores. At the time, I'd been seeing someone for a while. I was in control of me so I didn't let him get away with much or hurt me. But the more I talked about jerks in interviews, the more I recognized he was one. I'd been so busy, I hadn't had a chance to process his behavior. When I got home, he became my ex.

Many people are surprised that in this era of women's empowerment, a majority of young, vibrant women with great careers still make having a man and marriage a crucial component of their happiness. That approach gives men power to take advantage of you! I continue to hear from women of all ages saying this book changed their mindsets away from that conventional "wisdom" and they're now happily jerk-free. Once you read this book, it's hard to stay with someone who doesn't treat you well. Knowledge really can be power.

Big changes don't happen overnight, but once you learn the lessons in this book, you'll start to see improvements in your life and relationships right away. For example, Amy e-mailed to say that her boyfriend Tony was a jerk with a capital J. But she loved him and stuck it out until her friend insisted she read this book. When she finished, so was her relationship, but Tony lured her back with promises and romance. This time, Amy was so aware that she quickly dumped him when he reverted to jerky ways. She weakened and got lured back several more times, but left faster and faster until she ended it for good. She said, "After reading *All Men Are Jerks—Until Proven Otherwise* I could no longer delude myself about how Tony kept hurting me." This book does wake women up!

I believe that one woman's jerk can be another woman's treasure. You can't change a man, though women try hard to do that. But, you can respond to him in ways that tell him you expect to be treated with respect and honesty.

Often, the need for a man trumps common sense and you give your power to a guy you like, praying he'll be your Prince Charming, even though he keeps croaking like a frog instead. I hope by the end of this book you'll be prepared to control *yourself,* so any guy you're involved with knows he has no choice but to treat you well. Understanding how your response to men creates jerks gives you power to only be with a treasure.

Introduction

"Nor deem the irrevocable Past

As wholly wasted, wholly vain,

If, rising on its wrecks, at last

To something nobler we attain."

HENRY WADSWORTH LONGFELLOW

I've come a long way from the scared little girl I used to be. I've got great confidence, a ton of self-esteem, and a belief that I can handle almost any situation. So why did my intelligence turn into oatmeal, my resolve to take care of myself turn into Jell-O, and my trust in my ability to create my own happiness turn into shredded wheat when I got involved with a man I liked?

What is it about men that can make even a strong woman like me forget about taking care of herself? It's not like I don't know better. For years I've taught classes on taking care of oneself, and I run support groups. Women turn to me for guidance about handling men. Yet there I was, wanting to kick myself for being weak, for not heeding my own lessons. Scary!

The biggest complaint I get from women is having a weakness for the opposite sex. There are attorneys, housewives, corporate executives, teachers, secretaries, and psychologists in my groups, but no matter how successful they are, women still struggle with relationships. My students always admire how I seem to have it together. However, I explain that like them, my Achilles' heel is the opposite sex. They look surprised, not quite believing that someone like me could weaken over a man. For a year I'd been in total control of my life, very happily without a relationship, dating a little but enjoying my life solo too, and it was the most exhilarating feeling. And then I met HIM . . . the jerk . . . and all of a sudden I wasn't in control anymore.

Trapped by Your Needs

Who was this jerk who threw my life into turmoil? Was he my Prince Charming? No! Was he gorgeous? No! Was he rich? No! He was just a guy who seemed nice, said the right words, and satisfied the needs I'd been stifling for a while, the ones that get so many women into trouble emotionally: the need to be held, the need to be told nice things, the need to have great sex, the need to be in a relationship, the need to feel attractive to a man.

This pattern is common in women. We tell ourselves that we're strong; we're together; and we don't need a man. We stay resolute and unemotional, keeping all those nasty needs bottled up. We pride ourselves on no longer being needy and take pleasure in the fact that we can live without a man. We have our lives in such good order. And then it ticks us off when all it takes to crack our determination are a few nice words, some sweet affection, or promises that we don't really believe anyway.

What's wrong with us? Losing common sense over a man is a consistent complaint, both in my classes and from friends—as well as from me. Why does this happen? You're smart; you've had your share of combat training; and you 're supposed to learn from mistakes. Yet you weaken so easily. One taste of the goodies men can give and you fall into the trap they set. Then you wallow in disgust as you try to pull away from him in yet another round of the battle of the sexes.

How You Get Yourself in Trouble

You often get yourself in trouble by jumping into relationships too quickly. You trust him before he's earned it and assume he's a nice guy because that's how he appears on the surface. I fell into that trap again with HIM, a guy who knew what I needed. I trusted him because I wanted him to be nice and decent and everything he appeared to be. I wanted it so badly I ignored clear signs that could have warned me to slow down and give the relationship more time to develop. Many women do it at times, especially when they're vulnerable. Joann related this story in my class:

> I met John at a seminar. I hadn't had a boyfriend in a while, and it was nice finding someone with everything I'd wanted in a man. We shared many interests. He bought me lunch and called that night. He seemed so nice, always keeping his word about calling. We dated several times. I completely trusted him. He seemed perfect. Then he broke dates. I'd call and get his voice mail. He kept telling me everything was fine. I kept trying to believe him.
>
> John finally told me about his girlfriend. Then I understood why he never invited me to his apartment, and why I always got his voice mail. It had been in my face, but I didn't want to see it. What a jerk he turned out to be.

Joann didn't take the time to get to know John because she wanted to enjoy the front he put up. She let her need for the kind of man John seemed to be cloud her vision. Joann ignored little things that didn't add up because she wanted to see John as perfect. Nobody is perfect! Now she knows "All men are jerks until proven otherwise." Men need to prove themselves by their actions, not their words. It's lovely when a man does prove otherwise!

My Kind of Jerk

I used to routinely fall for men with problems. Once they hooked me, I stayed hooked and let them wring almost everything I had out of me before I accepted the relationship wasn't healthy. Bailing out was never my game plan. I always saw some good worth saving. Me, the Queen of Nurturers, would heal HIM!

My relationships might have been different had I not walked around on tiptoe from the beginning, always afraid to rock the boat. Often, the guy's attitude seemed to say: "Be a good girl or you'll be alone." And I was good, keeping my mouth shut about everything that bothered me. Placating my current HIM was my main objective. Each man I fell for knew he could do almost anything—and I'd still be there. I convinced myself that if I proved I could stick out the bad times, he'd change into the man I wanted him to be. It never happened. Yet lots of women do that!

As my self-esteem grew, it became clearer that a man who didn't satisfy my needs would never make me happy. I had to risk rocking the boat to express my needs. It was finally possible to accept that being in pain half the time wasn't worth the good I got from HIM. Hearing other women talking about the jerks they were hanging on to made me feel sick—because I was doing the same thing. I knew it was time to develop a new attitude toward men.

I was giving my need for a man too much importance in my quest for fulfillment and happiness. By working on myself more and shifting my focus away from meeting men, I've created a very satisfying life without one. It took time and work on my self-esteem. And therapy. It took the effort of developing interests that satisfy me and making more friends. And you know what? After finally reaching the point of feeling whole on my own, I attract more men than ever!

The Ultimate Test

I was put to the test after meeting a guy I really liked. It had been a while since I'd been involved with anyone, so it felt especially wonderful. He swept me away with romance, giving me a rush of desire for the things only a man can give—and he was very good! I ignored clear signs of trouble, using my old excuses to justify them. My resolve to keep my head above water in a relationship waned. Even knowing everything I know about the true nature of men, I thought he was different. But he wasn't.

I didn't like my schedule being all askew during our relationship. I couldn't do my writing because I was too distracted. Seeing him occupied a good chunk of my time. Hours were spent daydreaming about the good times, and even more hours complaining about him to friends. I didn't sleep well from the aggravation.

The lessons I've learned finally clicked in, making it obvious to me that he was a jerk—a delicious one, but not deserving of me. He wasn't worth the aggravation. So I reluctantly told him not to contact me anymore. Though I got caught up in it for a while, it was important that I recognized—much sooner than ever before—that he was no good for me, and bailed. My usual rationales for staying with him didn't work this time, thank goodness. I got out of it, and over him in record time, using the techniques and mindset emphasized in this book.

Are All Men Jerks?

All Men Are Jerks—Until Proven Otherwise is not about male bashing. It's about being on your guard when you meet someone you're attracted to but don't know well enough to trust. It's about protecting yourself against pain and bad treatment. I use the expression "All men are jerks until proven otherwise" as a way of keeping my guard up and reminding myself that men may not be who they seem. Basically, it means "don't trust a man until he's proven himself to be for real—over lots of time, with actions and follow through on his words." Repeating this cautionary statement to myself, over and over again, has kept me and many other women from making the same mistake with the next man encountered. I'd rather repeat the expression than repeat mistakes that bring pain and suffering.

I tell women in my classes to think "All men are jerks until proven otherwise" to themselves when they meet a man—as a survival technique. You must take care of yourself. You must make men earn your trust. You can't keep giving yourself away. The little saying "All men are jerks until proven otherwise" serves as a reminder not to trust men or take them seriously too soon. Repeating it until it becomes second nature to you can be like wearing an emotional suit of armor.

A Few Good Men?

It's time for women to develop defenses against jerks. Part of this means protecting yourself from the large number of men who understand how to manipulate women. They know how to play on your emotions and how little you need to let your guard down so that they can come into your life on their own terms. They know that when you want a man, you'll accept their problems and lack of consideration in exchange for getting some of your needs met.

"All men are jerks until proven otherwise." You can't say it often enough if you want to stay out of emotional trouble. But don't lose heart. In reality, there are many potentially good men available. You just need to learn how to handle them to prevent them from becoming jerks. There are also a lot of jerks who can learn to become wonderful partners—if you give them good reasons to do so. Men are often jerks because you allow them to be. By changing your responses to them, you may be able to change the way they treat you. By not accepting their unacceptable behavior, they may have to develop new approaches. No, not all men are jerks. Not even close! But give yourself lots of time to find out. Let time and his actions be your guide. Let his words go in one ear and at least partly out the other. Temper their sweetness by saying to yourself, "All men are jerks until proven otherwise." Cynical? Maybe. Practical? Definitely!

Know When to Quit

You also need to learn to know when it's time to call it quits and stop milking a bad relationship to the often very bitter end. Whether he dumps you or you decide to dump him, breakups should become a time of control and power, because you can move on with your life instead of falling apart and wasting time you could use for fun trying to get over him. And you need to stop setting yourself up to be caught again in the tempting, often too-good-to-be-true, seductive but heart-breaking clutches of a jerk. It's just not worth the price.

This Book Can Help You Deal with the Jerks in Your Life

There is life beyond a jerk. You can let go of him, get over him, and have a wonderful life without him. You don't need a jerk in your life, even if he's cute and endearing and sexy and great in bed and can really satisfy your needs (when he wants to). I've been through it and have talked with hundreds of other women who have, too. My friends, students, and clients were impressed watching me reclaim my life when I left the relationship with my last jerk. They've encouraged me to write this book and have given lots of support, feedback, and anecdotes. I've interviewed women and men from all walks of life. Most women have fallen for a jerk at least once. I'm sure every woman reading this will find a piece of herself in the examples.

One of my primary intentions is to help you understand why your behavior often encourages men to act, or keep on acting, in ways that drive you crazy. Why do you give up your control to the often calculating ways of the opposite sex? How do you get over yet another painful relationship? How do you protect yourself in the future? Answering these questions and more is what this book is about. Women often make major trade-offs, including compromising our self-respect, to be with a man. We'll complain and complain but make excuses at the thought of leaving him. It can take an awful lot of garbage to make us actually get up and leave!

I'll address many of the common complaints I hear from women. Being aware of these patterns can help us avoid making the same mistakes in the future. When I actually saw my actions and responses to men objectively, it sickened me at times. I'd been so sweet and accepting I felt like I was OD'ing on candy. Remembering that "All men are jerks until proven otherwise" is better than going back to my old ways of seeing him through rose-colored glasses, and giving my heart and soul away to yet another jerk.

But I *Love* Men

As cynical as I may sound, I do love men and get along well with them. My male friends are terrific. I'm still on good terms with my ex-husband and several ex-boyfriends. When I meet a man who's not a jerk, I thoroughly enjoy being with him. And you know what? Men love me too. They don't like being called jerks, but understand why I use the term. They know men can be jerks and that I'm just being realistic. And they know that if they treat me right, I'll treat them well in return.

I also teach classes for men and some of my support groups are coed. Believe it or not, these men encouraged me to write this book. Many think that men can act like jerks, but women need to change their approach to handling them as well. I've gained a much better understanding of men through these classes. I understand them—and they've asked me to spread the word!

Though I'm not trying to justify men's behavior, I will also give reasons why they do what they do. Men can be made to own up to inconsiderate behavior. They can even be taught to give you what you want. But it will rarely come from them voluntarily. Would you willingly give up a good thing? Why should men change if they don't have to? Why give up their old ways of doing and getting what they want? Why be on their best behavior if they don't have to be? Believe me, a jerk can learn to be a wonderful partner, if a woman knows how to take care of herself and not accept behavior that makes him a jerk.

I've evolved from a total wimpy doormat to a woman in control of her life. I used to settle for men, just to have someone. Now I blow off one jerk after another because I've learned that I'm happier on my own than with someone who's not good for me. Happiness can only come from yourself. Excessive energy shouldn't be wasted on those who don't deserve it. You need to take the emphasis of your energy off him and put it onto yourself. I've experienced and observed ways you can focus on yourself while dealing with some of the manipulative, often calculating ways of men. I'm so joyous these days, both from my own progress and from the major changes I see in many of the women who take my classes or work with me individually. I want to share the lessons we've put into practice. Read on to learn more about why men can be jerks, how to make them prove otherwise, and how to let go if all else fails. I'll even tell you how to get over—and stay over—them, and not weaken again so easily the next time.

PART ONE

HOW WE GET INTO TROUBLE

Chapter One

Do Women Create the Jerks We Complain About?

"Tis strange what a man may do, and a woman yet think him an angel."

WILLIAM THACKERAY

Yes, you often create the jerks you complain about. Many men do act like jerks, but you contribute to their being who they are. When you put your need for a man before your common sense, you selectively hear and see only what satisfies your needs, while ignoring signs that he may not be good for you. And if he's getting what he wants from you, why would he change his behavior? Only when you change your own attitude toward men will they have to change theirs.

COMPLAINT

Who do men think they are?

Let's take some responsibility here. Men weren't born with a predisposed desire to hurt women, as some of you may think. And they wouldn't have been getting away with their nonsense for so long had women not let them. Yes, we allow them to be spoiled little boys who can put us on guilt trips, or to melt our hearts with the curl of a smile, or to lower our resistance with a good dose of affection. And while we're apologizing from the guilt, melting from the smile, or letting our guard down from the sweetness of affection, they shoot straight for our hearts and get what they want with so little effort. And what do we end up with in the long run? Pain, disillusionment, and a cynical attitude about men.

Men Are Who We Tell Them They Are

We put men on pedestals. We give men too much credit and importance in our lives. And we often don't make men own up to their sometimes inconsiderate, selfish, cold, mean, etc., behavior. We tell them their behavior is all right by not saying anything. We tell them it's acceptable by still being there for them. Look at all the abused women who stay! They say it's okay to abuse them by not leaving. If you put up with things you don't like, you tell men that your need for what they give you is stronger than your need to take care of yourself!

It's *Your* Choice

My friend Judy commented that, "we create the monsters we always complain about." She sees women all the time who put up with things they don't like to have a man. We seem to be programmed to take the garbage in order to get the cream. We're so used to it that we often do it without thinking. I talked to Cindy, who giggled about how her boyfriend sometimes stands her up then is all apologetic the next day. Cindy resolves not to let this continue, but when he tells her he loves her, she forgives him. Cindy explains:

> Bobby is a good man. He just has lots of responsibilities. I hate when we have a date and he doesn't show or call. I always tell him I wish he'd call, and he promises to do it next time. He tells me how much he loves me and how much work he has to do. He accuses me of trying to keep him from his work, which he does partly to have money for me. I know he tries hard to be a good man, but I wish he'd at least text when he can't come over. I get so angry, but when he comes over and tells me how much he loves me, I can't stay mad. I just try to understand him. I love him. I don't want to lose him.

Cindy won't change until she truly wants to—and neither will Bobby. Right now, she's letting him get away with intolerable behavior just because he tells her he loves her. He plays on her need to be loved, and gets love without giving her anything back but words. You must remember that "All men are jerks until proven otherwise"—until their *actions* consistently prove their words over a long period of time.

COMPLAINT

We give men so much and they don't give it back.

Earlier I said that women give men too much credit, but we also don't give them enough. We talk about them like they just act inconsiderate.

I don't hear women describing them as manipulators, although it would fit many jerks. It's true—some men deliberately manipulate because they can get away with it. We don't want to think about a guy we like that way, because then we might have to take action, or leave.

The Cheap Apology

Spare me the excuses. Men have learned their lessons well. Many know exactly what they're doing when they manipulate you and play on your weaknesses. They know all the right moves. Think about how little it takes to weaken you. Remember the times you were duped by a kind word or sucked in by an apology. Men have it so easy! Many of you will excuse almost anything for a single rose they buy in a deli for a dollar or two. *How romantic*, you think. They know you too well. You're in la-la-land because of the wonderful glow from being given a rose, and he's thinking how cheaply he got over on you. Women can be such suckers.

Resolve Busters

Men have lots of secret weapons to weaken your resolve. These come in the form of words you want to hear and as romantic gestures you appreciate. I call these weapons *resolve busters*, because they break down your resolve to hold out for what you want. I asked women to think about some of the small things men had done to lower their guard and take advantage of them. The following responses are things women settled for to forgive men who hurt them. Look at how little men had to do to get back in their good graces. And you wonder why men like things just the way they are? Do you see yourself here?

PAM: He called and told me he missed me.

JUDY: Jim said everything he knew I wanted to hear. Even though I knew in my heart it was just to appease me, I liked hearing it so much I let him back into my life—again!

MARIA: He came over and was very affectionate. I tried to be angry, but I love when he's in that kind of mood. I feel so good when he hugs and kisses me, and he knows it. It's a no-win situation, a vicious cycle. He disrespects me. I throw him out. He comes over and gives me loving I need, and I melt. He's nice for maybe a day and then goes back to his old ways. Why don't I learn? I'm a respected corporate executive by day and a wimp by night.

JACKIE: I was very pissed at Bob, so he sent me an "I'm sorry" card. It was so sweet I called him right away. Afterward, I realized the card didn't make up for what he'd done.

LINDA: He played it kind and sweet. He brought me roses, took me out for a nice dinner, and gave me lots of compliments. It was the compliments that really got to me the most. I love hearing them and keep hoping he's being sincere.

ADRIAN: He told me I was beautiful. It took me by surprise and felt so good. What an actor he turned out to be.

LOIS: He came over looking very sexy. I couldn't resist him, even though he'd made me furious the day before. He has such a great body.

JUNE: He offered companionship.

ELANA: He made me dinner.

HARRIET: He made me feel like I am needed, sexy, and wanted.

Many women told me it was just a phone call or loving text message that broke their resistance. Many others fell for the sweet words, the apologies and promises, the tenderness, and the fear of losing him. Some said they succumbed to small gifts. I'll say it again and again: Men have it easy!

So what can you do to beat the resolve busters? Keep track of the difference between his behavior and make-up gifts relative to how much you really deserve. Remember how many times you gave in to him, how many times you got all sickeningly sweet over him, and how many times you kicked yourself afterward. Awareness is a great start. Learn from examples in this book. When I first paid careful attention to the way I spoke to a guy I liked, I felt disgusted. What a shock! I was a wimp! After that I became more conscious of my responses. When I was with HIM, I lost it for a while but woke up to my own needs fast! Being aware of the problem can do that for you.

COMPLAINT

Why do flowers weaken us so much?

When I surveyed women, I found that the ploy that worked best at winning women over was giving them flowers. We seem to just melt when we get them! Most women love flowers because they're pretty. I do, too. Women say flowers represent romance. You get a special feeling when you're expecting nothing and he walks in with some. They give you a dose of beauty and romance that makes you feel special for that moment. Men have it *so* easy. They can mistreat you, verbally abuse you, stand you up, not call, etc.—and get forgiven with *flowers*. Men can say things that hurt, insult, and turn you off, but can wipe it out with flowers. Who's the real jerk?

Flower Power

One example was given by Diane, who was determined to wait before going to bed with Michael. She'd known him for a while, but they had just started dating. She wanted time to see if he was sincere about their relationship. The chemistry was intense between them, but she felt very strongly about not going to bed with him until he arrived with the old female fix:

> I wasn't expecting the flowers. They were beautiful, more exotic than the usual ones in the deli. I was so excited I flew into his arms, feeling euphoric from having received them. I kept thanking him. Then we kissed. All my resolve went out the window, and we made love. Now I feel lousy about it. Even though I'm still seeing Michael, I feel uncomfortable knowing I weakened about going to bed with him for a stupid bouquet of flowers.

Flowers have that effect on us. What a *bargain* for men! Diane acted like she'd never gotten flowers before. It told Michael that she didn't value herself highly enough to wait and that it wouldn't take much to satisfy her romantic nature. Flowers take so little effort to give, and we make so much of them. We make it so easy for men!

A Substitute for the Right Thing

Men often bring flowers instead of "doing the right thing." Take the case of Jane, who experienced a scary flower incident in her hometown in England. (This is an international issue. Women all over the globe fall for flowers!)

I had an abortion. I went to a clinic where most of the women were young. While waiting my turn, I heard their stories of feeling abandoned by the men who'd gotten them pregnant. They felt guilty about giving up their babies—but their boyfriends had made them. Afterward, I watched in horror as each man arrived with flowers and each woman melted. I still carry the memory of these women all acting like everything was all right after getting the flowers. The flowers seemed to make losing their babies okay! And it told their boyfriends it was fine for them to leave them in an abortion clinic as long as they brought flowers afterward. Every single man knew the game! I was relieved when my boyfriend arrived without them. I figured he knew better but was amazed to find an orchid waiting for me at home. He thought he could erase all the pain of having to go for an abortion with an orchid. I hate admitting it, but on some levels, I did feel a little better. Women are the jerks. We let men know we'll happily accept so little from them.

An Exception: Abusive Men

Someone who abuses you regularly, whether physically, verbally, or mentally, falls into a much worse category than a jerk. No matter how much he says he loves you, no matter how sorry he is afterward, **abuse is completely unacceptable**! Each time you accept his apology and stay after being abused, physically, verbally, or mentally, you give him permission to do it again. You say you'll be there after he hurts you. If you're getting abused by someone you love or think you need, put this book down right now and get help. Call someone you trust—a minister, friend, or family member, for example—or call an agency or the police for help. Counseling might eventually help, but the first step has to be yours—out the door to a safe haven!

Chapter Two

The Allure of the Jerk

*"A man falls in love through his eyes,
a woman through her ears."*

WOODROW WYATT

You're not stupid. You know, at least deep down, when a man isn't treating you right. You've been burned before, so you know it can happen again. Yet you often don't learn from your mistakes. Why do you continuously set yourself up for disappointment with men? What attracts you to those jerks you complain so bitterly about?

I Know It's Not Good for Me, But . . .

You know that candy isn't good for you, but that doesn't stop you from enjoying your chocolate fixes and other treats. You complain about putting on weight but keep eating yummy treats you find it so hard to resist. We weaken easily for fried foods, cookies, candy, drinks—and jerks.

We're attracted to jerks, but eventually they drive us crazy. Your annoyance is often a well-kept secret, only divulged in complaints to girlfriends. But when you don't let men know how you feel in an appropriate manner, or you complain but do nothing about it, they *will* continue to do things that make you angry. Many men can be reprogrammed to give you what you want, if you learn not to accept unacceptable behavior; that is, if you get over your fear of losing HIM, and learn to set boundaries. The men worth keeping often can be taught to treat you right. After being in a support group for three weeks, Jen told us:

> Billy's always done what he pleased . . . calling me at the last minute to get together. I've told him it bothered me, but he knew I love seeing him . . . he's so cute . . . I made myself available. When he wants something, he can be arrogant and demanding. I don't like it, but he laughs off my complaints. Since being in this group, I've changed. I make plans with friends when I don't hear from him. When he gets obnoxious, I walk away, telling him I won't allow him to talk to me like that. I was sure it was over. But guess what? He does love me. I see him making more of an effort to give me what I want. I suppose when he saw I was serious, he took my complaints seriously. He actually didn't want to lose me!

The lesson? You're better off losing the ones who'll continue to bring you pain. Why continue to subject yourself to grief for crumbs of satisfaction? Gloria confided:

> Jerry drove me crazy! He always did exactly what he wanted and didn't show much respect for my feelings. He didn't keep his word about calling, coming over—you know. He'd attack me verbally for things I didn't do. Just when I'd get fed up, he knew exactly what to do or say to win me back. I was in pain most of

the time, but thought it was worth the times when he could be romantic and attentive. When he was in a good mood, it was the best. Unfortunately, that wasn't most of the time.

I finally put my foot down about specific things. I thought maybe he didn't understand how he hurt me, so I tried explaining. I wasn't mean but I started making plans without him, since he couldn't be counted on. I'd hoped he'd come around, but he just left. I miss him, but I'm in less pain now than when we were together. He would never have changed, and wasn't worth the pain.

Many men do things you don't like if you let them get away with it. Out of frustration, you label them jerks. So how do you change the pattern? Complaining probably won't stop a man's unacceptable behavior. Apologetically letting him know what bothers you won't either. Identifying the problem, putting a limit on what you'll tolerate, and *changing your response* when the limit is reached might get through to him. As I said earlier, if you complain but preserve the status quo, he'll put up with your whining to get his way. If you leave him, see him less, are less helpful, stop being available, etc., he may be motivated to change his style.

The Jerk Behind the Facade

We often label a man a jerk because he manipulates our feelings, actions, and attitudes after his facade has sucked us in. *There's something about a jerk that can be very attractive.* Many men can act as charming and nice as can be. They know they look good and have their routines down pat. These professional jerks are like fishermen. They regularly go on missions to get things from women by using their bait to get us hooked. Then they keep us dangling from their lines as they pick us clean. And they do it because we let them. They use us because we want to fall for their facades. Susan told us the following in a class:

Cary seemed perfect at the beginning. He was gorgeous and seemed so nice. I couldn't believe someone like him wanted to be with me. He started out being kind and giving me compliments that I wanted to hear. He romanced me a lot. I fell almost under a spell. I was so crazy about him.

Once he knew I was his, he slowly began to change. Everything became his way. He told me what he wanted, and that became most important. I wanted to stay with him so much that I went along with it for a while. But it hurt, and I told him what I wanted. He kept telling me what other women he'd been involved with did for him. I finally saw that Cary didn't care what made me happy, and I had to walk away. This gorgeous man began to look ugly to me.

Let's face it. Being with a man you're really attracted to is the best. And when he says things you've been waiting to hear, dying to hear, and thinking you may never hear, you become putty in his hands, without waiting to see if what you're hearing is for real. These men are manipulators, used to getting their way. And when they stop getting their way, they move on.

Which Came First, the Jerk or Your Desire for One?

Believe it or not, men ask me all the time why women are attracted to jerks. These are usually the nice guys, the ones you could have but don't want. They don't understand why women are attracted to men who don't treat them well. David asserted:

Women bring on these problems themselves. They encourage men to be jerks. I see it all the time . . . women being attracted to men considered bastards . . . the ones who treat them like crap . . . the ones who ignore them . . . the ones who talk down to them. . . . Why do women want those kind of men? And why do they complain about them and call them jerks? Women have created these monsters.

Paul's point of view was similar:

Women seem to love arrogant bastards who treat them poorly. Women feed into it by letting the men . . . no . . . they actually *encourage* men to treat them poorly by letting them know they find the bastards attractive anyway.

Yes. Women have encouraged a breed of men who get by on looks and charm but who aren't nice to us. We reinforce their unacceptable behavior by continuing to allow ourselves to be attracted to them—unconditionally. We let their looks be substitutes for emotional gratification. We let their smooth-talking ways take the place of decency. We accept the crumbs they give us for the honor of their company. We sell ourselves very short, while allowing these men to feel more and more important. And the nicer guys are motivated to work harder at becoming bastards so they can attract women too!

Buying Into Jerks

I met Rick at a bar. He was extremely good-looking! I watched for a while as he flirted with one woman after another. I asked him if he was able to use his looks and charming personality to get what he wanted from women. This is what he told me:

It's so easy to win over most women. I flirt with them, act like I'm interested, and I can often take them home. Getting sex is a piece of cake. If I let them think I want to see them again, I often get laid pretty quickly. Women want to be reassured . . . so I reassure them. They want to believe me.

I know I'm good-looking. I work on my body to keep it in shape. It helps me to have as much sex as I need. I like the variety of different women. I hurt most of them. Do I feel guilty? No. If they're too stupid to doubt my words, it's their fault, not mine. They want to believe me because they like my looks. So we both have a good night. Then I move on. I like to see how many women I can get in a week.

If you don't make men prove their words before you fall for them, who is the real jerk? If his looks and his saying the right words are more important to you than who he really is, then you'll continue to set yourself up for trouble. If you stop making it easy for these good-looking men to manipulate you, they'll have no choice but to treat you better. If you make them work harder to get what they want from you, they'll appreciate you more.

In subsequent chapters, I'll give you tools for getting rid of the jerks and for being happy in the process. Right now, keep remembering: "All men are jerks until proven otherwise."

What's Wrong with Nice Guys?

I've gotten to the point of truly appreciating a nice man instead of a jerk. The jerks often seem more exciting, but I don't find getting taken for granted exciting anymore. The jerks are more of a challenge. But I no longer find it challenging to see how much pain I can take from a man before cracking. The professional jerks have a wonderful "facade" that's nice to look at. But I no longer enjoy seeing a man who doesn't treat me with respect. Jerks say many wonderful things that I yearn to hear. But these days, my ears only want to hear what's for real. So in the long run, I'll personally take a nice guy over some gorgeous jerk any time. The one thing I've gotten out of being with too many jerks is an appreciation for nice guys. I can live without the excitement of wondering where the pain will come from next.

Men consistently ask me to tell women to give nice guys a chance. They complain women are too judgmental when they first meet men and don't give themselves a chance to get to know a nice guy. They feel a lot of good guys get passed over because they don't pass the initial test. I agree. I used to be more looks-oriented. A guy needed to have a perfect body if he wanted to date me. I attracted young, hot guys, but it didn't make me happy. The price of their egos was too high. That doesn't mean all good-looking guys are jerks. But when one is nice, too, you often wonder what's wrong. Why is he being so nice to me? What's the matter with him? You should wonder instead what's wrong with you for feeling this way. Don't you deserve to be given the best by a man, even if it comes easily? As Lea said in a support group:

> I was going out with Jake and found him attractive. But he was very good to me. Listen to me! I say, "*But* he was good to me" like it's a bad thing. When a man is very good to me, it puts me off, as it did with Jake. I'm more turned on by men who aren't as nice. It's sick. I dump the good men for ones I complain about constantly. Why can't I be happy with someone decent?

Many of you are like Lea—you don't want to be with a nice guy, even though the men you're attracted to may make you miserable. For years I did the same thing and wrote off nice guys. They didn't seem sexy. They seemed too easy. I wanted to work hard to keep a guy's interest. I blew off nice guy after nice guy as I fell for the jerks. How I wish I could get some of those nice guys back now! More and more men are trying to be jerks in order to attract women. Do we really want to create more monsters? As Greg admitted:

Most of the time when I treat a woman well, she dumps me. I'm a good guy. Why don't women appreciate that? These days my guard is up, and I'm hesitant to be nice. Sometimes I put on an attitude and don't do much for a woman I'm out with. But you know what? Then she wants me more. I'm working very hard to get myself to a point where I'm more of a bastard. If that's what women want, I'll give it to them!

Nice Guys Mean More Responsibility

Sometimes we avoid nice men because it puts pressure on us to recip-rocate. If you get involved with men who aren't jerks, you may have to deal with being in a relationship. Being with a jerk is safer: You know it won't last and you'll have excuses when it doesn't work out. It's less of a commitment and demands less responsibility on your part. With a nice guy, you know he'll call when he says he will. With a jerk, you never know. Nice guys are easier to trust. You may be afraid to give your trust to anyone, so you avoid them. Lexie confessed she's guilty of this:

I always complain about the bad boys hurting me, but when I meet a nice guy I run. My friends yelled at me when I stopped seeing Jordan. He was a very good guy. Good job. Good family. Treated me well. But something in me couldn't handle it. I think I've been burned so much that I feel more comfortable with a jerk than a good guy. I'm scared to trust anyone. I say I want a relationship but when it seems possible, I panic. With a jerk I can expect bad behavior and buffer myself. With someone like Jordan, I feel more vulnerable. Can I live up to how well he treats me? Do I deserve it? I don't know exactly what it is but I just can't handle being with a guy who treats me well. Yet the joke of it is I can't stay long with a jerk either.

I've finally grown up enough to know I don't need the excitement a jerk can create. In those scenarios, excitement and pain go hand in hand. A soothing, loving, constant relationship is healthier and more satisfying in the long run.

I will agree that a challenge is exciting. We like the thrill of the chase, the rollercoaster ride of the challenge. We like to feel we have to work a bit to get HIM to come our way. It's always more fun to try to attract a man than to have him easily. Open your eyes, sisters—avoiding nice guys is not necessarily healthy for you. If you want a thrill, take your nice guy to an amusement park and go on the rollercoaster!

You *Do* Deserve a Nice Guy!

Maybe you feel you don't deserve a nice guy. Subconsciously, you may not think you're worthy of someone decent. If someone is good to you, you may feel obligated to be good to him. Many women are more comfortable giving, in the sense of groveling to keep a jerk, than giving because they're getting good things from a man. Are you open to a healthy relationship? Being with a jerk can take the pressure off, because you don't have to take responsibility for your own happiness. If it doesn't work out, you can blame the jerk.

A man who lets you know he's interested can lead to wonderful feelings. How nice if he calls when he says he will. How sweet when he gives you compliments and means them. So what if he's not a jerk—he can still be very attractive. At the last in a series of support group sessions, Barbara came in all excited and told us:

> I met Steven a few months ago. We've been going out once in a while. I wasn't attracted to him because he was the typical nice guy. But I made the effort to give him a chance. I've been trying to appreciate his good qualities instead of wishing he were different.

We have a lot of fun together. I know now that if he were different, I'd probably be unhappy a lot of the time. I'm actually happy with Steven and can't believe it. Me, who always manages to get involved with the wrong man, is finally seeing a good one.

The most exciting thing is that I had sex with him this weekend. I honestly didn't expect much, but he turned out to be a sensual and very pleasing lover. I sold him short at first, but I'm glad I got to know him better. Nice guys can be *very* sexy.

After going through my phase of making snap decisions about whether there was instant chemistry between me and a new guy, I've learned to appreciate the good guys too. If you take the time to get to know a man, he may look much more attractive down the road. When you start by developing a friendship first, the rest may come later.

Chapter Three

Who Needs a Jerk?

"Women have served all these centuries as looking glasses possessing the magic and delicious power of reflecting the figure of man at twice its natural size."

VIRGINIA WOOLF

Needs and Neediness

I hate the word "needy." It has such a pathetic connotation. Self-help books tell you that if you're needy, you're weak, not in control, and in general, something that's not good. We've been conditioned to feel that being needy is a stigma. Well, I have news for you: *Everybody* is at least somewhat needy. That's what life is all about—looking to satisfy needs.

We all have desires. Being in need isn't always bad, but some needs—and how much you need them—are healthier than others. Needing something in a reasonable way doesn't make you the negative connotation of needy. But having an unrealistic or obsessive desire for something that affects many aspects of your life and peace of mind creates problems.

It's natural to want people in your life who you associate with providing comfort. We all have a need to be liked and to be secure. It's normal to have a strong desire for a special man as part of your life. There's nothing wrong with that. But when you're troubled by your behavior to fulfill these needs, it's time to re-evaluate yourself. Annie admitted:

> I want to be in a relationship. I want to get married. I used to attract worthwhile men. These days I don't meet any. Whenever I go out, one eye is looking around for men. I do it with my friends and anywhere there's people. I've become compulsive about looking for men. I don't enjoy doing things anymore because I'm too busy trying to find men. When I'm at the movies, I check out everyone around me. I linger in bookstores in hopes of spotting a cute guy. I date men who don't treat me right, but it's become better than nothing. I wonder if I'll ever be happy again.

Annie's life now completely revolves around searching for a man. This is too common among single women. "I have to meet a man" is a refrain from women wherever I lecture. It crosses racial lines; rich or poor; younger or older; educated, professional, blue collar, or white collar. It's a woman thing. It's hard for many women to imagine finding happiness without a man in their life.

Needs vs. Wants

There's a definite distinction between being needy and wanting something in your life. Women in my classes are apologetic about admitting they want a man. They believe it's a sign of weakness to desire being in a relationship, to be horny, to yearn for the closeness that only an intimate relationship can provide, etc. Well, I want a man too! I love the intimacy that being in a relationship provides. But I don't consider myself needy. I'd love cheesecake every day too, but I can live without it. It's perfectly normal to crave something that gives you pleasure, as long as it doesn't consume you. And you don't want to get obsessive in the other direction either, as Julie did:

> It's been a while since I've been in a relationship. I miss having one. Then I get angry with myself for being needy. I have a good career, lots of friends, and good health. Why can't I appreciate all I have and stop thinking about being with a man? It drives me crazy and I get angrier. I feel so weak.
>
> Most of the time I fight the urge to think of men. But then it comes over me—I want to be in a man's arms! I want to be loved. I get upset. Then I get angry at my weakness and I fight it. I'm becoming a mental case.

It's perfectly natural to want all the things Julie desires. We're often brought up being told that we're not complete without a man. Many of us see a man as a source of security. Let's face it: There are certain things that you cannot provide for yourself in the same way a partner can. That's just the way it is. But though I *want* a man, and at moments terribly *crave* a man, my life is full and satisfying enough that I can be very happy without one.

Seriously needing a man can be a major problem. Many women go through it at some point, me included. There are times when I wake up on a beautiful day and feel down, or even start to cry, because I wish I had a man to share it with; when my self-loving doesn't cut it as a substitute for sex with a man; or when I'd give a lot to roll over and be in the secure arms of an intimate partner. But, the moments pass quickly because I have other things that satisfy me. I've learned it's okay to want a man, as long as I don't get obsessed by it.

Through therapy, I learned it's good to have downtime, to allow my sadness and longing to surface and to grieve over what I miss. Then I get on with my life. I don't lower my standards for what I want out of a relationship in order to satisfy my needs. I accept that it's natural to want a man, and the right one will be worth waiting for. I don't feel guilty about wanting one. My wanting just has to be kept in perspective. No one can be more important than me. Developing good self-esteem and creating a productive and satisfying life for myself has been the key to going from *needing* to *wanting*. If you feel you need therapy —find the right professional for you. It's worth it.

Why Neediness Gets You Into Trouble

Too many women obsess over not having a man in their lives because they don't feel good about themselves if a man doesn't want them. They lower or even lose their standards and become perpetually unhappy. Their whole life becomes a mission to meet a man. Eventually the search for Mr. Right becomes a desperate attempt to find Mr. Not Too Wrong. I've been there too. I hear it at every lecture and from most of my single friends: Many of us can't be happy without a man.

Beautiful, intelligent, successful women that many of us would kill to be like tell me they completely lose it when it comes to men. They're just as wanting as other single women. Many think they're going crazy because they have their lives together on every level but the personal. These women seem self-assured and on top of their lives. The other women in my classes are shocked to hear these otherwise successful women whine about men as much as they do. It's a sobering experience. At the first class I ever taught, Laura, an extremely beautiful, young, well-spoken woman in her late twenties, stood up and said:

> I'm a psychologist. I counsel other women, yet I don't know how to handle men I like. Men complain I put too much pressure on them. I want to be in a relationship so badly, yet I always screw things up by trying too hard. I feel almost like a young girl when it comes to meeting men . . . so inadequate . . . so ner-

vous because I want it so badly. I don't feel happy without a man and keep wondering if I'll ever be able to find one and hold onto him in a healthy way. I'm a psychologist, yet I'm becoming irrational about needing a man. How can I advise my clients properly when I can't handle my own need?

Amazing, huh? And you thought only women who aren't gorgeous could lose their sanity yearning for a man. You can't control wanting to have a man in your life. But you can control whether you keep your desire in perspective or allow it to make you so needy it limits your ability to find happiness without one.

Women Need to Nurture and Love

It seems to be a woman's duty to nurture everyone. Why do we need to hug so much? For years I looked for stray puppies to use my nurturing instincts on. I gave lots of caring and support to any man I was seeing, whether he returned it or not. Inside of me, there was this great big, uncontrollable urge to love. I couldn't stop myself. Yet usually the recipient of my indulgence would take and take, while reciprocating only once in a while.

As crazy as it sounds, I believe the need to give a man affection can become an addiction. When I became single, not only was I starved to get affection from a man, I wanted to give it even more. He'd have no doubt that I cared. I literally couldn't stop myself from kissing HIM at every opportunity. It was definitely unhealthy. Women often tell me that they need to hug and kiss as much as a man can stand.

Men say that being hugged and kissed all the time can call up associations from their childhood, when they got smothered in Aunt Bessie's large breasts or had to constantly rub lipstick off their faces while attending family get-togethers. Women love to give love and affection to little boys too! So little boys try to squirm out of grandma's grip during a hug, learning to hate being smothered in affection. Peter recalled:

> I hated going to family parties as a kid. All the women in my family seemed on a mission to hug and kiss me while I tried to get away. They thought it was cute. I thought it was awful. So when a woman gets too huggy/kissy, I bristle. It reminds me of those times. I do like affection, but in moderation. When it gets excessive, I become that little boy at family parties and try to get away.

Giving love/nurturing is a form of assurance. By showing your feelings as much as possible, you think you're just assuring your man he's loved. Then he can deal with his own insecurities, knowing he has your undying support. You tell yourself that you're giving as much love as possible so he won't leave you. Unfortunately, this doesn't usually keep him around. A man loves the ego boost of having a woman all over him for a while, and then it gets tiring. As George said in my class:

> I don't know why women have to be *on* me so much. I do like getting and giving affection, but I tend to pull back when a woman I'm dating overdoes it. The one I'm dating now holds on to me when we're out. Whenever she can, she gives me a kiss or squeeze. It's nice, to a point. Then it makes me feel like I need breathing room . . . space. I've asked her to cool it a little, and she gets hurt. I don't want to hurt her, but I don't want to feel like a pet, always having to be touched. So I may just stop calling.

I had a boyfriend who hugged and kissed me all the time. When we walked down the street, he always kissed me. We had close calls almost bumping into poles and people. I was crazy about him, and at first I thought I had every woman's dream. I loved the attention and feeling of being loved and wanted. It was different to be on the receiving end of affection, but, surprisingly, it wasn't much fun after the first couple of weeks. I felt suffocated and finally understood how men feel receiving excessive affection. Trust me: As enticing as it sounds, it can get on one's nerves. Too much of anything is not good.

Needing to give love excessively is a form of losing control. Women argue when I tell them to hold back more with men. They call it game playing. I call it breaking an unhealthy habit. Their argument is, "Why should I stop being myself? If I'm affectionate, I shouldn't have to hold back. Then I'm playing games with my boyfriend." It's not game playing. An excessive need for almost anything doesn't create healthy grounds for a relationship. Conditioning yourself to give less affection can have positive effects. It may help you deal with your need to give affection so frequently. You'll be more in control of yourself when you break the habit of having to reach out and touch your man constantly.

Affection in moderation is more likely to inspire reciprocation. Many of the men I interviewed said that when a woman is overly affectionate, they're hesitant to give much in return, concerned it might encourage her even more. So they hold back. Conditioning your control can help you get more of what you want from a man. Katy related the following to my support group:

> Tyrone and I had a good relationship, except he was hardly ever affectionate. I made up for his lack. But it bothered me. Sometimes he squirmed when I'd kiss him spontaneously. I'd always snuggle up to him wherever we were, but he rarely snuggled back. After hearing things said in this group, I started holding back. I still gave affection but not nearly as much. He finally noticed. I was surprised when Tyrone asked why I wasn't snuggled up to him while we were watching TV. I told him, as I was advised in this group, I didn't think he wanted it much since he rarely initiated it. He said it wasn't true and pulled me over to him. Now we're getting more of a balance. And I feel more in control of myself.

David was also in this group. After Katy spoke, he added:

My current relationship is my longest yet. I may stay with Shawna forever because she's different from most women I've dated. She has more of a sense of self. And she doesn't smother me with too much. She likes to kiss and hug, but only some-times. That makes it special. When we first got involved, I waited for her to be all over me. It didn't happen. Of course part of me—my ego, I guess—was disappointed. But I feel so much more comfortable with her and would rather have it this way. She's really got control over her emotions. So many women are out of control about affection. It's like they can't stop.

Control. That's what we often lose when the need to give love over-whelms us. When I was a compulsive love-giver, I'd sometimes get angry at myself for always needing to hug and kiss. But I couldn't stop. It was like smoking—a bad habit. As my self-esteem grew, so did my resolve to get my habit under control. Rather than getting down on myself for being weak, I saw my kissy/huggy need as a habit to break. It started with developing a clear consciousness of how many times I'd hug and kiss the man I was involved with.

Breaking habits isn't easy. We kissy/huggy types have probably been doing it our whole lives, but we can stop. After becoming aware of how often I'd reach out and touch, I'd postpone my gratification for five minutes. (I use this technique with dieting too. If those cookies call, I wait five or ten minutes and then sometimes don't need them at all.) Postponing gratification works with affection too. When I wanted to hug him, I'd wait five minutes. Then I'd try to wait five more. I didn't stop giving affection, but I postponed my gratification to do it less fre-quently. Gradually I got my affection habit under control. Postponing rather than canceling made it easier. Eventually, I didn't need to give affection so much. I still want to, but I enjoy the control over myself more. When you take control, revel in it. Pat yourself on the back. Let the power help keep you strong.

They'll Take What You Give

Men tend to put their own needs first, which many women haven't learned to do yet. How many times have you cooked a man dinner? How about cleaning his apartment or washing his clothes? It's amazing what we do for them. Our upbringing may have told us that we're supposed to please, so we cook and clean and bake, and in general do all sorts of loving things for these men when they haven't earned it. We spoil men and then wonder why they act like spoiled little boys!

Men have come to expect this royal treatment because so many women give it to them. Why shouldn't they take it if they can get it? We think men will like us more if we do a lot for them. We think they'll need us more if we make them dependent on us for their basic needs. We think they'll never want to leave us if we make it so pleasant for them to stay. Trust me: It doesn't work that way. They can hire a maid, eat out, and do their own laundry if they have to. None of those chores equals love.

Victoria was an independent, self-assured woman, but she was struggling with her feelings for Vince, the man she'd been seeing for a year. He'd gotten distant, so she had pulled back too, focusing on other things. Victoria came to my group all excited because Vince had expressed more feelings for her, and she told us:

> He said he missed me and wanted us to spend more time together. I spent the whole weekend in his apartment. I was so happy about what Vince said that I cleaned his whole place. I even did his laundry. And I cooked all weekend. It was so nice doing these things for him. He's trying hard to give me what I want.

We all looked at Victoria in shock. Some of the women were downright horrified that this normally independent, cool woman was cooking and cleaning and laundering for a man, just because he'd said he missed her. That was all he did. The following week Vince pulled back again. He wanted to be alone more. Victoria tried to figure out what she'd done wrong and why he'd made the effort in the first place. Maybe he needed his apartment cleaned and couldn't afford a maid. A few nice words were cheaper than paying someone to clean. Marvin laughed when this topic was discussed in a coed group. The women were talking about what they did for men, while the men just sat quietly. He told the women:

If you give, we'll take. If you don't give, we can't take. You're the ones with the power, but you don't use it. Women are the ones who spoil us. My mother spoiled me as a kid, but when she got a job, I had no choice but to do things for myself. I may stick around longer with a woman who spoils me, but it's for the wrong reasons. If I like a woman a lot, I'll stay with her even if she doesn't spoil me. I may even spoil her.

Some women are so insecure that they think the only way a man might want to stay with them is if they make themselves indispensable. Shana explained:

I always wondered what Brad saw in me. He was extremely good-looking, and I felt he could get better than me. Because of this, I bent over backwards to please him. He told me he had no ability around the house and expected me to do it all. I kept our house in good order and had a good meal when he came home. I felt if I took care of him, I could be assured of always having him in my life. Wrong! Brad left me for another woman. From what I hear, she does nothing for him. Brad takes care of himself now. I don't know who's the bigger jerk, him or me!

Men are capable of taking care of themselves. If you make him a household cripple, he'll gladly take the crutch. If you put his needs before yours, he'll gladly go first. If you assume he can't do things, he'll gladly let you take care of them. But if you put your own needs first, he'll have no choice but to do things on his own.

Some women say they cater to their men as an act of love. Sacrificing yourself isn't love. It's a show of insecurity, and men know it. In the short run, they may find being pampered good for their egos. In the long run, it's a turn-off. I rarely do chores for men I date, but when I do, they appreciate it. When you do things all the time, there's often little appreciation. That's how you get taken for granted. When you give it as a gift, as I do, you can get much more mileage out of it.

We All Need to Be Loved

Love is one of the necessities of life. No matter how strong you are—no matter how successful and independent—we all need love for our well-being. It's just healthier to keep your need for love in perspective. It may sound hokey, but love *is* all around, if you'll just open yourself up to it. When you can turn your attention away from your man or from finding your man, you may have the vision to see and experience the other wonderful people in your life. And while you're enjoying a good relationship with *these* people, a man who's not a jerk may appear *because* you're happy and filled with good vibes. Being loved by a man can be the best, if the relationship is good. But love that makes you feel good doesn't always have to come from someone of the opposite sex. By being loving, you attract love into your lives. Don't sell the love of family, friends, pets, etc., short.

Nurturing is another basic need. It's nice to feel that someone is willing to take care of you. My last boyfriend wasn't a jerk, and I knew if I ever needed him, he'd be over. Being able to count on someone is a blessing. Building a support network of good friends can provide some of that security. My parents were always happy to nurture me when I visited. When you stop thinking that only a man can satisfy your needs, your enjoyment of the world and the people in it can expand dramatically.

Most important, I never forget that the most important person I can get love and nurturing from is myself (see Chapter Seventeen). It feels so great knowing I can take care of me. And when the right man comes into my life and wants to pamper me, I'll relax and enjoy it. Until then, I'll relax and enjoy the other loving people in my world.

Meeting Your Needs

Often a man satisfies very specific needs you have. If there's something you've been needing, you may be attracted to that aspect of him. You may focus on the need he's filling and accept what bothers you as a trade-off. You may fall in love because he gives you what you've been lacking. If your need for love, sex, security, romance, etc., is intense, you may only concern yourself with getting that piece of your needs satisfied. If the rest of him turns abusive, disrespectful, just not right for you, and so on, you may be afraid to risk losing the piece he does give you. So you hold on for the side dishes while the man makes you his main course.

I found myself doing the same thing with my last HIM. When his problems weren't getting to him, he could be delicious. I got romance, great sex, and fun times, when he could give it. He was a very decent person. I always got respect, and he kept his word. But there were things in his life that caused problems that hurt, frustrated, and distracted me. While telling a friend about him, I defended his shortcomings by reciting all his wonderful qualities. She cut me off, telling me to stop settling. She said, "You deserve the whole enchilada!" I realized she was right. I let him know what I wanted from him. When he couldn't give it to me, I let go.

You shouldn't settle for pieces of goodies from a man or trade your happiness and self-respect for the opportunity to be held, cuddled, and given tenderness. You shouldn't give yourself away for the words you want to hear if there's no action behind them. You deserve a healthy man who can make you happy. Keep remembering: "All men are jerks until proven otherwise." Until he proves otherwise, don't get too caught up in his "goodies."

Be Realistic about Men

While you shouldn't settle, you have to be realistic and not expect to have every need satisfied. It's hard to get that from any human being, so it's imperative to decide what's most important and stick to it when meeting a new man. The biggest factor shouldn't just be that you're getting something good—you also have to consider the price you're paying to get those needs met and it shouldn't be too high. Are you putting up with pain and frustration in exchange for intermittent romance? That's where you need to set a boundary. Saying "All men are jerks until proven otherwise" will help you draw the line.

By resolving to only get involved with men who give you most of what you want or need, you'll be more open to attracting that sort of man. (Remember, let's not expect perfection. This is life, not Fantasy Island.) If you only accept acceptable behavior, that's what you'll get. There are men out there who are quite capable of giving you *everything* you need! One woman's jerk can be your treasure—if he knows behaving well is the only way he'll have you.

Chapter Four

Setting Yourself Up for Disappointment

"The hardest task in a girl's life is to prove to a man that his intentions are serious."

HELEN ROWLAND

Relax and Have Fun!

One very basic difference between men and women is that men often try to keep dating simple, while women can make it complicated. A consistent male pattern goes like this: A man meets a woman he finds attractive and thinks, "She seems nice and is attractive. It would be fun to go out with her." They don't necessarily have any agenda beyond that, except maybe the desire to take her to bed. Here's the same scenario from a woman's side: A woman meets a man she finds attractive, who asks her to dinner. She calls all her friends. They discuss his potential, wondering where it will lead. The poor guy thinks he's just having dinner with an attractive woman, while she's analyzing the possibilities of their future together!

Women tend to take men too seriously at the beginning. I'll keep repeating this: We need to relax and just try to have fun. Men tend to do this already. I asked both men and women what they think about before a first date. A majority of the women said they think beyond the first date, many far beyond. Many men said they don't think about anything. The majority of men's answers were simple versions of, "I hope I have fun." Only a small percentage thought about the future.

When you meet a man, you're better off if you relax. Think of him as someone to enjoy, instead of picturing him in your future. If a relationship is meant to be, it will happen. If not, you *might* still have fun.

Take Him at Face Value

We also set ourselves up for disappointment by having too many expectations of a man we're not seriously involved with. Our hopes get mixed up with reality. We read too much into his words and actions, often taking them way beyond his intention. Of course, our friends don't help. They feed into our speculation, which inflates our hopes for this man in the future. Ilene told my class:

> I had the greatest time with Ron when I met him at a work-related party. We were definitely on the same wavelength. I told my friends about Ron, and they got excited. We went out for dinner, and he was a perfect gentleman and said he'd like to hang out with me again. We did, several times. He kissed me "hello" and "goodbye" on the cheek. We talked on the phone a lot.
>
> My friends were sure he liked me and must be shy for not going beyond a kiss. They encouraged me to set up a romantic scenario. I finally did and felt stupid when he said he was gay. He thought I'd figured it out. Ron was surprised when I told him

I hadn't realized that. He'd never acted like more than a good friend. My friends helped me blow everything out of proportion.

Just because a man smiles at you, it doesn't mean he's interested in romance. Just because he seems to enjoy your company, it doesn't mean he wants to date you. Just because a man tells you something complimentary, it doesn't mean he wants to see you again. Try not to read too much into men's responses. If you take anything positive they say too seriously, you set yourself up to be let down. Many men just enjoy being in a woman's company. Period. They may show enthusiasm when you're together, but it doesn't mean anything until it develops into a relationship. Enjoy the moment but don't dwell on it. Stop overanalyzing the details!

You set yourself up for disappointment by judging a man on the basis of the good behavior most of us try to have at the beginning. You don't allow enough time to decide if you like him or not as a person, beyond his potential to be a husband. You set yourself up for disappointment by forgetting that "All men are jerks until proven otherwise." Yoko related the following story:

> I met Leo last year. He was always trying to please me. I couldn't believe how lucky I was to have him . . . at the beginning. The first month Leo was always sweet, saying he'd never had it so good with another woman. Then he shocked me by losing his temper and calling me a bitch. Later he apologized and was very good . . . for a few days. Then he was in a bad mood again and said awful things. I talked to him about it the next day, and he said if I had a problem he'd leave. He acted very cold to me. I reminded him of how special it was between us and he laughed . . . a mean laugh. I didn't know him at all. What a disappointment.

All men *are* jerks until proven otherwise. Yoko found out the hard way. Leo put up a nice front, when it suited him. Jerks can be delicious in the beginning, but *consistent* decent behavior is proven over time. You all know that, at least deep down. You've all had at least one (or a hundred and one) experience that proves it. You've all seen that it's hard to know if a person is for real before knowing him well. But you push that knowledge aside as you become yet another target for a man with a good opening act.

While it may sound harsh, the best way to weed out jerks and set yourself up for a healthy relationship is to have *no* expectations of a man you don't know well yet. And, remember that it takes time for a guy to earn your trust. When he says he'll call, don't expect it. Then you won't be as disappointed if he doesn't. Let it be a nice surprise if he does. When he talks about future plans on your second date, silently sing "la-dee-da-dee" and tune it out on an emotional level. It will help you avoid getting sucked into premature enthusiasm. Say to yourself, "All men are jerks until proven otherwise." I know this sounds awful, but it's more awful to be let down later. Not taking him seriously until he proves himself is better than getting excited and then deflated if he turns out to be all talk or someone who changes his mind quickly.

Why Do Men Run?

Why do men get carried away? I asked men what makes them sweep a woman off her feet and then under the rug. They admitted they sometimes come on strong at first and never cease to be amazed at how seriously women take them. Here are examples of what makes a man *act* like he's seriously interested:

TODD: I love attractive women. And when I'm with one, for the moment I could fall in love with her. But it's just a high for that moment.

JERRY: I'm a hopeless flirt. That's it. I can't have a relationship with everyone.

VICTOR: When I meet a woman who has many of the qualities I find attractive, it excites me. But then I think that I don't really know her or that she'll have more expectations of me than I can fulfill, so I leave.

HECTOR: I love women. And I love to give them what they want . . . for a short period of time. When they start to take it seriously, I'm outta there!

MICHAEL: Interaction with women is a game I enjoy. Why not have fun when I'm with one? I relax and enjoy and then usually forget about her. I can't help it that women take the game too seriously.

LEE: When I meet a lovely woman and she seems like she could be a soulmate, I get carried away. I enjoy the rush of new feelings and excitement. But then I usually see things in her that I don't like, and it cools me off fast.

Not all men are like these examples, but I wanted to show that most men don't consider their emotions as much as many women do. Nor do they think about the future as much. They very often just want to live for the moment and have fun. That doesn't necessarily make them jerks, but it's up to you to make them prove otherwise. These men do fall in love eventually, often with a woman who makes them own up to their behavior.

The Benefits of Holding Back

When men promise wonderful things at the beginning, it's easy to get caught up in the romance. But three weeks into a relationship is too soon to talk about going on vacation together next year. It's ridiculous to think about living together or being in love after one month. But men throw us promises with passion, followed by a dispassionate withdrawal. Lynn told my class:

> Paul and I had been dating for two weeks when he gave me the key to his apartment and insisted I leave clothes and cosmetics. We did everything together. He talked about the future. I was swept away by how perfect it seemed. After six weeks, he coldly came over to say he wasn't ready for a relationship, nothing personal. He demanded his keys back and left me crying. Two days later my things came in the mail, pushed into a box! I don't know what went wrong.

It takes time for feelings to become real. If Lynn hadn't taken Paul so seriously, she might have spared herself some of the pain. It's hard. I've been there. Nothing is more delicious than getting carried away by a romantic interlude. But the sweetness isn't worth the pain. I almost always temper my feelings with "All men are jerks until proven otherwise," telling myself he probably doesn't mean everything he says. How he makes you feel at the moment shouldn't be more important than who he really is. You often assume that if he makes you *feel* wonderful, that's how he must *be*. WRONG!! If happiness is your goal, hold back, no matter how sincere he seems.

Eileen came to my support group enthusiastic about Bobby, whom she'd just met. He was coming on strong, and Eileen was falling for the lines. We made her promise to say, "All men are jerks until proven otherwise." Then next week she confided in us:

Bobby was extremely romantic and gave lots of compliments. I started to get sucked into it, but remembered my promise and said the phrase to myself when getting carried away. It helped me keep my cool. I asked Bobby to slow down, and he was surprised. So was I—I was able to keep some distance for the first time when crazy about a guy.

Bobby phoned a few days later to see me again. He said he was confused because usually he gets scared when things go very well, as they did with us. He knows he has a tendency to get carried away too soon, and then he usually doesn't follow through. But because I didn't respond as most women do, getting carried away too, and because I didn't take him too seriously, he wanted to see me again. He felt comfortable with me. Bobby said he's usually a typical jerk with women but felt differently because I was different. He still hasn't proven otherwise, so I'm still seeing him as a jerk. But I feel more in control than ever, and things are getting better. What a nice situation for a change!!

"I'll Call You"

This scenario probably sounds familiar: You have a great time on a date. He seems to be enjoying himself, and you have much in common. He kisses you tenderly goodnight and says he'll call. You anxiously wait for a phone call, e-mail, or text—three days, a week. You text to remind him what a great time you had. Ten days, two weeks— he doesn't call. What happened? Why did he act so sweet? What did you do wrong? Why did he have to be such a jerk?!

I've asked men about this particular pattern, and a majority admit to being guilty of it, at least once. One reason was that while they often mean what they say at the moment, they get busy; time passes; and they feel funny getting in touch, so they don't. That's it. They may meet someone else, get distracted and forget to call, or get scared, and never give you another thought. Remember, many men don't take dating that seriously at the beginning. Meanwhile, you wait around dwelling on HIM.

If you think, "All men are jerks until proven otherwise" when he says, "I'll call," you might not take it seriously until he does. Men shouldn't be labeled jerks because they lose interest. No matter how pleasant the time you spend together, if you develop major expectations after only one, or even a few, evenings out, then you're the jerk.

The most common answer I got from men who admitted to saying "I'll call/text you" when they knew they probably won't was that they don't know what else to say. Saying "I'll call you" is out of obligation. They assume it's polite or expected. I agree with them to a large extent. When you're with a man whom you had a good time with and are interested in seeing again, you may look at him expectantly because you WANT him to say he'll call. When he sees that expectation in your eyes, rather than let you down to your face, he says "I'll call or text," then "loses" your number. This is awful, right? Wrong! Okay, there are other ways to handle it, but men are basically chickens. It's difficult for them to face someone who they may not want to continue to have contact with, but she's smiling, waiting for reassurance. I've looked at men with that, "Please say you'll call" look in my eyes. Men just don't know what else to do.

It's human nature to take the easy way out. Men don't own that bad habit. Women do it, too. When a guy you don't want to date asks for your number, how many times do you say, "Don't bother since I'm not interested?" Not often! You've probably given him the wrong number, or taken his number and not called, or given him your number and then avoided his calls or made excuses for not seeing him. Is that better than what men do? Let's not be hypocritical in judgments or create double standards. Both sexes say things they don't mean because there's no nice way to tell someone you're not interested.

Neil agrees—he said he feels guilty and promises to call "because it might be hard for me to put into words why I think we may not be right for each other." Yes, men take the easy way out, but women do too. I repeat: "All men are jerks until proven otherwise." Give them time to prove otherwise.

Looking for Approval in All the Wrong Places

Many women don't have a strong sense of self. They only know who they are, and if they're worthy, when someone says something nice about them. Since we're brought up judging ourselves by how others see us, you only feel validated as a woman when a man lets you know he likes you, finds you attractive, or wants to be with/marry you, etc. That's why you need to hear compliments. That's why you want to please everyone. Men know this and use sugarcoated words to manipulate. Matt asserted:

> Women love to be sweet-talked. I tell them what they want to hear ... you know, that they're beautiful, special, sexy, smart. They eat it up ... lap it up. It's amazing how much I can get from just smiling at a woman like I'm interested in her. I tell a woman I love being with her and she opens up to me. Why do they fall for it all?

Why do we fall for it all? Because we love hearing it. Even when you know it's a line, a part of you enjoys it. Women need approval. Sometimes we'll sell our souls to a man for it. We love feeling attractive. But no matter how much we like the way we look in the mirror, we don't truly feel attractive until someone, preferably a man, confirms it. So we're suckers for the approval of those around us. We crave approval from those we most want to like us, especially the opposite sex. Cheryl admitted to my group:

> Before a date, I fix myself up a lot. But I'm never comfortable with how I look unless HE tells me I look good. If a man doesn't give me a compliment quickly, I start to lose my confidence. I can put on my favorite outfit that I know makes me look thin; my hair can come out perfect; and my roommate can tell me I look terrific. But if my date doesn't comment, all night I'll wonder what is wrong with me. What's wrong with me that I need a guy to tell me I look good to feel attractive?

If you haven't learned to trust your own opinions, you may look outside instead of within to decide if you're okay. That gives men a very powerful weapon to manipulate you with—their words of approval. When you need to hear them, you rarely make men prove themselves through their actions, even though you know better. Unless you make a serious effort to work on your self-esteem (see especially Chapter Seventeen), you'll always fall for the kind words men throw at you like throwing bones to a dog.

Chapter Five

Ms. Fix-It

"There's nothing so stubborn as a man when
you want him to do something."

JEAN GIRAUDOUX

"I Know What I Want"

I always go around the room at the beginning of a class, asking attendees what he or she wants to learn. Women consistently say they want to learn how to get what they want from men. How can they change men so they are who they want them to be? Women often come with a complete agenda of what they want in a man, and just as many complaints.

In contrast, men in my classes aren't looking to change anyone. They want to know what women want from them. They're clueless and complain that women make demands but never seem happy with what men do. Nothing ever seems to be enough. They want to get along with and please the women they're involved with, without losing themselves in the process. Men's biggest gripes aren't about what they're *not* getting. Getting something specific from a woman isn't their primary concern. They feel some women are unreasonable in their expectations, and they just want their relationships to have fewer hassles. Men are very confused! Dwayne told me:

Why can't more women just go with the flow? I get exasperated when I try to please a woman I'm involved with and it's never good enough. My last girlfriend told me I wasn't romantic. I thought I was. So I brought her flowers. She said that was too easy. I asked her to spell it out and she started crying, saying I make everything unromantic by having to ask. I gave up! I liked her a lot and honestly thought I was being romantic. Women! Why can't they just relax and have fun? If something more serious is there, it'll happen whether she plans it or not. I'm more likely to stay in a relationship if a woman is not on my back.

Men in my classes, and many whom I've interviewed, see women as often irrational, demanding, desperate for security, money-hungry, on a crusade for the father of their children, and other unattractive descriptions. The guys just want to have fun. When they start dating someone, they'd be happy to go out, have a good time, and, if possible, have good sex. They're simpler than women, their needs more basic. They can't or don't want to deal with all the needs women throw at them, especially at the beginning. When it eventually becomes too complicated, or too much of a hassle, they bail out. Then we complain about them to all our friends, calling them jerks. Remember, a man isn't a jerk just because he won't do things your way. That's unfair.

If He's Not Broken, Don't Fix Him

Men consistently ask me to tell women that they're not broken and therefore don't need to be fixed. They want women to be more accepting of them *as they are* when they meet. What seems to get many women into trouble is that they consider qualities in men that they don't agree with as wrong instead of just different. They believe that if they keep working on a man they like, he'll see the error of his ways.

Then they go on a mission to fix/change/upgrade him. Whether you like it or not, this isn't fair. Men have a right to have their own ways.

You might believe that if you meet what you think are a man's needs, he'll want to please you by becoming the man you think he should be. This rarely happens. Usually both parts of the couple get frustrated: he, because of the pressure to change; she, because of his refusal to bend. So what may have had potential to be a satisfying relationship ends. Kim admitted to my support group:

> Every man I go out with does things I don't like. What's wrong with men? Why can't they have a relationship the right way? When I meet a man I like, I give him a chance. Then, when he does things I don't like, I tell him how I want it. I don't think it's anything terrible. Like, why does he have to always watch those dumb football games? Or why doesn't he like getting dressed up? To me these are such little things to correct, but men don't want to. Are there any decent men?

Does his not doing things your way make a man wrong or bad? No. I repeat: Men are different and are entitled to their differences. They aren't machines that need repair. No, they may not do things in what you see as the best possible way. Yes, they may behave in ways that you'd think any rational person might label stupid. More often than not, what you want to change the most are things that don't live up to your expectations of how you think a relationship should be. But men shouldn't have to adjust to your expectations unless they want to.

Your Own Agendas for Men

Often we get ourselves in trouble by setting an agenda, mandating how things should be with a man. With strong determination, we set out to live by it. We know how we want him to be and what we want out of a relationship, and we even have a time frame of where the relationship should be after different time intervals. Since the agenda is so pleasant, it's commonly shared by our friends. We get together and reinforce each other's need to find a man who'll provide what we think we should have. When this particular man doesn't seem to exist, we get angry with all men. As Merry told my class:

All my friends want a man who's reliable, romantic, and communicates well. We believe when people are in a relationship, they should spend most of their free time together. After six months, there should be a formal commitment. Jim drove me crazy spending so much time with sports. I wanted him on Sunday mornings for brunch, but he was playing softball with his league. My friends all agreed it was terrible. Why can't I find the right man?

Then I was so happy to meet Michael. He loved leisurely weekends with me. But I couldn't get him to talk about himself. I told him everything about me, but he wouldn't open up and share. I wanted to know everything, and he avoided talking. My friends couldn't believe he was like that. Why can't men do it the right way? If we tell them what we want, they should at least try. Why don't men understand this? Why can't they be more sensitive? If you care about someone, you should want to be with her, right?

Wrong! Men get judged and sentenced by juries of women who have nothing better to do than set unrealistic standards for relationships. Women should instead go with the flow more, and either get used to him and his routines or find someone else. No man will have everything you want. It's impossible. Having other interests besides HIM is healthier. You often spend too much energy on HIM and not enough on yourself. You can turn this around!

Expending unnecessary energy on deciding how you think men *should* be gets you nowhere. I believe a large percentage of you have problems with men because you won't accept them as they are (there's more on this in Chapter Sixteen). All that does is make you crazy!

I've seen a vicious cycle with women. We spend an inordinate amount of time trying to change men, instead of using that time to find other ways to satisfy ourselves. We get frustrated, burned, angry, etc. Then we get desperate. Eventually we put up with too much we don't like and complain about it. Later these men become jerks in our eyes. There's often no middle ground. But who really has the problem?

Commitment-Phobic or Just Phobic?

Men can't fall in love on schedule. They try to enjoy themselves and see what happens. The timetables you sometimes present them with can be a source of resentment. Men don't analyze relationships, so they often simply don't understand where you get your timetables and expectations from. They get put off when confronted with your needs, and who can blame them? I listened in amazement when Sharon related her story:

> Phil and I dated for a year. I have rules about where things should be in a relationship after a certain amount of time. After we'd been involved for six months, I told him I expected to be with him more often. That's how it should be. After nine months, I insisted he call me more and let him know I expected him to open up more about himself. After all, when you've been together for nine months, you should be sharing more. He did try. But after a year, I told him I should know what he planned for our future. After all, we'd been together for a year. Phil told me he wasn't sure. I couldn't accept that, so we broke up. No need to waste my time. I do this in all my relationships. Men

need to understand what I expect at different times in the relationship. I don't know why they make it so difficult.

Why not learn to relax and have fun? You can't expect rules that you apply to someone else's emotions to work the way you plan. Hearts don't have clocks built in. The alarm doesn't go off after a year to signal "love forever." Often the pressure put on men backs them into a defensive position, depriving them of the breathing room they need to be happy in a relationship. The defenses they put up against your demands/needs/inability to accept them as they are can drive you crazy. So unnecessary!

Setting Men Up to Lie

Sometimes women's agendas motivate men to lie. Men say they lie to protect themselves. They've often been conditioned into bad habits like lying by their experiences with women before you, or directly by you, and sometimes they avoid the truth because they don't trust you to handle it. Besides being jerks, men can be chickens. Since they don't have the coping skills women have, they avoid emotional confrontation at all costs. Jess explained in a coed group:

> "Yesing" women and doing what I wanted started in childhood. My mother always gave me problems when I told her the truth. She wanted everything her way. She'd forbid me to do things I told her about. I learned that sometimes what she didn't know wouldn't hurt her.
>
> I used to be straight with women I dated, but they'd react negatively. It drove me crazy how they seemed to be on a mission to have things their way, reminding me of my mother. So I got into the habit of telling half-truths. Okay, sometimes it wasn't even half true. It made my life easier than going through

the wringer every time I did something that wasn't the way they wanted it. Now I automatically don't tell the whole truth. I don't want to go through that wringer if I don't have to.

I'm certainly not condoning lying, but sometimes your attitudes or response to the truth give men no pleasant alternative but to lie. Your sometimes nagging, suspicious selves have to take at least some responsibility for their telling lies. Men say that they're sometimes hesitant to tell their wives or girlfriends the truth because they may take it the wrong way. When you don't understand a man's needs or actions, you may have a bad reaction to the truth. So men lie rather than risk an argument about something they think is harmless.

Lying isn't right, but think for a moment. Can you truthfully say that you've never gotten on a man's case because he told you the truth about something that bothered you? Sometimes you may get possessive or feel threatened if your partner wants to be with someone other than you for an evening. If you don't understand why he feels this way, what might you do? Give him an argument and blow what he's told you out of proportion! Take Gwen's story, for instance:

> When I started seeing Lenny, he spent time with Pam, an old friend from school who he regularly got together with. I got jealous and made a fuss when he saw her. I couldn't understand why he had to see another woman and told him to cool it with her. I gave him a hard time so he'd stop. He started seeing his male friends more often, and I felt better. Months later I found out he was lying and seeing Pam all along. I was hurt he'd lied. He said it was easier than telling the truth.

I spoke with Lenny about what happened. Here's what he said:

> Pam was just a good platonic friend. It had nothing to do with her being a woman. Gwen was so jealous of her, I couldn't

mention Pam's name without getting a rise out of her. It wasn't fair to ask me to stop seeing a friend. So I let her think I was with guys instead. It got Gwen off my back and made our relationship better. I hated lying, but I hated her harping on me more. Women do that to us. They make us miserable when we tell the truth. I'm not saying lying is right, but neither is jumping down our throats when we're honest about things.

Insecurity may cause you to feel threatened about things going on in your man's life. Usually when a man tells the truth, he has nothing to hide. If you don't accept that, you may encourage a man to lie. If you don't accept things in his life that you don't like, you may not hear about them, but they'll still be there. Men don't have to give up their lives for you, even if you do it for them.

Judd said in a men's class that he felt that talking to a woman could be a lose/lose situation. Other men readily agreed, asking me how they could be expected to tell the truth when it often got them, to quote several, "crap." Judd explained:

> I play softball on a team from work, and an important game was scheduled for one of the nights Suzy and I usually spend together. I told her I couldn't come over but invited her to the game, and she got all upset. "What will I do if I don't see you? I don't see why you can't miss it. Friday is our night together." And Saturday and Sunday and Tuesday. Yet she got bent out of shape because I wanted to play in my game. I told her I'd come over after the game, and she said I'm supposed to be over at 6:00.
>
> The next time I had a game on one of our nights, I told her I had to stay late at work. She accepted that better. So what can I do? Be chewed out every time I deviate from her plan? Feel like I'm on trial when I break rules? Suzy isn't the first woman to

do this. If women don't want us to lie, they have to accept the truth, nicely.

Other men had similar stories. So who's to blame? Is it up to you to make rules? To judge him? To punish him if he deviates from your game plan? I insist on honesty in my relationships and have heard plenty of things I didn't like. But I'd rather hear them and know they're in the open than wonder what he's not telling me. Sometimes I have to bite my tongue to prevent making a sarcastic comment or expressing displeasure because I know I have to accept his life as is. If I don't like what I hear, it's always my choice to walk out. But it's never my choice to forbid him to do something I don't like. I express my opinion once, in an unemotional, straightforward way, and then decide if I want to deal or walk. There's no third choice. Nagging just forces a man to make one of two choices too: either lie or leave. If you listen without judging, he may trust you enough to be honest. If you get upset or try manipulating him when he's honest, you have to be prepared to not always hear the truth.

Would You Rather Be His Girlfriend—or His Therapist?

From stories I hear, many men can be labeled the walking wounded, with scars from their childhood, previous relationships, and whatever they can't handle. So there you are, with your nurturing hats on, ready to help HIM, heal HIM, support HIM, and let HIM take it out on you. Rubbish!!! You must take care of yourself first. His problems aren't more important than your own. His scars don't hurt more than the pain he can inflict as you try to heal HIM. Amy gave a good example in a class:

Nick was so sweet when I first met him. My heart opened to him when he told me his father died when he was a boy. He told me about his bad relationships and the women who hurt him. I was determined to erase the pain by being loving and kind. Sometimes Nick got nasty when I hadn't done anything wrong. Later he'd apologize, telling me it was because of what other women had done. He even cried a few times.

At first I loved how he became dependent on me for support. But then I became paranoid, afraid I'd upset him. I realized if I did the slightest thing that wasn't his way, he'd get bent out of shape. He did little for me except tell me nice things like he loved me, when he was in a good mood. I was unhappy most of the time and had to break up with Nick. He'll probably complain to his next victim about me.

We Ms. Fix-Its should be careful. Being supportive must have its limits. Usually we have none. Just as you don't want to change a man who doesn't need his habits and preferences changed, neither do you want to try to heal his deep-seated emotional wounds, which you're not qualified to handle. Many of you love having a man emotionally dependent on you, thinking it'll provide insurance that he won't leave. But that's being needed for the wrong reasons. Do you want to be his therapist or mother instead of his girlfriend? Do you really want him to stay because he's dependent on your emotional support? Can you be happy in that scenario indefinitely? I doubt it! If you see these issues with a man, encourage him to get professional help.

Men Get Hurt Too!

Many men are terrified of getting hurt. Even after a satisfying date, a man may get home and remember something that makes him feel vulnerable. He may see you as the kind of woman he'd like to marry, except that he's not ready to marry. He may feel too much too soon and get scared of falling in love. Men who've been hurt badly like staying in control. Opening up to a woman, feeling comfortable enough to trust her, and thoroughly enjoying her company scares them. Warren told me:

> Seeing Janine was wonderful. I felt good being with her. She was nice; I could really talk to her. On our second date we shared feelings. She told me a lot of personal stuff, and I did the same. We felt close that night. When I got home I panicked, feeling like I'd opened up too soon. Janine knew so much about me and trusted me. I couldn't handle it, and stopped calling. She left a few messages on my machine and that was it. I knew it was rotten but didn't know what to do.

When a man reveals himself to you at night, he may not be able to face you in the morning. Men hook you with a false sense of intimacy by sharing their woes. We think we can make them feel better, and love being needed. Danny related the following in a group:

> Women love to hear my problems. They're much easier to talk to than my guy friends, so what the heck. I know women I'm dating feel more comfortable with me when I tell them how I was hurt in the past. They get more affectionate and happy when I lay my troubles on thick. I like it when it gets them into bed sooner! But then I lose interest most of the time. What is it with women? Sometimes I feel like I'm out with a shrink!

Men don't easily trust a woman enough to open up. When a man meets that special woman and finally lets his guard down, he becomes vulnerable. It's a bigger thing for him than for a woman. We do it all the time and open up more easily, so we're more used to getting hurt by someone we trust. But often when a man opens up to a woman, it's a special occasion. So if she hurts him, he may see it as a major betrayal. It can make him determined not to set himself up for getting hurt again by trusting a woman. These men end up hurting everyone they get involved with, in an effort to spare themselves pain. Richard told my class:

> I'd been a player before I met Jody. I fell for her hard. She seemed so sweet. I was faithful to her for two years . . . very unlike me . . . I let her see the real me, not the arrogant guy most see. I confided in her, and we shared everything. I planned to marry her.
>
> During our second year, I was out of town a lot. She didn't like me being away but coped. It was wonderful when we were together. Was I shocked when she confessed to seeing someone else when I was gone. I'd trusted her so much and never cheated on my trips, though I could have.
>
> I've vowed to never trust another woman. I trusted Jody so much. What a fool! Now I don't treat women nearly as well. I keep my distance. Do I care if I hurt them? No. It's just a payback for what Jody did to me. If I meet someone I feel I could fall in love with, I stop calling her. I don't want to get hurt again.

Richard got vehement telling his story. Other men agreed. When they get hurt, they'll do almost anything to avoid more pain. If that includes hurting you, they will. So be careful of men who've been hurt badly. They may need more space than you can comfortably give them. Women are pros at handling this stuff. Our friends are always sharing —that's part of being a female. Men aren't like that. They may let their guard down during a sweet moment. You may revel in how nice it is that he trusts you. But in the long run (or in the morning), he may decide to bail out because he feels too exposed. The best way to avoid this situation is to avoid intimate conversations until you know him well enough to guess how he'll respond.

Men, Women, and Therapy

You must understand a key difference between men and women: therapy. I don't necessarily mean therapy with a professional. Most women have been in a form of therapy since childhood. Growing up, you probably found someone to talk to—an older sister, cousin, neighbor, mother, etc.—so you didn't have to deal with problems and confusions alone. As you grew up, most likely you talked things out with friends. And many more women than men do go for professional therapy. We're used to dealing with life's ups and downs. We may talk about problems too much, but at least we have outlets for them.

Then there's men, who were more likely taught to work things out for themselves. Most men I know who confide in friends mainly choose female ones. They wouldn't dream of sharing a problem or insecurity with a male. It might seem unmanly. When these guys were younger, they may not have had a female to talk to, so men tend to keep more things to themselves. Rather than dealing with problems, they bury them, hoping they'll go away. Grant admitted:

> I don't know how women do it, talking to their friends about everything. I'm a private person. When I was a kid, I had no one to talk to. My dad told me to be a man when I came crying to him with a problem. So I got into the habit of handling my problems. I'd never dream of talking to a friend about feelings. It just wasn't done where I grew up. It would feel unmanly to show that I can't handle my own affairs. I'd die before telling a male friend my problems. Some things just don't need to be dealt with. Emotional crap is better off put aside. Women always want me to open up. Don't they know men don't like to do that? That's for wusses and women.

It's healthier to deal with troubles than to stuff them in a closet of the mind. I believe the imbalance between the way women and men learned to handle/not handle their emotional baggage contributes heavily to the problems between the sexes. There are large numbers of women with numerous outlets for dealing with what bothers them interacting with large numbers of men whose concept of handling their emotional trash is not to. So these very (or over-) therapied women try to develop relationships with these men in denial, who make believe things are fine rather than get involved with emotions. We talk with friends and/or a therapist to work out problems, whereas men keep withdrawing. And we wonder why there are so many problems between men and women!

Playing therapist isn't the answer. Men know that when they're dating a nice, sympathetic, nurturing female, they have an outlet to lighten their load. They may play on your emotions to manipulate you. Be careful. Even if he needs to make changes to be in a healthy relationship, don't be the one to facilitate them. Decide if you want to be a therapist or a girlfriend. It's hard to be both.

Chapter Six

Wanted:
The Perfect Man

*"It is a woman's business to get married as soon as possible,
and a man's to keep unmarried as long as he can."*

GEORGE BERNARD SHAW

Marry Me, Marry Me—If You Have Enough Money

A woman I was friendly with said she'd placed a profile on a dating website and asked me to guess which was hers. I guessed wrong because I'd never have expected her to emphasize "financially secure." She responded, "I don't plan to work forever. I want a husband to support me in style." I've heard variations of this from an inordinate number of women who are counting on finding someone to take care of them. For them, the amount of money a man earns is as important, if not more so, than the person he is. What does this attitude tell men?

It tells men you're looking for a keeper and that who they are may not be as important as how much money they make. Most men with a reasonable sense of self won't be looking for a woman who wants them for financial security. Ali asked men in my class if they have this problem, explaining:

> It seems like every woman I meet these days has a list of requirements in a man. When I first meet someone, I think about taking her out and having fun. I want to know what her interests are. But women start asking personal questions before you even know each other: What's your job? Are you financially secure? Do you own the condo you live in? Do you want children? What was your last relationship like? To me, these questions come much too soon. I often feel more like I'm on a job interview than a date. It completely turns me off. I don't want to be viewed as a potential husband until it's appropriate. Let them check these things out when they've gotten to know me better as a person. Then at least I know they're interested in who I am, rather than just my money. I may start giving them resumes to save time.

As Ali spoke, the men bobbed their heads "yes" in unison. Some expressed anger at women who seem almost mercenary. Think about it. Women send mixed signals as we take control of our lives. You want more independence and demand equal treatment. But if your date doesn't treat you to dinner, you may not want to see him again! What does that tell men? It says that we have our own double standards, that we go along with equality only when it's in our favor. Here's how women looking for a man with money justified this attitude:

> FRAN: I'm accustomed to a certain lifestyle. I like to eat in expensive restaurants and go to fine places. I need a man who can accommodate my preferences. It's very important to me.

> BARBARA: I'm ready to get married. I know what I want in a husband and lots of money is one quality. Of course, I'd like him to be

good-looking and fun. But if I meet a man I'm attracted to and he doesn't have money or seem a good candidate for a husband, I'll stop seeing him.

LORRAINE: I want to get married and have children. I'm willing to settle for a reasonably decent man who's financially secure enough to meet these needs.

Men know why many women are anxious for a committed relationship. They understand that their wallet may be more important than who they are, which creates a resistance to committing to anyone. It certainly puts men on their guard. Gerald said in a class:

I do want to be in a committed relationship. But I'm afraid to open up until I'm sure of her motives. More guys would commit sooner if they didn't have a doubt in the back of their minds about what each woman they meet is really after. If I fall in love with a woman who makes me feel sure that I'm who she wants to be with, instead of me just being a man who can give her security, I'm hers! Otherwise, I keep my feelings in check.

Charlton added, "The women I date wouldn't believe this, but I really do want to get married. I just don't want to marry someone who only wants to get married. I know a lot of men who feel this way." Few men want to be just somebody's meal ticket. Finding a man who's happy with his career may be a healthier, more realistic goal than finding one who earns a lot. I definitely wouldn't want a partner who just did things to get by, with little interest in his work or advancement. A man who enjoys his job can be more attractive because he's usually happier and more interesting. In general, though, it's not productive to treat each dating situation as a trial for marriage. Take it easy and just have fun. If you're attracted to his money now, don't label him a jerk later when you find yourself unhappily married to him.

Tick, Tick, Tick: The Biological Clock

This topic is hard for me to discuss. I tell men that no one has the right to judge a woman for wanting a child, even if she seems irrational about it. I have no right to do so, since I've been blessed with a daughter. Men have no right to judge because they can marry a younger woman and have kids when they're older. Single women don't have as many options. As the years pass without a possible father for their children in sight, some women get panicky. Julia admitted:

> I'm desperate for a baby. I'm thirty-eight years old and don't know how many more years I have left before I'm too old. But I want to be married if I have a child. These days I feel like I screen men. I am looking for the father of my child and know it's not a good way to approach men. But what can I do? I'm at the point where I'd settle for almost any man who had a job that could support me and a child. I used to want to fall in love with a sexy guy. Now I'd take a fertile nerd. Isn't it awful?

Julia is going through an emotional time that many women experience. It can feel like time is running out when you want a baby, but marrying a man for the sake of having a baby probably won't bring you happiness in the long run. Being married to a man you're not in love with or turned on by isn't satisfying, especially on those nights when the baby is driving you crazy. It's a lose/lose situation. I wish there was a reasonable solution besides learning to accept that you may not have a child. But going on a manhunt with your clock ticking definitely isn't the answer.

When you give off the vibe that you're anxious for a man, you usually don't attract one. It can come through in the way you present yourself. Even when you think you're keeping your cool and masking your anxiety, it's there. That clock is ticking like the crocodile in *Peter Pan*, and just as Captain Hook ran, so will most men. I've learned that I'm more likely to get something I want when I relax than when I'm uptight. Even if you're dying for a baby, try to accept for your own peace of mind that if it's meant to be, it will happen. Being anxious about it hasn't helped, has it?

I've advised some women to go for therapy to help them cope with this situation. Therapy can help you accept that you may not find a man in time. It can also help you expand your options. Single women are having babies, and they're also adopting. If you want a traditional family, those options won't cut it. But, as hard as it is, you can come to terms with the fact that not all women can find a man to have a baby with. If you'll let yourself accept your situation, you may get what you want. By going out with men just to have fun, your life will flow more naturally. In fact, by creating a life for yourself and focusing on being happy, you might attract the man you wanted all along.

Perfect Men and Other Fantasies

Have you ever known a couple that had everything you'd like in a relationship? Couples I've known who seem ideally happy usually end up divorced. You never know what goes on behind closed doors. The few couples I'm aware of where both partners consider themselves happy and blessed do not make love every night. Their existence isn't swathed in romance, nor do they always get along. But they love and respect each other enough to accept each other, despite their differences and imperfections. They're smart enough to appreciate what they have in each other. But most women want more. As Marcia complained in my class:

> What's wrong with wanting it all? My parents were barely civil to each other. I want more, a relationship filled with romance. I want a man who totally adores me, who brings me flowers and wants to make love a lot. I want to be spoiled. It's not unrealistic to try to find the perfect man. I know it's

possible. Other women have those kind of men, don't they? At least I hope so.

Too many women want perfection. That's why we create the agendas I discussed earlier. But that's not real life. Nobody's perfect. You want Prince Charming, but end up with the frog. And no matter how often you kiss him, the frog won't turn into a prince. So you feel disappointed, try to change him (unsuccessfully), or move on to find other frogs who *might* be the prince. But there is no Prince Charming. No person or relationship can meet every need. No man will live up to all your expectations. You need to identify the qualities in a man that are most important to you and learn to accept a few "warts" you'd prefer to avoid.

Brainwashed by the Media

Where do your expectations come from? Did you grow up seeing your parents continuously immersed in romantic bliss? I doubt it. Were members of your family, neighbors, or close friends examples of a perfect marriage? Probably not. So if reality didn't provide a model for the type of relationship women strive for, where do we get our ideas from? From romance novels, movies, soap operas, etc. Your idea for a perfect mate is probably actually a fictional character!

As children, my friends and I talked about how we didn't want marriages like our parents had, which seemed boring. Instead, we planned to fall in love the way people did in movies. Our husbands would always be romantic, faithful, and attentive. We'd have excitement like the couples on soap operas. As we got older, we read books that glorified how perfect a man could be in love. Yes, we were convinced that this was how it should be between men and women. My friends and I were raised on these fantasies.

But that kind of romance and those kinds of men exist only in fiction. Deborah told my class:

> I love going to the movies. That's where the real men are. I especially love Brad Pitt. You can tell he'd be a wonderful husband. He just seems so nice and is a wonderful father. I see all his movies. Why can't I meet men like that? Why don't men understand women want them to be more romantic . . . more caring . . . more sincere. Sometimes I wish I could jump into the movie screen or into a book I'm reading and be the leading lady to experience a good man. Where are all these men? The men I meet seem so, so, so . . .

Deborah couldn't find the right word to finish her sentence, so I did: human. In other words, they're fallible, imperfect, and all those other human qualities you don't want your man to be. Believing a man should be perfect puts a lot of pressure on the average guy. He can't live up to your leading man expectations. As Joe said:

> I was dating Rochelle until recently and thought it was going well until she started getting on me for not . . . I guess . . . being perfect. She got angry when I wasn't being loving during a basketball game . . . what's her problem? I was with her, wasn't I? I could have watched with my friends, but I wanted to be with her. She complained I wasn't romantic enough . . . or attentive enough . . . I didn't call enough. What's enough? I cared about Rochelle and tried my best. I called when I could . . . when I had something to say. She always wanted to linger on the phone when I had work to do. Texting isn't enough for her. She reads too many of those damned romance novels. They put ideas in her head. I finally stopped seeing her because I couldn't be the man she wanted. I can't imagine anyone being that.

It's taken me almost a lifetime to realize that my parents had an enviable marriage for more than fifty years. They held hands and kissed. I never viewed their marriage as perfect or romantic. They argued regularly and complained about each other. But they'd do anything for each other. The illusions created in books, on TV, and in movies distort the reality of love, showing that everyone is romantic and that all men are passionate. The fictitious men become every woman's dream. But we need to wake up from our dreams. Is this book waking you up yet?

It's impossible to develop and sustain the perfect relationship created by screenwriters. You may enjoy it for a short time, but it rarely lasts. No man can concentrate so much on loving a woman and still maintain his sense of self. And think about it this way: If he works hard all day to make that money you want, how can he be totally attentive to all your needs?

Listen carefully. Stop waiting for Rob Pattinson or Brad Pitt or Ryan Reynolds clones to enter your life. They probably can be jerks too. As Nick shared with me:

> My wife gets on my case constantly, accusing me of not wanting to take her out very often. I work six days a week managing a restaurant in order to support her and our daughter. When I get home I'm tired . . . wiped out . . . kaput. I just don't have much to give. Margo takes it personally. She doesn't understand how much I love her . . . or how much I'd love to have more energy. She complains I don't give her enough attention while I doze off in exhaustion. What can I do? It's going to kill our marriage.

Women want the works. After all, in the movies, men come home from a long day and make love all night. They remember the little romantic touches. Why can't our men be like that? I can almost guarantee, given some time, you'd find a guy like that boring! Jessie related the following story to me:

I thought I'd met Mr. Right when I met Charles. He was handsome and sweet. He was also extremely romantic. I thought I'd died and gone to heaven. But I also saw he was a pushover for everyone. As I got to know him better, I realized how insecure he was. Charles was very devoted to me, but I didn't respect him after a while. I got the feeling he was pleasing me so I would like him . . . kind of what women do to men. It became a turn-off. I got bored fast. I'd rather be with a man with a mind of his own. I guess a little romance from a strong man is more appealing than a lot from a weak one.

There's always a trade-off. If you get what you think you want, there'll be another complaint. Be realistic. Appreciate a good man when you meet one. My last real boyfriend was much more practical than romantic. When I wanted flowers, he bought me a water filter to keep me healthy. Thank goodness I was smart enough at that point to appreciate that he was showing how much he cared about me. While flowers are more romantic, the water filter was more sincere. Ideally, I'd have liked both. But, this is real life.

Maybe This One Will Be Different

You know what happened with the last guy who hurt you. You remember those who came before him, too. You're intelligent and know the signs, symptoms, and lines. Yet if you really want to meet the "right man," you may not bother to stop and learn from your mistakes. You hope each new guy isn't a jerk and give him the benefit of the doubt, praying, "Maybe this time will be different." It often isn't, yet you don't learn that "All men are jerks until proven otherwise." You get caught up in the relationship before they prove otherwise.

I used to convince myself that every man I met would somehow turn out to be different—*he'd* be the perfect one. He always seemed special. Why should I prejudge him just because I'd been burned by others? So I'd be trusting and get my hopes up about this man who seemed so wonderful and appeared to fit all the requirements I had of a perfect guy. Mr. Wonderful inevitably turned into Mr. Belongs in a Toilet Bowl when he started to resemble those before him. It got to the point where all the men I met seemed like clones of each other. How discouraging!

Had I changed my own patterns like I have now, things might have been different. Had I realized I was harboring unrealistic expectations, I could have reframed my idea of what a great guy or a happy relationship would look like. Had I believed "All men are jerks until proven otherwise," I might have held back and given them a chance to prove otherwise and avoided a lot of disappointment and pain.

Chapter Seven

Jerks Online

"Deceiving others.
That is what the world calls a romance."

OSCAR WILDE

Why am I often let down meeting a guy in person who I met online?

The popularity of dating and socializing via the Internet adds a huge new playing field for men to be jerks. Anonymity facilitates men in being any kind of guy they choose online and takes being jerks to a whole other level. Men can create romantic personas that make you tingle, say wonderful things that get your hopes up, lead you on in ways beyond what they do in real life, and disappear instantly if they get tired of playing with you. All of the online social media outlets allow the Prince Charming desire to flourish since men can be whoever they think will get and keep your attention.

Cyber Prince Charming

More women than ever get duped by guys who sound sooooo good in e-mails, messages, chats, and other forms of communication that you think he's your Prince Charming. But, they often turn out to be worse than frogs when they hide who they really are behind a user name. They might even send or post appealing photos, except they may be someone else's! A jerk can be whomever you want him to be for as long as you let him get away with it. I talked to Jerry, who meets women online for sport and acts out fantasies he can't have in the real world. He said:

> I love meeting ladies on the Internet! In person, I rarely have my flirting reciprocated. Women don't appreciate the great guy I am and dump their problems about a jerk they're dating on me, or pay me no attention. But online I'm a stud! Since they can't see me, I can take them on romantic mental excursions. I've become very good at knowing what to say to make a woman want me on dating sites.
>
> Online, I'm 6'2" and weigh 210, but in real life, I'm 5'8" and out of shape. Right now, I have ten women falling for me from our correspondence. It's fun and turns me on, which adds to my pleasure, if you know what I mean. When someone pushes to meet in person, I stop writing. I use several e-mail addresses and names and don't feel guilty because I know these women wouldn't speak to me in person . . . and a guy's got to get his pleasure from somewhere, right?

It's up to you to go slow when meeting someone online and not fall for words you love from a man you don't know. When you get lured by the thrill of this "wonderful" guy of your dreams, potential problems and pain down the road can be much worse than getting sucked in by a jerk in person. The online fantasy can go on for as long as you let it. You can get so carried away that you're sure you can relocate from your great Manhattan apartment to a cabin in Wyoming or give up you dream job in London for a small Detroit studio with a guy you never met. A picture is one-dimensional and doesn't tell much. Even a short in-person meeting won't allow you to really know someone. Sara learned the hard way, explaining:

Aiden responded to my profile on a dating website, though he's in LA and I'm in Baltimore. I looked forward to his e-mails. Our "relationship" escalated to phone calls and we spent days sharing feelings. By the third month I was hooked. Aiden was my Prince Charming and I wanted my fantasy to happen! He had a layover here on a business trip and we spent three romantic hours together. When he asked me to move to the West Coast, my friends thought I was crazy. But I was sure I'd found "the one" and quit the job I'd worked hard to get and went.

It's hard to explain that first moment when I felt like I was with a stranger. After eight months of intimate conversations, I thought we knew each other well. But as I unpacked, I began to question what I was doing. Real life was different from our fantasy world. I knew Aiden's philosophies but didn't know *him*. It got awkward quickly and I learned he had a bad temper and no patience for how hard it was for me to adjust. I headed home a month later.

I must emphasize this: No matter how much you share by e-mail, no matter how sincere he sounds, no matter how sure you are that you've found Prince Charming, no matter what he says:

- ALL CYBER-MEN ARE JERKS UNTIL PROVEN OTHERWISE— in person over a long period of time.
- It's almost impossible to build a relationship with someone you only know from the Internet.

I'm not saying you can't meet great guys online. I have; you can too. But you need to be more vigilant than in person. Even if you talk on the phone, or via Skype, you still can't know who he really is until you spend lots of time with him, meet some of his friends, and experience real life with him. Jerks can make themselves sound delicious electronically. Proceed carefully!

Unfair Expectations

I once heard a colleague lecture about online dating. She emphasized that people tend to lie in their profiles, ads, or their response to one. It's true—and it's universal. Both sexes take liberties. People use *very* old photos. Men often add inches to their height as if you won't notice in person. Women minimize their weight. She advised lowering your age five years and your weight, 10 pounds if necessary, in your profile since "it's expected." I was surprised to hear a therapist encouraging people to lie since "everyone does it." But that's why it's imperative to be wary of getting your hopes up about someone you don't know. No matter how many times you speak, he's still a guy you may not like in real life. Britney's online romance crashed and burned in person:

> Jared responded to my online dating profile and I thought I'd found the perfect man. We shared a lot in e-mails and talked on the phone for hours. He called often. Each time I asked to meet, though, he had an excuse. I kept pushing and we finally did. After all the intimacy we'd shared, he was a stranger in person. We just stared at each other. I think there was mutual embarrassment about sharing so many personal details and expressing deep feelings for each other. Awkward! It was our last date. So much for getting to know a guy without meeting him.

While men don't share personal feelings nearly as much as we'd like them too, many are much more open online since it feels safer. Sharing personal stuff more than you do in person escalates your cyber-relationship faster. It can feel lovely to hear details from this cyber-man but it creates a false bond—closeness based on just words. Some women refer to cyber-man as their boyfriends or soulmates. My response is usually "ridiculous!" A boyfriend/soulmate relationship is built from in-person interactions over a long period of time. Yours and his online personas might not hold up in person, as Diane learned:

> I have a sexy phone voice. Nick fell for me hard when we spoke. I told him not to judge me by my voice, which makes me sound much younger than I am. Nick insisted it was me that mattered. We talked several times a day before meeting a week later. By then Nick was excited beyond belief about it. He'd fallen hard for me. But from the moment we met, I saw disappointment. It was excruciatingly uncomfortable. Nick had created a fantasy that I couldn't live up to. We began a stiff conversation. Suddenly he screamed—"You're a fraud! You look ten years older than you said and I can't look at you." He stormed out, leaving me embarrassed as I skulked out. I haven't done Internet dating since.

Communicating electronically can create fantasies that most can't live up to. It's much easier to open up without the person being there than face-to-face. The Internet brings down people's walls but you do have to eventually meet. That's where fantasies can end. If you're fine with a fairy-tale electronic guy, indulge in e-mail and phone intimacy. But if you want a real-life relationship, don't get sucked in by a cyber-man. No matter what he *says*, you can't really know him from cyber-communication. Be extra vigilant about not getting carried away until you get to know him for a long time—in person!

Technology Disconnect

I already addressed how men communicate differently from women and many don't like speaking on the phone, and that's okay. But, technology makes it too easy for guys to disconnect from the kind of personal contact we crave by limiting it to texts or e-mails. Some of that is fine. It's your guy's right, to a degree. And you might be fine with just electronic communication in between personal contact. Many women, especially young ones, prefer to text or e-mail too. But if you've made it clear you want to speak occasionally, and he ignores you, you only have two choices:

1. Learn to live with it.

2. Move on if it's not what you want since nagging won't change him.

You have a right to ask for phone calls, no matter what he says. Electronic communication disconnects you somewhat and isn't as satisfying as verbal interactions. That's why many of us still want to speak. If you see him many times a week, cut him some slack. But if you just see him on the weekend or less, asking to speak on the phone is not unreasonable, as long as you don't try to hold him hostage for longer than he's comfortable with. Many men resort to electronic communication because it's short and sweet. That's what they like.

And speaking of short and sweet, keep electronic communication that way. Don't tell him every detail of life in an e-mail or text him constantly just to connect. And don't take it personally if he sends short, abrupt messages. That's what men do, so it's unnecessary to read anything into it and think it means he's not that into you. Electronic communication can get misconstrued, so be careful what you say and interpret.

He's not a jerk for not calling, but you should ask for a compromise about communication. Nagging probably won't work. Using the communications skills I shared earlier, nicely explain why it means a lot for him to call in between texts and e-mails. If he says it's stupid or he doesn't want to do it, calmly explain that you want to be with a man who respects your needs, just as you're trying to respect his. Ask if he can he please try because it means a lot to you. If he refuses, it's your choice to stay with a guy who wants it all his way.

> **WARNING:**
> Never, ever, ever send a photo of you naked or in a position that's very personal or a very overt sexual message to *any* guy, even if you're in a committed relationship with him. Anything you say can be used against you in the future, so be careful. Things change, fights happen, and the baggage gets out on the Internet. You might do it for fun to entice him, but it can get sticky if others see it after you break up. Of course, you like to think you'll never break up . . . but it happens. DO NOT RISK IT!

Protecting Yourself from Cyber-Jerks

Be much more vigilant about how you get to know someone online and control yourself against falling for an electronic image. After getting a message from a guy with potential, I ask for his phone number. If he insists on getting to know me better through e-mail or messaging, I refuse. Talking on the phone tells me much more. If the call goes well, I suggest meeting, and refuse to continue building a fantasy with more phone calls. I'm busy and don't want to waste time writing or talking to a guy who may not work out. Many people drag it out, feeding the fantasy instead of meeting in person to see if anything real is there.

Coffee shops are the best place to meet. Don't plan a long evening or day. Just go for a cup of coffee and if you hit it off, have another date soon. I've met for coffee, liked the guy and he liked me, and agreed to continue the evening with dinner. That's fine. But you shouldn't commit to a full date until you've met and are both interested in getting to know each other better. Before meeting, be especially careful to watch for these signs that something might be awry. For example, if he:

- Gets very intense quickly. Just like in person, guys who jump in quickly will also leave quickly. People don't fall in real love fast from just words or calls. Until you meet, you fall for a fantasy, and fantasies aren't real.
- Talks more about his feelings for you than about his life. All that just stirs the fantasy. Don't talk intimately when you don't get to know who he is for real.
- Makes sexual innuendos fast. That's unacceptable in my view! Until you know each other in person, it's the fantasy that turns him on, not you.
- Stalls about meeting in person. Some men just enjoy the online game. He may not want to meet. Hiding behind a computer or a phone allows him to be the man of your dreams. He may disappear if you push (which you should do anyway!).
- Says the kind of things I've already warned you about. Cyberjerks take compliments and promises up several notches. Don't buy them until you spend lots of face-to-face time together.
- Sounds too perfect to be real. In this case, he probably isn't. Perfect is easy to create online but doesn't transfer to real life.

When you begin communicating with someone online and start to fall for what he says, remind yourself, "All cyber-men are jerks until proven otherwise" with more conviction than for a man in person. Add, "I don't know him!" to remind yourself it's not real until you get to know each other in real life. For months you may think you're writing to your thirty-year-old, tall, fit, handsome "Prince Charming" who's actually sixty, balding, short, fat, and unattractive, using your correspondence to get his rocks off. There are many good men online and you can weed out jerks if you go slowly and give him lots of time to prove he's a good guy.

PART TWO

SEX AND THE SINGLE JERK

Chapter Eight

Thinking with the Wrong Side of His Brain

"You mustn't force sex to do the work of love or love to do the work of sex."

MARY MCCARTHY

COMPLAINT

Why do men think about sex all the time?

Men can be total jerks when it comes to sex. Testosterone, which is known to be responsible for everyone's sex drive, is much higher in men than in women. Men often physically crave sex more often than women do. If sexual gratification is their goal, they may say what you want to hear and treat you how you want to be treated. When they've gotten what they want, they may move on without looking back. Some men act totally different in and out of bed. They'll truly enjoy giving you pleasure but forget about you after sex is over. The bottom line is that too many men think with the wrong part of their body.

Men can be two-headed monsters, depending on whether their head or their penis is guiding them. They can get into you fast if you let them, and be gone just as quickly, when their upper head takes over. If you let them get you into bed with a hot intro, you'd better be prepared to see a cool exit.

My Erection Made Me Do It!

When men feel the need to be satisfied, they might think about just that one thing. Women can't always relate to this. Yes, we get horny too. And this horniness can drive us up the wall sometimes. I'm sure many of you get as horny as any man—but you don't get erections. Try as you might, you can never put yourself in a man's shoes, or should I say pants, to understand what it feels like to have this visible proof of your sexual need/desire. It can be more difficult to deal with. Brett admitted in a class:

> I can't control when I get turned on. Sometimes when I see a peek of cleavage, great legs, or a zillion other things, I get an erection. There's nothing I can do about it. Most of the time it goes away by itself. But sometimes I stay turned on for a while. Women don't understand what a pain it can be. So yeah . . . I want to get relief when it gets bad. If God didn't want us to have sex, he wouldn't have given us erections. If I meet a woman and charm her enough, we have sex and I'm satisfied. I have no patience for romance. That's what I use to get women into bed. When it's over, romance isn't necessary. What's the big deal?

Many of the men agreed, saying sweet-talking/romance/compliments were a good prelude to sex. They also discussed how difficult it can be when they get horny and have regular erections that don't get relieved. Gregory added:

> Sometimes a situation or visual turns me on. It could be a woman, a scene in a movie, a new fantasy, whatever. I think about it all day . . . and get an erection each time. I can't stop them. I try to think about other things, but it doesn't always help. The vision returns . . . and the erection. It makes me very horny, so I want to be with a woman. It's a physical thing . . . caused by the mental. I don't know why. If I have the opportunity, I'll be on my best behavior to score. Screwing a woman is the best relief. So why not give them what they want. They want a perfect man, they've got it . . . but that can't last all night.

Hard Body, Soft Brain

A man's sexuality is often held in high esteem. His private parts at times have almost been immortalized. Men have "family jewels" while we have "down there." A person displaying courage is said to have balls. I don't hear such glowing metaphors for female genitals. Society has made it much more acceptable for a man to flaunt his sexuality. Women are supposed to be more ladylike, more subtle. Men wear their sexuality like a badge of honor. Women whisper about it to their friends. It's considered normal for a man to have a strong desire for sex. Only in recent years has there been more openness about a woman's needs. When a man flaunts his sexual libido, it's considered macho, a very positive statement. When a woman expresses hers, she may be looked upon as a slut, or something else negative. By almost idealizing men's sexual exploits, they feel encouraged to sometimes let their penises be their guide. And women wonder why they meet so many men preoccupied by their sexual needs.

The brain is the center of our intelligence system. We usually use it to make intelligent choices. So when men think with their penises, it's not going to be the most rational decision. The best way to deal with a man's sexuality is to understand it from the beginning and approach him with your eyes open. Try not to be too judgmental. If men can go in the direction their penises point them and get away with it, why not? There's not necessarily anything wrong with him if he thinks along sexual lines, as long as he treats you fairly. But it's always your choice to decide whether to sleep with him or not. Remembering that "All men are jerks until proven otherwise" can help you decide to get to know him much better out of bed, before having sex.

COMPLAINT

Why don't men take their actions in bed seriously?

"But He Was So Loving in Bed"

Men and women often make love to each other for different reasons. Someone once told me that men make love with their penises and women make love with their hearts. I think in many cases this is true. Men may want to make love more for the physical gratification, while women may be looking to satisfy their emotional needs. We want to be held, loved, touched tenderly. We love the kisses, the caresses, the sweet words. Men love the act of sex. While you may be thinking how wonderful it is to make love to him, he may be reveling in the pleasures of "getting some," "getting laid," "screwing," etc. When it's finished, men often switch gears, while women want to continue the romantic mood. Marvin said:

I love sex and love finding a woman who loves sex. It doesn't have to be someone I want a serious relationship with. I wish women would treat sex more casually and enjoy it for the great feelings it can give. Sex can be so much fun, but women spoil it when they get all heavy afterwards. My advice to women? Relax and enjoy it. Stop thinking so much.

How can you tell what a man is thinking? Give yourself plenty of time to get to know him *out* of bed first. I recommend not having sex with a man until you know him well, unless you just want physical gratification. The longer you wait, the better the chance that he's with you because he likes you as a person and not just because he's horny. All men are jerks until proven otherwise. Give him some time to prove otherwise!

While men are thinking about the physical release of sex, you may be thinking way beyond that. This isn't true of all men, nor of all women. And I emphasize that men having a different perspective than you have about sex doesn't make them wrong, bad or a jerk. Please accept this. They have a right to different needs, whether you like it or not. Many men have wonderful intentions, whether you see them or not.

Based on the response of men I've interviewed, I believe that no matter how much a man wants to make love to a woman because he likes her, the act is often less emotional for him than for her. Flo was very disappointed when she told a support group:

Bob and I made love Saturday night. He was so loving and caring while we were doing it. It was wonderful. But what a let-down when, right after we were finished, he got up and made himself a sandwich. I wanted to hold him for a while and enjoy the afterglow of lovemaking. I asked him to come back. He said he didn't feel like it and didn't understand at all. I don't either. How can the jerk switch moods so quickly?

While men give sex itself more importance, you may have over-blown romantic expectations. When you attach high hopes to sex, you often set yourself up for disappointment or heartache. We romanticize the intimacy of the act and hold it in high esteem. Ideally, sex is special and should be treated that way. Ideally, it should be done with someone you care about, who you want to enjoy mutual pleasure with. It would be ideal if everyone felt this way, and would make your emotional lives easier.

Unfortunately, life isn't ideal. But you want ideal. As I said earlier, you see how beautiful it is in the romance novels. You drool over the romantic lead in the movies. But this sort of romance isn't reality so you want make-believe. You crave the man who loves you passionately, that wonderfully attentive man who does everything right to satisfy your every physical and emotional need, with little thought to his own. Don't hold your breath—those men don't really exist. And I'm sure the off-screen partners of the delicious actors making love so tenderly in the movies have as many complaints as you do.

Giving You What You Want— But Only Momentarily

Men know what women want and try to give it to us, when they can. But we take it too seriously, which can get us into trouble. Sometimes they lay it on real thick in an effort to be what you want them to be at that moment. But if it's not real, it hurts afterward. You don't understand how a man can treat you so lovingly and tenderly if he doesn't have strong feelings. I actually tell the men in my classes to ease up on the tenderness and sweet talk in bed if they're not sure how they feel about the woman, to make it easier on her if the liaison ends after sex.

Get out of the habit of giving much credence to what a man says or does in the heat of passion, especially one you haven't known very long.

He cannot be held accountable for his thoughts just before or during an orgasm. Ben explained to me, "I can't control what comes out of my mouth during sex. I've said many things that I meant at the moment, sort of, that I didn't mean afterward. When sex is over, so are those feelings." Men continuously assure me that most of the time they don't mean to deceive their lover. Words they don't mean aren't necessarily said consciously. Ben continued, "They just come out, like moaning. I can't control my thoughts or words when I'm overwhelmed by sex." Shem told me:

I've gotten myself into trouble a few times by saying things I don't mean when I'm enjoying a sexual encounter. When the sex is feeling incredible, I get carried away. For that moment, I love the partner I'm with. I've actually told a girlfriend I wanted to marry her because I was so into her at that moment. It ruined our relationship when I had to take back the words I'd said during an intense orgasm. Why do women take it so seriously? Why can't they understand we can't be held accountable during sex?

In my classes, men have consistently admitted to saying, "I love you" at least once accidentally. Many wish they could control it. Victor was embarrassed to tell us:

I tell most of my girlfriends I love them when I'm about to come. I must love them for bringing me to that point. But I don't love them the way they want me to. I can't believe how they throw those words said in passion in my face later on. Why do women take it so seriously? Don't they know we're not responsible during that time? They can't expect to hold us to those words. It's not fair.

Why argue with a man who goes back on what he says in bed? I'm blown away by how many women in my classes try to find ways to hold a man to his promises and words during sex. You don't really want to force those feelings. You can't hold onto promises or "I love you's" said because he got carried away. If he really does love you, he'll say it out of bed too. Remembering that all men are jerks until proven otherwise helps you not take the words seriously. As long as you don't take them seriously, you can at least have fun making him squirm once it's over, if he wonders how far you'll take his words.

Women ask me all the time: "How can a man seem so into me in bed and then disappear/change/become cool/lose interest?" Men *are* into you when sex is going on, but it's not always for the reasons you'd like to believe. For him, it may be for the moment. For you, it may be thoughts of long-term romance. It's just as unfair for you to have long-term expectations at the beginning as it is for him not to call after sex. Men's and women's needs are definitely unbalanced. Larry admitted:

> I love sex. Of course I don't want to just go to bed with any-one. But I don't need to be in love, and it doesn't have to be a relationship with major potential. If I'm with a woman who I find attractive and whose company I enjoy, I'd have sex with her in a minute. I need regular releases, and it's more fun with a woman than alone. I don't think I'm unfair. That's the way men are.

Men seem surprised when I tell them how seriously many women take them. During sex he might be thinking, "This sex is great. I'm enjoying it," as he strokes your face and tells you how great it is. And you're thinking how great it is to make love to him. The difference is that men tend to focus more on the *act*, while you focus on the *man*. You make too much of every touch, sweet word, or expression of plea-sure. You assume his feelings for you are responsible for it, yet he's simply enjoying the sex. Did you ever wonder why sex is sometimes referred to as the *act* of making love? Start thinking.

Chapter Nine

Double Standards

"The difference between sex and love is that sex relieves tension and love causes it."

WOODY ALLEN

COMPLAINT

Men don't always call after they have sex with me.

I've heard many women complain they've felt used sexually at least once by men who misled them. What happens? You to go to bed quickly with a man you click with in order to satisfy your sexual needs or his, and then you don't hear from him again. Then you experience regret, doubt, guilt, and confusion.

There's still a terrible double standard when it comes to sex. Men consistently say that when a woman goes to bed with them on the first date, or even on the second and third, they automatically wonder about her. Some assume she's an out-and-out slut, or they have it in the back of their minds that she may do this with others. It's an ego thing. Men like believing you're having sex with them because they're special, not because they're available. If you sleep with them before allowing time to get the full gist of how wonderful they are, they may assume it's casual for you and wonder how many others you've slept with as quickly. Susan told me:

Bruce and I had an instant chemistry. He was very romantic on our first date. We started at the museum in the afternoon. Then we had dinner and were so into each other. We took a long walk after and then had coffee. By the time we returned to my place, it felt like we'd had three or four dates. We made out for a while and got aroused. I thought it was too soon to have sex, but Bruce told me how special it was between us. He reminded me we'd been together for many hours. I broke down and we made love. It was wonderful.

When he left, he promised to call soon. After three weeks I called him to ask why he hadn't called. After beating around the bush, he finally admitted concern that I'd gone to bed with him so fast. Yet he did it too! I thought those double standards were a thing of the past.

Beware, ladies: Many men I interviewed said when they truly like and respect a woman, they often don't make moves too soon. Going to bed quickly is considered a "man thing" by many. It's terribly unfair, but many men think nice girls still don't do that! Don't think for a minute that sleeping with a guy will make him want you more. Fair or not, you have a better chance at a relationship if you hold sex over his head like a prize he has to earn. Richie explained:

Jen was a woman I could have gotten into big-time. She was pretty and very sexy. We had fun when we first met. When we went out for dinner, there was chemistry between us all night. When we got back to her place, we ended up in bed. The next morning I felt uncomfortable. I know it was unfair, but she was just too easy. I couldn't see her again, though I liked her a lot. How can I explain it? I want someone who doesn't give it away. Is that a double standard? I guess it is, but that's the way I am. Women should understand a man will always make the attempt. It's up to her to keep things in check.

Men want sex, but don't necessarily feel it should come too soon. This situation is approach/avoidance. Their sex drives push the moves, but their head and heart may reject the woman who gives in too soon. No matter what your needs, if he's pushing you to go to bed, try to keep your legs crossed and say to yourself, "All men are jerks until proven otherwise," unless it won't bother you if he doesn't call afterward. If you don't want to go to bed with a jerk, wait until he's proven otherwise, at least a little, no matter how much your hormones are raging!

Raging Hormones

When you don't know a potential partner well, going to bed with him can set you up for disappointment. You come home with stories about how sweet and tender he was, revel in the memory of his touch, and get carried away. Then he disappears. As Debbie in my group said:

I met Donald through a personal ad. We talked for hours on several nights before we met. He seemed to have all the qualities I wanted in a man. I fell for him on the phone. When we met, the chemistry was there. He was very romantic. When saying goodbye, we kissed for a long time. Then he asked me over the next night for dinner. It was a perfect evening. I stayed the night, and we made love. In the morning he made break-fast and waited on me hand and foot. When I left, he promised to call but never did. I tried several times but got hemming and hawing. I finally left it alone, realizing too late that I hadn't known Donald at all when I went to bed with him.

This wasn't the end of Donald. Months later, he called Debbie, all sweet again, wanting to see her right away. She'd been in the support group for a while and was better equipped for dealing with it. Instead of jumping right back in, she took her time and waited to see where he was coming from:

> Donald said he'd felt bad about how things ended with us and invited me over. This time I said "All men are jerks until proven otherwise" to myself. Normally I'd have given him a second chance immediately because I had enjoyed the passion between us. Instead, I told him I'd think about it. I left him a message a few days later, but he didn't get back to me.
>
> After two weeks, I called and got Donald. I wanted to know why he'd done that. He said he'd been feeling horny when he'd called, but since I hadn't been available at that moment, he lost interest right away. "All men are jerks until proven other-wise." Donald never proved otherwise. Good riddance to him!

When the chemistry seems there but he hasn't yet earned your trust, keep in mind that chemistry isn't everything. When your horn-iness motivates you to see only the good in a man, get a vibrator. Do what you have to do to keep your eyes open and yourself out of his bed until he's earned your trust. The good stuff they give in that very intimate way can make you lose your good judgment. Make him want you so much that you're in control instead. Then you can work on getting *all* of your needs satisfied.

Poor Little Scaredy-Jerks

Some men get scared after they've had sex with a woman, no matter how long you wait. They've told me they feel vulnerable. Perhaps it's the intimacy. Perhaps great sex increases the attraction and that makes them uncomfortable. Perhaps they're afraid, heaven forbid, that they'll want to see you more because they enjoy the sex. Who knows? Men don't seem to. They give evasive answers about exactly what makes them stop calling after a wonderful night in bed. Andy told me:

> When I'm with a woman I like, I'm always anxious to get her into bed. But sometimes when it's been very good, I get nervous afterwards . . . I may feel too close to her . . . I don't know what she'll expect of me. I'm not ready for commitment with anyone yet, and women seem to want more from guys once they sleep with them. One woman acted like she owned me after sex. She became possessive. So when I see a woman looking at me all lovey-dovey after sex, I panic. Then I may have to stop seeing her. I don't know how else to get her to slow down.

Sometimes people open up more during sex. Women are usually thrilled when this happens. We'll take any show of enthusiasm and intimacy. Men don't always like us to see their more vulnerable side. Or they may see something that scares them. Molly told my support group about Bill. They'd been dating steadily and got intimate. It was going well when she invited Bill for dinner:

> I'm very independent and had been pretty distant with Bill up until then, even in bed. But that night was special. He was very romantic, and I let go a bit. I enjoyed the intimacy between us so much. We both love crossword puzzles, and after dinner we did some together in bed. I was excited about that. I even returned some of his affection.

When Bill called a few days later, he was distant. We talked a while, but he didn't ask to see me again. After two more of these calls, I asked him why. I was shocked when he said I'd seemed clingy that night and it scared him. I reminded him that the affection he gave me was still about ten times as much as what I gave him. He said I seemed nervous because I was giggling a lot. I told him that was from having fun and from the bottle of wine we'd finished—nothing more. I couldn't believe I had to reassure him.

What a nerve! He was always smothering me, but I didn't get on his case. Poor baby was scared of a terrible, affectionate, happy woman. He's bye-bye.

Men can be brave when it comes to killing bugs, chasing a burglar, and millions of other manly things. But these usually brave souls can lose their nerve with women. I once dated a guy who tried to get me to his place after our first date. Something special was happening between us all evening. We had to sit in the car for some time to wait out a sudden rainstorm, and he got amorous. I liked him a lot but was uncomfortable getting too intimate. I gently kept pushing him away. He kept trying to convince me to go back to his place to make love, telling me it wouldn't change things between us. I refused.

The next day he admitted he did have a double standard and would have thought me a slut had I gone. He wanted to get to know me slowly but acknowledged being frightened of the passion he felt. Unfortunately, he felt he was so uncomfortable with declaring his desire for me that he couldn't go back. He felt vulnerable.

Things deteriorated quickly. It was ridiculous because I had asked nothing of him. I always felt bad that he was such a chicken because there was something very nice between us. Feeling vulnerable was his own creation.

Vulnerable. What does it mean? It could be that men don't like you knowing they have feelings. Sex can make them emotional. It could mean that they actually need you for something specific for a change.

Men don't want to be needy—it's very unmanly. They can get a maid or go out for dinner with friends, etc., but it's hard to replace a good sexual partner. So they run away before it gets too good. Oscar admitted:

> I was very attracted to Sybil. We got along in so many ways. Making love was like heaven. Only I didn't want to be in heaven. I'm exceptionally busy and wasn't ready to be too close to a woman. I admit, I panicked. The better it got, the more I pulled away. I didn't want to want her so much.

Men's feelings may show more during sex. When you make love, you trust that person to let go, if only for a minute. Your guard goes down. Men usually try to maintain the upper hand, but when he needs his sexual release, he also loses control.

Vulnerability: It's something you face all the time as you search for that one man who's not a jerk. You're more used to putting yourself on the line to be hurt. Men aren't so conditioned. *Vulnerable.* So they do have feelings after all!

COMPLAINT

Men can be so heartless when it comes to sex.

You must understand some basic facts about the differences in the way men and women think about sex. You know men and women are quite different emotionally (see Chapter Sixteen). While men do have emotional needs, many have been taught to suppress them. Women have always been encouraged to express them. Very unbalanced, don't you think? Men may go into a relationship more focused on the pleasure of the moment, whereas women have their hearts primed for something special.

Sex and the Fragile Male Ego

Men are achievement-oriented, seeing themselves more in terms of their successes. Taking a woman to bed may be an affirmation of one's manhood, an achievement of sorts, as unpleasant as that sounds to the "object of his desire" (another term to ponder). When you have sex, your concern may be more about feeling that you're attracting a man. Both sexes get an ego boost in bed. The trouble is that many men think of it as a short-range achievement, while you may play for keeps. You often want longevity after you sleep with a man. Again, it becomes more emotional for women. Men are more concerned with knowing they've gotten someone into bed to get their immediate needs satisfied. Though a majority of men prefer a connection with the women they sleep with, it may not be as relevant to them as it is to you. Phil said:

> Men do have to prove something to our egos. We want to know we can get women. It's always nice to be with a special one, but if she's not available, we'll sometimes go with someone who is. I don't keep count of every woman I sleep with, but I like knowing there have been a number of them.

Men can separate sex from love, and when you get down to it, there's nothing wrong with that. Sex with love can be the best there is, but sex without it can be satisfying too. Sex is a physical hunger that many need satisfied, apart from any emotional need. If you want the emotional too, give yourself ample time to see if something special is there before going to bed with a man. Most men who are just looking for the physical won't hang around indefinitely waiting for you to give in. See who stands the test of time. Rashida told my class:

> I met Derrick at a party. We started dating and seemed to get very into each other. He pushed to go to bed with me from the first date. I wanted to give it some time. Derrick agreed

to be patient but kept pressing. We had great times when we were out. Our connection on all levels was intense. But after the fifth date, he increased the pressure for sex. I refused. He never called me again. Maybe I should have slept with him. Or maybe it was better to see what was most important to him.

Some men turn to sex to make themselves feel better when their lives aren't going well. Graham explained, "Men can be pigs. We can't help it. When we're feeling down about ourselves, we may turn to a woman for a boost." Sex can be a terrific self-esteem pick-me-up when nothing is going right. If someone just dumped them, men can validate their desirability by getting another woman to have sex with. If their job isn't going well, doing a job on a woman might perk up their egos. When men feel down about themselves, they can validate their manhood by getting laid. Not all men think like this, but many do, at least once in their lives. That's just the way it is.

Never forget, even during the heat of torrid passion, even while experiencing excruciating tenderness, even when you're hearing ear-titillating "sweet nothings" (another term to ponder), and even with all the other wonderful motions of the moment, "All men are jerks until proven otherwise!" Don't take what goes on in bed seriously. Expect not to hear from him. Expect nothing until something is really there. When there is, you can relax and enjoy it on your terms, not his.

Chapter Ten

Nice Girls Can Be Sexual

"In my sex fantasy, nobody ever loves me for my mind."

NORA EPHRON

COMPLAINT

Why shouldn't women love sex as much as men do?

Although women may hesitate to admit it, many of us love sex for more than just the emotional gratification. Our reluctance to acknowledge this basic natural pleasure is related to messages that taught us it's unladylike to enjoy sex too much. Men who are judgmental or intimidated by women who aren't demure in bed can add to our reticence. When I was growing up, sex was only discussed in the street, where nothing was accurate. The rule of thumb for females was to go to bed only after you were married and tolerate the icky parts of sex to satisfy him. In exchange, we'd hopefully be kissed and cuddled: Then our needs could be met too. We were never told the twain were supposed to meet. Some women learned to enjoy sex right away, despite the naughty implications. Other women took a long time to wake up and see that sex can be wonderful for a woman too. A large number haven't quite found that out yet.

As a teenager, I read that the best kind of woman is a lady in the parlor and a whore in the bedroom. It sounded good to me, though I was still too young to completely understand. Now I do, and I think this combination can be the most fun in a relationship. You can be more creative than men and bring the potential for new dimensions into the bedroom, when men can accept it. But not all men can handle being with a woman who truly wants to let go in bed, nor can they understand that even though you're enthusiastic about sex, you're not a slut. Most women are much more selective about who we have sex with and don't sleep around nearly as much as men do, even if we're just as horny.

Let's get something straight here. It's not just okay for women to love and crave sex. It's absolutely, positively normal, healthy, and terrific for you to love and crave sex. I used to feel uncomfortable with my sexuality, until I talked with more and more women who love sex too. We're just coming into our own and understanding that it's acceptable to explore our sexuality. Thank God for Nancy Friday's books on sexual fantasies. They've helped so many women understand that it's normal to get those hot thoughts, those wicked ideas, those desires to masturbate and have multiple orgasms. By reading about other women's sexual odysseys, you can feel more comfortable developing your own.

If anyone reading this feels embarrassed, dirty, or uncomfortable about feeling sexual, please try to relax. No matter what anyone tells you and no matter how guilty you're made to feel by someone's ignorance, you're supposed to enjoy sex. So—relax and enjoy. I acknowledge that when we do like sex, it's better to expose a man to that fact in small doses at the beginning, for his sake.

Madonna Ain't What She Used to Be

Men lust after sexual women. They fantasize about a woman taking the sexual initiative and being insatiable. They fantasize about a woman talking dirty, wearing a garter belt and stockings, and knowing all the right moves. But in reality, on an emotional level, many men can't handle these qualities in a woman they're involved with. It's an incredible double standard, but some men have a problem having a committed relationship with a sexual woman.

Attitudes are more enlightened these days, but women are still hampered by what's referred to as the madonna/whore syndrome. Men don't know what they want. Ideally, they want a woman who'll be hot, sexy, enthusiastic, and insatiable. But, they also want to feel their partner is pure, sweet, and innocent. So they crave all the sexual qualities, while wanting a woman who seems relatively pure. Yet many men can't see a sexual woman as pure. They don't understand that just because you're enthusiastic about sex, you won't sleep around as a man might because of that enthusiasm. So, sexual women sometimes feel a need to put a lid on it. You learn to manipulate men to think that many of the things you do in bed are their ideas, or you stifle your sexuality.

I asked Steven to explain a man's position to me. He said:

> When a man finds a special woman, he wants to feel like he's her first real good sex. I know it's not right, but it's our egos. We want to be the one who opens up this beautiful flower. An inexperienced woman makes us feel more like we're her first real lover. It makes us feel more special. Although we love sexual women, they remind us more clearly there were men before us.

Some men love the combination of the madonna and the whore, but it intimidates others. Younger men seem to be more accepting of a sexual woman. It's not fair, but men can't help the way they were conditioned. Sexual women in the movies and on TV are often characters who fit negative stereotypes: a bitch, a domineering temptress, etc. When you think of *Sex and the City*, it's Samantha who's remembered for being sexual and she really slept around! The other women liked sex but seemed more demure about it. The bad girl may be the primary image men have of a sexual woman. Pay attention to what's out there. Do you see nice girls being portrayed as very sexual? Do you hear nice girls talking about being sexual? Do mothers encourage their sons to find a nice, sexual wife?

So some men see a sexual woman as being desirable, but not as the "nice girl" they want a relationship with. It's a fine line to walk. You can't completely blame men. To some degree, we're all conditioned early on by the media and other outside influences. But the bottom line is, if you're not subtle about your sexuality, he may think you're loose. And if he thinks you're loose, he may be gone, if only emotionally. Alicia told me:

> Alex and I had an active sex life. As I got comfortable with him, I opened up more. I eventually started initiating sex and tried some new things on him. One day Alex asked me how many lovers I'd had before him. He asked many other questions too. He wanted to know where I'd gotten so much experience. I thought he'd like the excitement, but he seemed very uncomfortable with it. He said he wanted it to be special with us. I told him it was. He said it didn't feel special for him if I'd already done everything with someone else.
>
> Why is it okay for men to have sex as a physical outlet, but women must save that for one man? We're still together, but things haven't been the same and I'm too self-conscious to let go anymore, so sex isn't as much fun.

Here are double standards in your face again. Men can be ignorant jerks when it comes to your sexuality. So, how do we sexual women stay true to ourselves in bed, without alienating HIM? First, you should never give it all away at the beginning. It's better to get to know a man before opening up too much, both in and out of bed. Being overly assertive at the onset of sex may turn him off, even though a part of him would love it. I've seen surveys that reveal that a majority of men would love to be seduced by a woman. Yes, men would love that on one level: It builds their egos and fulfills their fantasies. But those fantasies aren't always about a woman they want a relationship with. In reality, they still want control, especially in the beginning.

Those darn egos! We're ruled by our needs, and men are ruled by their egos. What a mess both sexes can get into! When you finally step away from your need to please HIM and express your sexuality, his ego might be wounded. If you do something different, he wonders why. If you try something kinky, he wonders if you're bored. He needs to feel that he's a brilliant stud and what he does is all you need. Your initiative can threaten his masculinity. Elliot explained in a coed support group:

> I had been sexually involved with Dana for two months when she arrived at my place in a raincoat, dressed only in a garter belt and stockings underneath. At first I was turned on like crazy. She came in, and we had great sex. But afterwards, I began to wonder what made her do it. Did she find me dull? Didn't I turn her on enough? And where did she get her ideas from? Is this something she does with all boyfriends?
>
> She was annoyed by my questions, but I couldn't help it. On the one hand, it was very exciting. On the other hand, I felt inadequate. If I had initiated kinkier sex first, I'd have felt better. My doubts eventually killed our relationship. I couldn't help wondering what made her do what she did. Isn't that stupid? It was one of the best sexual encounters of my life, until after my orgasm. I don't know why I couldn't handle it.

Managing Men's Insecurities

Nowadays, men express concern that women who love sex may just want them for their bodies, as opposed to wanting them for who they are. A little role reversal seems to be happening: This used to be almost purely a woman's concern. Now, however, men want to be liked for themselves, for their stimulating company, for their witty sense of humor. They don't want to feel like sex machines. When they know we love sex, they may feel the pressure of being obligated to do it for you, instead of just when they want it. That's another reason men can be almost irrational about sexual women. John shared:

> When I'm seeing a woman who loves sex a lot, I feel more pressure to perform. Okay, it's my own edict. But that's the way it is. I assume she needs me to be better, go longer, and in general, be a sexual superman. So I try harder and then resent her. I've had women tell me they enjoy it as is. But the self-imposed pressure is always there. So then I stop caring about pleasing her in other areas. That's sick, isn't it? But I can't help it. I'm not used to women who get that enthusiastic about sex. It's what I want, yet I can't always handle it. I guess it's my upbringing, or maybe my need to be thought of as great in bed.

The trick with a man who is uncomfortable with too much sexuality is to go very slowly. Let him adjust. Remember, he can't help being ignorant, and he may just be insecure. Don't cut an attitude, because it won't get you satisfied. Hold back (I know that's hard, not to mention unfair) and encourage him to lead you at first. Start with less enthusiasm and let it build through him so that he'll feel responsible. Once you've "learned" from him, anything goes. He'll be happy now, loving the idea of having a "pure whore" of his own creation. Danny revealed:

> I'm never sure if I'm a good lover. I want to be. Men aren't born with skills. We bumble along until we think we get it right. I'm always insecure about what a woman thinks of me as a lover. When I'm with a woman who seems experienced or knows what she wants, I get nervous about what to do and what she'll think. A lot of men are much more insecure in bed than women think.

Some men think that when they're with a sexual woman they have to live up to a certain standard with them. They're afraid that a more uninhibited or experienced woman may find out they're not studs, and they take it personally when you suggest something new to try in bed. As I keep emphasizing, if you want to try something you learned before him, it's easier to initiate it slowly. I hate saying this, but it may be the best way to get him comfortable with new ideas. If you coyly act like you learned it from a book or on TV and let him lead, he may be more comfortable.

Whether you like it or not, it will take many men a long time before they get comfortable with sexual women. They can't help it. William admitted in a class:

> I used to get flustered with a woman who seemed very sexual. Maybe I was afraid I'd never be able to please her. I didn't know how to handle a woman who seemed to know what she wanted, or who took the initiative during sex. But I've had some good experiences lately with women who didn't take my awkwardness for rejection, and now I appreciate a sexually liberated woman. It took me getting to know several good women who were open-minded in bed to show me that it was okay.

And in that same class, Bernie advised the men:

> Develop friendships with women. When you can get to know a woman as a friend and see her as a sexual being too, it can help you understand that it's normal . . . no, good, for a woman to be sexually aware of herself and what she wants. It was very helpful to me to hear my female friends talking about sex.

Some men need to know it's all right for you to need sex and to initiate the act or method of stimulation. Many still don't understand that your being creative or assertive doesn't mean you're not happy with their moves. As more women get comfortable with their own sexuality, more men will accept that sexual women can be nice girls too! Give it time. But don't always worry about HIM at the expense of your own needs. When that happens, you need to accept he may not be right for you.

COMPLAINT

Why do men take advantage of my sexual drive?

Stay in Control of Your Own Sex Drive

Some women weaken for sex, and men take advantage of it. Women tell me that men have held sex over their heads. Sometimes you can get so carried away by your own sexual needs that you can be as bad as men (heaven forbid!). As Donna told my class:

> I was at Marc's house when I found out he'd cheated on me. We'd just made love. I told him it was over, and he held me, whispering "don't go." We talked, and he offered me the back rub he'd promised before I left. Here I was with a man I'd just told I didn't want to see anymore, and I rolled over for a rub. He knew I couldn't resist his hands.
>
> Of course the massage became more, and I actually made love to him after he'd told me he'd cheated on me. I had to get it one more time. I know he did it purposely to keep me there. What a jerk I was, succumbing to the jerk's sexual maneuvers.

If you want sex that way, go for it. But accept that if you become needy for his body, he may take advantage. Be prepared to deal with it. It's wonderful that so many women are learning to enjoy the fulfillment that only men owned until recently. But you can't get carried away to the other extreme—trading your good sense for an orgasm. I hear from too many women that they've been sexually hooked. Vicki admitted to my group:

> He was an excellent lover and he knew it . . . very loving. After getting me hooked on him sexually, he held sex over my head to get me to do things his way. At first I didn't mind, but I felt like he was a drug I couldn't do without. It's taken a lot of solace from my friends to get away from him.

You should never need someone too much on any level or sell yourself short for a passionate evening, even if he gives you many orgasms. I know, a good sexual partner can be hard to find, and you may be hesitant to risk losing him. It's hard letting go of a great lover, but I've learned there are other men who can provide satisfaction—or you can do it yourself. If you feel HE's the only one who can please you, he can become an addiction. Then you lose your power. His ability to give you orgasms controls your life. Cat related her story:

> I was a virgin when I got married. My husband took about five minutes for sex. I didn't know I was supposed to physically enjoy it. After fifteen years, I met Lenny. We became friends, and then I went to bed with him. Wow! I saw stars. I had my first orgasm with Lenny.
>
> After that, I couldn't get enough of him. I didn't care about cheating on my husband. It eventually killed my marriage. But I would have done anything to be with Lenny as much as possible. I don't even find him attractive. But I left my husband and am still living with this man who drives me crazy in bed. I would still do almost anything to keep him, and he knows it. After fifteen years with my husband, I'm terrified of never finding another man who can please me like Lenny.

No addiction is good for you. Some women get addicted to sex and take almost any line a man gives as an excuse to get it. Many men definitely are clueless when it comes to satisfying you, but you can't lose control with those who can. Too many women say they've hung onto a man who's no good for them out of fear of never finding someone else who can satisfy them as well. Once you give a man the power of needing him badly for sex, you lose control of the relationship. At that point, you may never be happy, except for those moments in bed.

Trading your self-esteem for great sex isn't worth it. That doesn't mean you have to give up a good lover. He may find you more attractive if you don't give in to his whims. By keeping the upper hand and not letting him know how much you need sex, you may keep a good lover on your terms. Then you can get what you need. You want to own your sexuality, not give it away.

Sometimes men you crave sexually don't just take you for granted. They use your desire for their skills in bed to manipulate you. If you've been with one man after another who only motivates you to fake enthusiasm, you're highly receptive to one who can push your sexual buttons effectively. Finding a man who can stimulate you to real pleasure, to intense satisfaction, can make you never want to let him go, at any cost. And good lovers know it. Theo told me:

> I'm excellent in bed, and I know it. I was taught well. It was worth the education because I know that most women I sleep with will want more. It puts me in a position of power, which I love. Once I've gotten them in bed, I call the shots. I get women who insist on taking me out. They make me dinner, clean my apartment, and let me get away with a lot in order to sleep with me.

I said he sounded like a glorified prostitute to me. Theo laughed and said he didn't care what he was labeled. He liked the position he was in. Too many women sell themselves short in bed. If you want to be happy in the long run, you can't let sex rule you.

Chapter Eleven

Female Performance Anxiety

"You know guys. They never want to stop and ask directions."

JAY LENO

COMPLAINT

Why are men so hung up on my having an orgasm?

What do men expect to hear when they ask "Did you come?" after a beautiful session of lovemaking? He just had his orgasm; he's just given you his all; he's done everything he can to please you. He's smiling—sure he's satisfied you, but wants a confirmation to top off his stupid ego. So what are you going to say if you didn't have an orgasm? Are you going to burst his bubble and ruin the moment? Probably not. There's a good chance you'll say "yes" to please him.

Now he's completely satiated, and you feel cheated because you had to lie or possibly deny yourself the chance to really have one.

A man's need for achievement may motivate him to be overly concerned about whether or not he's brought you to a climax. Whether you're satisfied or not isn't necessarily his issue. Women regularly complain that some men put more importance on giving them orgasms than on other things they ask for. In the past, men didn't care enough about our orgasms because they weren't as aware of them. Now you're supposed to be grateful that they've changed, but many women find that a man's desire to give them one can be counterproductive. Beverly explained in a support group:

> I've had lovers who threw me off from having an orgasm by asking me about it. Sometimes I'm just about there, and he'll say something like, "Are you almost there, because I am," or "How much longer do you need?" Why do they do that? Most of the time it just stops everything from happening. It's so unfair. Are they really concerned with me when they do that? I wonder.

When you're building up to an orgasm, it's nice to be able to lose yourself in the moment. You may fantasize or just revel in the delicious sensations your body is being treated to. Your thoughts may be variations of, "It feels good. I don't want these feelings to end. I'm getting closer." And then he breaks your reverie by asking, "Are you there yet?" In that second, all can be lost. Like sticking a pin in a balloon, you can get deflated very fast by a man's need to know. And you silently get angry.

Women have told me that their lovers have given so much importance to their climaxing that they felt threatened about being caught not having an orgasm. Not having one every time (or ever) can become a source of failure for you, making you scared of losing HIM. Men have actually left women who didn't always have orgasms from their stimulation. Too many women don't understand that you don't owe HIM an orgasm. And too many men put the pressure on you: If it doesn't happen, you're to blame or something is wrong with you. Shirley told a support group:

> Bert and I had a good relationship, except that I didn't have orgasms during sex. He always wanted to know if it happened. I told him that I loved sex with him and was completely satisfied afterwards, without an orgasm. I never had a chance to relax and possibly open up to him. He got so fed up at not being able to make me come, he couldn't enjoy sex. It killed our relationship. Now I fake it. I don't want to take the chance of having another man think there's something wrong with me. But I feel cheated and don't enjoy sex as much.

If you don't have orgasms with your partner, you might take it personally and think something is wrong with you. But a lot more of you than you'd think don't climax with a man. Often it's because you go along with him instead of guiding him. Or you may need more time than you feel comfortable asking for, so you don't ask, afraid that if he sees it takes a while, he may not want to be bothered. And it's true, jerks might blow off a woman because they feel inadequate if they don't accomplish their task. So women continue faking it, and men accept it. What does that make us? Frustrated women.

Over the last few years, I've given several hundred men of all ages questionnaires about sex, including the question "Can you tell if a woman is faking?" Over two-thirds of them said they couldn't tell. In answer to "How important to your pleasure is it whether your partner has an orgasm?" well over 50 percent answered "very important." I asked some of the men individually why the orgasm was so important to them. Here's a sample of the answers:

MARTY: We're supposed to give women orgasms.

IRA: I get upset if the woman I have sex with doesn't have an orgasm. I wonder if I'm inept. Is something wrong with her?

Maybe she doesn't like me. I always ask and am very disappointed if she doesn't say yes.

JAMES: Every time I feel a woman building to her orgasm, it turns me on like crazy . . . the moaning, the arching of her back . . . that all intensifies my own orgasm. What if the woman is faking? If she's doing that good a job, who cares?

A large number of the men were under the impression that if you don't come, you're not satisfied. Since an orgasm is what men need, they assume you need one too—every time—or you're not happy. But actually, many women can enjoy sex without one. Yet some men can't enjoy it unless they know you had one too, no matter what you tell them.

Performance Anxiety

We're now caught in a paradox. Men alone used to suffer from the pressure of expectation known as performance anxiety: Can I get an erection when she wants it? Can I last long enough? Can I get it up again? Am I big enough? It used to be simpler for women. All we did was lie back and take what men gave us. They never cared if we came. Now that they know we can have orgasms, there's more pressure. Many men have made it their job to give them to us. And we're supposed to have them all the time so that men can feel they've achieved their goal, proven their capabilities as men, fulfilled their responsibilities.

Okay, maybe at least a nice percentage of the time, their concern about giving you orgasms is for no other reason than to make you feel good. But many men aren't making you feel good *or* achieving their goal. Reaching an orgasm involves a lot of mental stimulation. You may take a long time to reach it, which is okay. Men will eventually understand that. But if you know a man is waiting for your orgasm to happen, it can keep you from having one. When he's waiting, almost impatiently, and you know he's anxious to hear the magic words "I'm coming," you get too self-conscious. Your pleasing nature may kick in, and you want to give him what he wants. You try too hard. You hope and pray. You wonder if there's something wrong with you. After all, men seem to come so easily. And some let you know that it never took their other lovers as long to reach an orgasm. Unfortunately, their other lovers could easily have been faking!

Men don't understand that we're physically different from them and have individual needs. If you rub a man's penis long enough, most likely he'll climax. We don't have a sex organ that's easily visible, one that responds to most any stimulation. A clitoris can be hard to find. Many women have trouble finding their own! Men can have difficulty comprehending that every woman needs to be stimulated a bit differently. Some like it hard; some like it gentle. And rather than tell him, you fake it, thinking he'll like you more if he thinks he's given you an orgasm.

There are men who assume that since they have an orgasm from sexual intercourse with no foreplay, their partner should too. They need to be educated, but you often don't want to risk turning him off. Marla told me:

> I moan and groan during sex. It's part of the act for me. No matter if he's good or not, I make noise because they love it! I rarely have orgasms . . . I'm too busy making him excited by thinking I'm having many. But that's the game. When I enjoy sex a lot, I actually get more quiet, which is ironic. But I keep it up for the guy's sake. He thinks he's the most macho stud as I lay it on thick.
>
> No one's ever questioned if it's real. They don't want to know. The ones I get very loud for are hilarious because they tell me how good we are together . . . for no other reason than I make a lot of noise. I want to get out of the habit so I can see what I actually do when I'm turned on.

Many women don't have problems climaxing and could care less if he asks about it because the answer is usually positive. More of you are becoming increasingly attuned to your bodies, and therefore can climax easily. But for those of you who experience female performance anxiety, gentle, supportive, yet specific communication is the key. You have to know yourself and your needs. It's important to accept that it's okay not to come on cue and that you have a right to let him know your needs. Only then can you communicate to him effectively.

My pat answer to "Did you come?" is, "When you ask with that type of expectation, I will always lie. I'd rather not lie, so please concern yourself with whether or not I'm satisfied or need more stimulation." They usually take it quite well because it's logical. When we're out of bed, I explain why I prefer that they don't ask. They get the point. Men aren't totally insensitive, but they can be a bit dense if they haven't been clued in. Many need an education about what satisfies you, and many need to detach *their* egos from *your* orgasms.

Some men manipulate us to satisfy their egos, and we allow them to. A man's ego needs to know that he's accomplished his task by giving you an orgasm. The need for approval, and to please him, leads some of us to fake orgasms to keep his ego intact. What might easily be rectified if he kept an open mind becomes a problem based on a combination of his ignorance and his ego. We're afraid to tell him we need it more or different or longer. And often he doesn't really quite want to know. This ignorance keeps him from feeling inadequate and unconcerned about learning the truth.

COMPLAINT

Can men ever learn to give me satisfaction?

Most of the men I interviewed who admitted that they can't tell if a woman is faking an orgasm said they did care about their partner really having one. Men aren't unfeeling creeps. They do care . . . but they don't. Sure, they'd like a woman to be truly satisfied, but many still don't want to go the distance to achieve that goal. Men complain they get tired before it happens and that stimulating you with their hand or mouth is a chore when it goes on for too long. Let's be fair: It gets tiring. How many of you would like to give a man oral sex for hours? It's the same difference, except that men don't need that lengthy pleasuring to climax the way we do. Ricky complained in a class:

> It's funny how women complain we don't do them long enough. Yet when a lady gives me a hand job, she usually starts complaining soon after about her hand hurting. And blow jobs! Boy, women try to get out of that quickly. Since they get so tired all the time, how come they get upset when I get tired? Am I supposed to be a machine? It takes two, you know. Tell that to women.

It's true. Put yourself in his place. Many men love giving oral sex and other stimulation for a long time, but others do it out of obligation, just as many of us do. If they don't know what they're doing in the first place, it's even harder to satisfy you. If you don't find a way to give directions, stop complaining and take at least some responsibility for not getting satisfied. Darryl said:

I think I know where a woman's clit is, but I'm not 100 percent sure. Each woman seems to respond to something else. But it's hard to get tuned in on my current partner if she doesn't let me know what she wants. They never tell me anything. I've asked women what they want, and they don't give me answers. So I try my best. But I'd feel better if I got some real feedback.

Many men would like to be, and have the potential to be, satisfying lovers. Some fail because they're clueless, and we don't know how to give clues. We call them jerks when they grope around the area of our clitoris, not quite finding it. Yet do we help them most of the time? No! We expect them to know what to do and get mad if they don't. There are no road maps to a woman's body, since each of us is a little different. Part of the problem is that some of you aren't familiar enough with your own bodies to guide men. Candace told her story:

I asked my last boyfriend if he knew where my clit was. He said "maybe." I asked if he wanted guidance. He said "yes." Then I started laughing and crying as I told him that I wasn't sure where my clit was either. I got a mirror, and together we looked for it. It was funny. It kind of broke the tension over his trying to learn to please me. He was amazed that I knew so little about my own body. Men have it so easy. Their organ is right up front. We eventually did find my clit!

Be kind and gentle, but men need to be educated. If every woman reading my book guided each new lover, men might get used to taking directions from us. They'd actually come to like it because it could lead to giving us more real orgasms and in a shorter amount of time. This will never happen if you all lay back and fake it. Nor can you educate them if you don't educate yourself (see Chapter Twelve).

Getting Your Needs Met
Without Hurting Their Egos

It's hard to tell your lover he's not satisfying you, but it's possible. Sensitivity is essential. Build up his good qualities. You may even have to tell a few white lies to assuage his fragile ego. If his asking "Did you come?" throws you off, tell him it puts pressure on you and that you can enjoy sex whether you climax or not. The key to getting more relaxed in your lovemaking is focusing on feeling good and being satisfied, instead of on the elusive orgasm. His concern should be your satisfaction—in whatever way it works for you, not for him.

What can you do to educate him or change his habits? Be aware that some of his lack of assertiveness in bed may come from a fear of your reaction or because of scars from previous girlfriends. Many women have specific rules about what is and is not acceptable. Too many men have said they don't know how far to go sexually because former girlfriends got upset in the past when they made overt moves. Tony revealed:

> My last three girlfriends objected to sex in the morning and would protest if I made an advance anytime before dinner. The last one in particular used the word "inappropriate" a lot when it came to sex. After a while, I got paranoid and tried to stick with a very traditional way to make love. We broke up, and I'm still paranoid. I've just gotten involved with a woman I like a lot and am terrified if I try something new, she'll get offended and it'll ruin everything. So I'm low-key in bed. I wish she'd take some initiative, but she doesn't. I want to do more but don't know how to approach her.

Sometimes men need cues that it's okay to experiment. One thing you don't want to do is come right out and tell him that you aren't satisfied. In Chapter Twenty, I give suggestions for introducing some more oomph into your sex life. That's often the best way. Start by saying positive things. Rather than telling him what he's not doing right, I always focus on what I need. For example:

ME: It's good to be with you. You make me feel wonderful. Can I show you my most sensitive spot? This is mine and mine alone. You know all women have their own little thing that turns them on the most.

HE: I guess so. I thought you liked what I do to you.

ME: I do. It's just that how can you possibly know all the different ways I like to be stimulated if I don't tell you? I would love you to try _____ or _____. I want you to get to know my body better and my personal preferences, just as I'd like to know yours. Don't tell me you only like to be touched one way?

HE: Well, I do like certain things better. Are you sure you enjoy making love to me?

ME: Of course. I get turned on just by being with you. But wouldn't you prefer me to let you know early on how to make sex between us as good as possible, for both of us? I want you to tell me what you like best too!

Sometimes, men take it well. Sometimes they don't. For your own sake, communicate gently. There's no need to batter egos, but there's also no need to sacrifice yourself for those egos. Find your own variation for giving him directions. If he hits the right spot accidentally, let him know immediately how great his touch there is. Maybe he'll try to find it again!

Keep your directions light and playful. Don't forget: Sex is supposed to be fun. Saying things like "Ooo, could you try touching me here, please?" are less threatening than complaining that you need something else. When he gets it, tell him how wonderful he makes you feel. Give him creative compliments—instead of saying that it feels great, tell him he's a human dynamo, that he makes you tingle all over. Most men will get turned on and try even harder. Make it a team effort. Try something new, and encourage him to try something new. If he just can't handle suggestions, it's your decision whether to stay with him.

Some men don't care about what they're doing during sex. These are the jerks you may want to discard if they don't prove otherwise in a reasonable amount of time, unless you don't like sex. It's your call whether to label him a jerk if he doesn't meet your needs in bed. Sex is more important to some women than to others. If he tries to please you but has a hard time, be patient. I know lots of women who almost left a good man because he wasn't great in bed at the beginning. These men eventually learned. His sincere caring for you can make up for a lack of skills. A comfortable, warm relationship can be more meaningful than instant great, hot sex. I love great, hot sex, but would rather be with a man I feel good about being with, who treats me well both in and out of bed, and who I can communicate with. Hot sex cools off over time anyway. Other qualities are more lasting.

I don't recommend deluding yourself that you can change a man whose ego puts cotton in his ears. If he continuously has sex his way, it's indicative of his personality, which may not satisfy you out of bed either. You can talk to those types forever and not get through. Some men just won't get it. It's better if you let them go. Why go around complaining and horny all the time? There really are many, many, many men who'll be happy to listen to your needs and heed them. Sticking it out with a man who doesn't make you feel good won't help you find one who will.

Here's something you should know: Men who talk about being good lovers often aren't. The good ones don't have to tell you—they'll show you! And they'll ask you to let them know what you like, since they know that all women are different. It's only the jerks who think they know the formula for all women.

Chapter Twelve

Pleasing Yourself

"Pleasure's a sin, and sometimes sin's a pleasure."

LORD BYRON

Do Nice Girls Masturbate?

Before you can experience an orgasm with a man, you might need to learn how to please yourself. Many women feel guilty about masturbating. Believe it or not, many men do too. Masturbation does have a bit of a stigma attached to it, for both sexes. Many boys are told their penises will fall off or they'll go blind if they "play with it." Some girls grow up feeling icky about "down there" and are scared of touching themselves.

Mothers often panic when they see their children putting their hands near their genitals. To be fair, most of your parents didn't know better. But many of you are still uncomfortable touching yourself because of old messages from childhood that remain stuck in your memory. In her book, *Women on Top*, Nancy Friday, who recognizes the need for girls to be given permission to explore their bodies, ends Part II with "Mother, let your little girl masturbate." I recommend her books on sexual fantasies for everyone. It can be reassuring to know how many other women experience sexual fears and fantasies that are similar to your own. No matter where you are in your sexuality, her books can be enlightening. And you can always use more enlightening!

Boys get easy cues about their sexuality—they get erections, which make the risks they've been warned about secondary to experimenting with themselves and feeling pleasure. Eventually they realize that nobody's penis has fallen off and no one's gone blind from masturbation. Boys have an easier time accepting masturbation, while many women still don't feel comfortable with their bodies. There's a lot less accessible information about female masturbation. While I was growing up, I thought of masturbation as a boy's thing. Many women found their sexuality by accidentally touching themselves or rubbing their vaginas against fabric (or a pillow or another inanimate item). When discovering they could feel pleasure, perhaps they made masturbation part of their repertoire. Unfortunately, many women didn't discover their pleasure zones during their youth, and many still haven't struck gold.

It's hard to find someone to talk to for confirmation that there's nothing wrong with giving yourself sexual pleasure. It's not something you ask your mother or even your friends about. Masturbation is one of the few topics that we, the usually sharing, verbal, and curious women, don't discuss much.

Ignorance of Bliss

I talk about masturbation freely in my classes and groups. Large numbers of women have asked evasive, roundabout questions about orgasms, or speak to me privately. Some of the more common things I've been asked are variations of these examples:

SUSAN: I'm 43 and have had an active sex life. I enjoy sex and think I must have had orgasms. I feel good from sex. I'm not sure, though. My boyfriend is sure I have. Can he tell that I've had one if I can't?

KANDY: I love sex. Sometimes I think I let it rule me too much. Yet I'm not sure if I have full orgasms. What do they feel like? I've never known who to ask, "How can you tell if you've had one?" I'd like to think I do because it feels abnormal not to. If I don't, how come I enjoy sex so much?

And so on and so on. Susan and Kandy aren't alone. I told them that I believe if they'd had an orgasm, they'd know. I also assured them, and the many other women with the same dilemma, that it's okay to acknowledge not having orgasms. I encouraged them to go home and get to know their own bodies. Most of the women who weren't sure if they had orgasms had never masturbated. They felt uncomfortable doing it because it has a negative connotation. But hey: It really is normal, healthy, and fun! Gert told me after class:

> I didn't learn to masturbate until I was 38. Until then I thought something was wrong with me. I hoped each man in my life would be the one to push the right button because I never had an orgasm, but it never happened. When I finally gave myself my first orgasm, I felt powerful. It's helped me to open up with my partner. Maybe it's because I started so late, but I enjoy masturbation as a separate pleasure. I look forward to time alone!

Why Do We Masturbate?

In *Women on Top*, Nancy Friday says, "Giving ourselves an orgasm is the sexual equivalent of being able to pay our own rent." It gives you sexual independence and a choice. Contrary to old messages, masturbation is good for you! There are a lot of great reasons to learn to pleasure yourself.

1. If you don't have an orgasm with a man, you can make up for it on your own. Learning how to give yourself pleasure helps you feel in control of your sexuality. Being able to give yourself orgasms makes you less dependent on your partner for sexual release and pleasure. It can alleviate some of the anger you may feel when he doesn't satisfy you. Sometimes you may have a partner who you adore, but who doesn't quite satisfy you in bed, no matter how hard he tries. If his other qualities make him worth hanging on to, masturbation can be a good side dish to his main course. It can be fun when he's not around. And it can be fun when he is around.

2. Masturbation is a safe way to have sex. You can't get pregnant or catch diseases from yourself. You can fool around and kiss a man and get all worked up. Then you can send him home and finish on your own, without worrying about getting a souvenir from him that you don't want.

3. Masturbation is relaxing. An orgasm releases chemicals that make you more at ease. Releasing your sexual tension takes the edge (or more) off horniness. It can make you feel wonderful, help you sleep better, and relieve stress. Women have told me it can even relieve menstrual cramps. Masturbation can alleviate problems you may otherwise have to take drugs for. Now that's a good reason to do it!

4. Masturbation is a great way of getting to know your own body. Until you know your own body and learn what you like, you'll have a hard time guiding a man. It's easier to experiment when you're alone. Stimulating yourself teaches you what you like and how you like it. The more you do it, the more your body may open up and become receptive to stimulation. This can enable you to enjoy sex much more with your partner. When you discover your pleasure zones on your own, you can more accurately tell your partner what you like: how fast or slow; how hard or gentle; what kind of variations. Then when a lover asks how you like to be stimulated, you won't be clueless. Try it; you may like it!

5. Masturbation is another form of stimulation, a treat that you can enjoy anytime. It isn't a substitute for a live partner. But it can be a separate entity, something nice you can do with or without someone in your life. I love a well-put-together salad as well as a meat dish. Though the meat dish may be more satisfying, I enjoy my salads too. I think of men as the meat dishes. Meat can be delicious, but some meat dishes aren't good for me. So I stick to the salads and enjoy them until I can have a meat dish that's healthier. And I can make a salad for myself anytime, which gives me satisfaction too! Masturbation can be the same once you start appreciating the orgasms you can give yourself. While you'd rather have a man, you can still have pleasure without one.

6. Masturbation enables you to get more comfortable with your body in its natural state. It allows you to embrace your womanhood and helps you let go of fears of being dirty and smelly. By touching yourself for pleasure, you can slowly lift the stigma and fear of that private area between your legs.

I asked women who said that they masturbated why and how often they do it. Here's a sampling of their responses:

CARRIE: I learned to masturbate in puberty. My mother would have been horrified. One day I got a tingle down there and touched myself to see what would happen. Lo and behold! This wonderful warm sensation occurred. Of course I followed up on it and still give myself orgasms almost every day. It's always made me feel a bit independent.

ELIZABETH: I masturbate whenever I have time. It's such a great stress release. My friend and I discovered how to do it when we were pretty young. Sharon was sleeping over and she told me she had noticed it felt funny . . . funny good when she washed between her legs and touched inside. So I put my finger inside my panties and started rubbing around. I found my clit pretty soon and had an orgasm. Sharon watched and then we did it to her. We did it together for years.

MICHELE: I love when my husband works late because it gives me the opportunity to have orgasms on my own. He'd probably feel threatened if he knew how much I enjoy it. But I do! I love sex with him, but it's nice on my own too.

DONNA: I don't masturbate often, but I enjoy it when I do. I used to feel weird when a lover didn't give me an orgasm. But now that I've learned my own body, I know I can give them to myself whenever it suits me. I like knowing that.

LAVONNE: I probably do it to myself three or four times a week. It settles me down. I do it with or without a man in my life.

Learning to Please Yourself

I think of masturbation as self-loving. It's control over myself and my pleasure. It's my outlet when a man isn't around. It's the sprinkles on my ice cream cone when there is a man in my life. I don't think of masturbation in heavy terms. It's just fun to be able to give myself pleasure and not depend on someone else all the time.

Women who've never masturbated regularly ask me how to do it. I explain that everyone has to experiment to find what makes them comfortable. I wasn't one of those lucky ones who found their sexuality at a young age. Instead, I had to go looking for it! Having never had an orgasm with a man, I eventually learned it was up to me to give myself the first one. I'd always assumed it was up to HIM to give me an orgasm. And yet I never quite trusted any of the HIMs I got involved with enough to relax and let go. I wanted an orgasm so badly, but I was hindered by a combination of my female performance anxiety, a lack of total trust for my partner, and the absence of information about orgasms. I never quite understood what happened during one. At times, I got close but was always afraid of what would happen if I let go. Would I embarrass myself? There was no one I felt comfortable enough with to ask.

I finally accepted that before I could trust a man enough to let go, I had to trust myself. My first orgasm had to be experienced without the fear of someone else seeing that unknown result and find out what would happen to my body before I could share it with someone else. So I had no choice but to go for it on my own. After some experimentation, I gave myself an orgasm and have been going strong ever since! What a great feeling of power to gain control over my sexuality. Now I know what I want.

Getting in Touch with Your Own Body

So how do you get started on the path to self-loving? I recommend getting your mental state sorted out before attempting to get to know your body. A nervous or guilty attitude won't make it easy to relax and enjoy. Here are five mental exercises to help you sort through your feelings and anxieties so that you can get into the active steps.

1. Think of what you're about to do as self-loving. The word "masturbation" may be too hard a label for you to be comfortable with. Keep in mind that you're just going to give yourself the pleasure you deserve, labels notwithstanding.

2. Relax! I know it's hard to relax in the beginning. But this is supposed to be done for fun, for pleasure, so there's no need to stress out about it. If you make sure to do it in total privacy, no one has to know what you're doing, unless you want to share it with someone.

3. Don't expect an orgasm at first. Just think of what you're doing as getting used to exploring your own body. You don't want to give yourself performance anxiety. A climax will happen when you're ready, so don't put pressure on yourself. You have the rest of your life to have orgasms! The important thing is to get comfortable with your womanhood.

4. Fight any doubts by remembering that although most women don't talk about self-pleasuring, a very large number do it. It's natural, normal, and can't hurt you. Read Nancy Friday's books about sexual fantasies before you do it, and even during if you like! There are loads of anecdotes from women about their feelings, fears, and guilt about masturbation. Seeing you're not in the minority can help.

5. Try to minimize any guilt by understanding that self-pleasuring isn't a substitute for a man, nor should it be a threat to someone you're involved with. It's a separate form of stimulation and satisfaction and should be viewed as such. You can enjoy pleasure given by a man and pleasure provided by yourself as separate treats.

Ice cream and chocolate chip cookies are two separate and satisfying desserts. Each might satisfy you in a different way, but both are delicious. If you're in the mood for ice cream but can't get to the store, a bag of cookies will probably give you at least partial satisfaction. The same is true for self-pleasuring versus sex with a man. You may really want a man, but if you don't have one to make love to, you can still get pleasure and a release on your own. Or, if you have a lover, you may look forward to his leaving so that you can have your own pleasure as well!! Sometimes it's nice to have both cookies and ice cream!

When you feel mentally ready, follow these steps or make up your own to prepare yourself to become familiar with your body. Make this a time of enjoyment by creating a very lovely atmosphere. Later on you might not care about these things, as you get more comfortable with the act itself. But it's always nice to put yourself in as delicious a mood as possible.

1. Pick a time when you're alone. It's hard to experiment in a sexual way if you know a family member might walk in on you or a roommate might knock on your door. Privacy is essential for comfort. Unless it turns you on, I'd recommend not trying it when your husband/boyfriend/lover is around.

2. Do whatever makes you feel sexy and luxurious. Get comfortable. Take a shower or a bath first. Put on your favorite cologne or lotion. Pamper yourself. Allow yourself to feel delicious, soft, and sensual. Wear something that makes you feel good. Sexy lingerie feels lovely on the skin, even when you're alone. Learn to enjoy feeling sexy on your own.

3. Set a sexy, comfortable mood. Find a place where you feel relaxed. It can be your bed, the couch, the floor, anywhere. Turn down the lights or use candles. Play some music that puts you in a good mood. Music can also help you feel less self-conscious if you're concerned about someone hearing you. The right music can really be relaxing, so choose it carefully.

So now you're soft and comfy and cozy, in your bed, or on a sofa, or sprawled out before your fireplace, or wherever you want to make love to yourself. And you're probably nervous. I was the first time. I remember feeling very awkward, knowing what I was about to do. I longed to have the elusive orgasm that I knew I was capable of giving myself. Getting there seemed very difficult at the time. But I took it slowly, not getting uptight when an orgasm didn't come during the first few attempts. I learned to enjoy the time I spent pampering myself. This focus on my womanhood contributed to the development of my self-esteem.

Every woman is different, so there's no one way I can tell you to touch yourself. It's best to start by locating your clitoris. Get familiar with it. You may even want to use a mirror to see it. It's the little round thing at the front of your vagina. Most have a hood covering it, to various degrees. Pull the hood back if you need to. That little love button can be the source of incredible pleasure, so take a good look at it and respect it.

When touching yourself, try different techniques. Use your finger, a vibrator, or any other thing to stimulate it. It's good to have a lubricant on hand in case you need it before you get warmed up, especially early in your experimentation. Try different types of rubbing or pressure. See if it feels better to touch yourself in a gentle manner or faster and rougher. Touch and caress your whole body lovingly. Many women play with their breasts. Really try to make love to yourself. It might seem weird at first, but it can end up being a loving experience. Caressing yourself is very healthy.

Experimenting can teach you how to reach orgasm faster, or slower. There's definitely more than one way to have one. Did you know you can intensify yours? For example, by doing many repetitions of kegel exercises (squeezing your muscles as if you had to go to the bathroom but had to wait, and then releasing them) on a regular basis, you can strengthen and make the muscles more limber in your genital area, which can improve the sensations. Men may notice it too! These exercises benefit both partners. Try tightening those muscles while you're stimulating yourself. It can bring on an orgasm. To intensify your orgasm, hold your muscles tight until the climax just can't be put off any longer. You have many tools available, once you want to learn!

Did you know that women are multiorgasmic? You are! You're capable of having many, I mean many, orgasms in one session. Of course, a majority of women probably don't have more than one because they don't know they can. Someone told me about it, and I tried for two and succeeded. Eventually I learned to keep going and going and going. This works on your own or with a partner. Try it. You may love it! If you do it to yourself, you may not get tired as quickly as HE might. So you can have many more on your own.

Yes, there are advantages to not having an accessible penis. Taking the time to get to know and love your own body can open up doors that you never knew existed.

Chapter Thirteen

Unsafe-Sex Jerks

"When a person has sex, they're not just having it with that partner; they're having it with everybody that partner has had it with for the past ten years."

OTIS RAY BOWEN

A large percentage of men can be jerks when it comes to safe sex. Women tell me over and over about how few men push to use a condom on their own. Too many men do whatever they can to convince their partner to skip them. The men I've interviewed who do use condoms expressed more concern about pregnancy than about diseases.

We're living in an age of serious denial. Men who consider themselves nice people don't want to recognize that they could be at risk. AIDS and other diseases seem like low-class conditions to have, so many people assume that people like them won't catch anything. Even though warnings are all over the place, too many men choose to ignore them. And many women go along with them. Stupidity is rampant these days in both sexes.

Many men just want to have sex, with no concern for diseases.

Why do men show so little regard for safe sex? Michael told me it was "because women are letting us get away with it!" A large percentage of the men I've interviewed said that in the last year they had unprotected sex at least once, many with several partners. They also admitted they'd lied to women, rationalizing that they use condoms most of the time. Men are good at giving excuses for skipping condoms. You can be too accepting of their rationales when you're horny or want to please them, but don't give in. And getting drunk is no excuse! Alcohol doesn't kill diseases. Carry condoms to avoid the excuses that men try to get away with. Beware: Too many men told me that most men are jerks when it comes to using condoms all the time. And that kind of jerk can kill you!

Though people talk about safe sex all the time, the biological urge can make one's memory fade. It's absolutely astounding how many men acknowledged that they don't think twice about not using condoms. I've encountered it personally. Most of the men I've been involved with wore a condom just for me. Had I not insisted, they'd have never offered. Scary! Bert told me in a class:

> I know I'm probably stupid. But I'd do anything not to wear a condom. I hear stories on the news about the spread of HIV and other diseases and ignore them. I tell myself it can't happen to me. Every once in a while, I think about the possibility but try to get rid of the thought quickly. I guess intellectually I know I'm an idiot, but I don't want to face reality. Then I wouldn't enjoy sex so much. It's a guy thing. Most of my friends feel the same way. We all try to get away without the condom if we can.

Not using a condom is like playing Russian roulette. Not everyone gets AIDS from sleeping with someone who has it, but it only takes one incident to be infected. Are you willing to take the chance? Haven't you ever won money when you gambled at a casino, even though the odds were against you? A *small* chance doesn't mean *no* chance. You never know whether that "just one time" has exposed you to something that can be with you for the rest of your life, or even kill you. Men like to think they're invincible. But they're not. Raz admitted:

I was very much in love with Cindy. I wanted to be inside of her without a condom. After a few months, she gave in. I recently found out I have AIDS. It was probably from one night I spent with a woman when I was in the service. Not only will my fling eventually kill me; it might kill Cindy too. We're still waiting to see if she's infected. Now I tell my friends that if they're not careful for themselves, at least be careful for their partner's sake. I would never have thought I could get AIDS. And now there's no way to undo it.

Playing Games

Women I've interviewed said they find that men still aren't too conscious about AIDS and other STDs (sexually transmitted diseases). If they don't obviously fall into a high-risk group, men don't take the threat of disease seriously. They either don't want to be bothered with condoms in the first place, or they take them off if there's a problem. Surprisingly, many, many women go along with not using them, rather than risk not pleasing HIM. I don't think this is what your mother meant when she taught you to be a nice girl! Here are examples of unsafe-sex jerks:

DIONNE: My new lover was from a small town. When I expressed surprise at his lack of concern about condoms and mentioned

AIDS, he said, "We don't worry about AIDS where I come from." I've never heard of a town that doesn't get the news! Is that a good example of a jerk? All he wanted to do was stick it in, with no regard for my life or his own.

ANGELA: Jim said he didn't like condoms. Who does? But I insisted on them. When I put it on him, he lost his erection. What a drag. I wanted him so badly, and he pushed me. So I had sex without protection. What's wrong with me? I know better. I was just as bad as Jim.

THERESA: I met Harold at a party. We started dating and eventually ended up in bed. He seemed very paranoid about getting AIDS, taking precautions for himself that seemed extreme. He made me feel like he didn't trust me. Yet he balked about the precautions I took during oral sex. Weeks after we started having sex he told me, "By the way, I have herpes and am having a flare-up now, so we can't have sex this week." Can you imagine? He waited weeks to tell me. He fought me on my use of condoms for oral sex when he knew all along I could catch something from him. What a jerk! Afterward he kept telling me it wasn't that serious.

Instead of putting on condoms, men put on blinders. They don't want to know better because that knowledge could dampen their sex life. So they choose to ignore the warnings and risk their lives for a night of sex. And they take you down with them if they're convincing enough. Joe told me, "Why should I miss some of the pleasure from sex because a bunch of lowlifes are getting AIDS? I don't associate with those kinds of people." We are *all* at risk. Nice people are HIV-positive. Intelligent, educated people have STDs. And when you have sex without protection, you can get those diseases too. Pay attention to the media. This is one instance when you must believe the hype!

COMPLAINT

Why are men so stupid when it comes to safe sex?

I've talked with many men about why they aren't as condom-conscious as women. Many said that "it doesn't feel as good with a rubber." I can understand that the sensation is less when the penis is encased in a condom. Men told me they feel anywhere from a little less sensation to feeling little sensation at all when wearing one. Wendell told us in a coed support group:

> Having sex with a condom is like watching a concert from so far back in a large stadium that you can only see the band on a screen, even though you're there in person. What's the point? A lot of my feelings about condoms are probably mental, but it's how I feel. I'd rather not have sex if I can't directly make contact with the woman I'm screwing. I want to feel all the sensations. I'm a man. I'd rather skip sex than use a condom. But I want sex, so I just work on the woman I'm with until she gives in. Most of them do.

Granted, a condom takes away more sensation from a man than from a woman, but neither sex likes them. They take away spontaneity. They have a funny odor. It's definitely more fun without them. I know few women who prefer the feel of latex to skin inside of them. Condoms can even physically irritate a woman and also get expensive if you have an active sex life. Hey, I know: Condoms are a pain to use!

But, your life is worth more than a night of sex. Women seem to be more aware of this. Men like to feel they're invincible. Many would prefer to quote statistics about straight men being in the low-risk category and trust the woman they sleep with. They'd prefer almost anything but to acknowledge that they could be at risk if they don't use a condom. If they could be made to acknowledge the real risks, they'd have to use one! Claude said in a group:

> What's the big deal? I'm not in a high-risk group. I don't even know anyone who has any disease. I've been having sex without condoms for forty-seven years and don't intend to change now. I can't. It wouldn't be sex anymore, for me at least. I'm too used to not using anything. I'm too old to change my sexual ways. If I'm gonna die, I'll die with a smile. I know . . . that's stupid, but I don't intend to die. I'm careful about who I sleep with.

How can one be careful about whom one sleeps with unless they insist on their partner getting tested before instigating sex? There's no other way to be careful. People with diseases in the beginning stages still look healthy. Just because someone says they've been careful, how can you know for sure? If someone isn't careful with you, it could be a pattern. You can't give in to the insistence of men. Value yourself enough to hold your ground about condoms! If men aren't serious about them, that's all the more reason to worry.

Younger men seem a bit more up-to-date about safe sex. That's probably because they started their sex lives with more knowledge of AIDS than older men, so they're more used to condoms. The older people are, the more ingrained habits they have. They may not be used to relying on condoms. Older guys are more used to a woman taking care of birth control for herself, so condoms weren't as necessary years ago. When you've spent your most lusty years without using them, it's hard to start. But they have to—or you can't sleep with them!

"Don't You Trust Me?"

Some men take it personally when you ask them to use a condom. I've been asked "Don't you trust me?" when I've insisted on their using one.

No, I don't trust anyone to that extent these days. I value myself too much. Men have a different idea of sexual trust. In the last ten years, every boyfriend I've had has insisted he trusted me enough not to use condoms. That's idiotic! No one can know who's safe and who isn't. But men think they know. Clarence boasted:

> I pride myself on having good judgment when it comes to women. I'm much more careful than I used to be and try to avoid one-night stands. So when I meet a woman I like and we get to the point of sleeping together, I feel I know her well enough to trust her. If someone insists I wear a condom, I will. But I always feel better when she trusts me enough to have sex without one. I hate using condoms. If I'm careful about choosing the women I sleep with, why bother? We should be able to trust each other.

Before I got my HIV test, I couldn't swear that I was safe. Yet my boyfriends would reassure me that they were sure I was. Their trust was presented to me like a gift—a gift of stupidity. I'd warn them that they didn't want to take the chance on me, and they'd insist I was okay. Even the ones I made get tested never made *me* go. Although I didn't trust them, they wanted me to know they trusted me. Foolish, foolish men!

Women tell me that they're more careful about safe sex when they're sleeping with a man they don't know that well. When they're in a relationship, they feel safer. Alison told me, "I always try to use condoms, but sometimes I let it slide when I'm with someone I know well." How can you know anyone that well? Just because you're in a monogamous relationship with the same person for a while doesn't mean you can't catch something from him. When you care about someone a lot, you feel like you should trust him. When you hope this man will be yours forever, how can you break the spell by showing a lack of trust?

I had a friend who got herpes from her live-in boyfriend. She trusted him completely and will pay for it for the rest of her life. But you know what? Since they broke up, she never tells men she sleeps with that she has it because she's afraid they won't want to have sex. Her rationale is that she can usually tell when the disease is flaring up and avoid sex during those times. When I reminded her that her ex-boyfriend had no visible outbreaks, she shrugged and said, "I don't like the fact that I caught it, and other men who don't protect themselves will have to take their chances, too. Why should I pay for this alone?"

Some men take it personally when you don't trust them enough to forgo the condom. Their egos can be damned! Of course, I don't say that to a man. I try to be nice about firmly insisting on putting rubber between him and me. Or, we abstain. We can hug and kiss and do everything but have sex. An orgasm isn't worth the price of AIDS. Anyway, I can give myself as many as I want!

Condom Performance Anxiety

Men don't avoid using condoms just because of the loss of sensation or spontaneity. Another major reason is that they know condoms can affect their erections. Women can fake orgasms. If a man can't get an erection, he feels embarrassed, like a failure, unmanly, and generally inadequate. When a man is with a woman for the first time, there often is some anxiety simply because it's the first time. Men want it to go as smoothly as possible. A large number of men told me that while they've often been able to use condoms successfully, the times they lost their erections are more pronounced in their memories. They admit to being more concerned with getting it up and keeping it up than they are about covering it up. Don told me:

> Women think we can get it up on cue . . . like we get hard whenever we choose . . . like our dicks are erections waiting to happen. Not true. Even when I feel turned on, I don't always get

hard easily. Alcohol, stress, lack of sleep, a cold . . . many things can affect me. Sometimes the anticipation itself can make me self-destruct. Add a condom to any of the above and forget it!

We can fake being turned on. We can't fake a hard-on. That's why I try to avoid condoms. Sometimes I need all the stimulation I can get. I don't want to risk not being able to get it up. That's humiliating. So I delude myself about disease to avoid being a failure in bed. Do I qualify as a jerk?

Wearing a condom makes some men nervous about keeping their erections. Hence, they prefer leaving it off. They'd rather risk their health than risk embarrassment. If they have a problem just one time while using condoms, there's a negative association with using them. Flynn admitted:

When I made love to Laura for the first time, she insisted on condoms. I'm always nervous the first time. That can cause a problem right there. Anything can throw my erection off. So I reached over to get a condom and went soft. She got it up again and opened the condom. I lost it again. So I played on her emotions until she let me in her without protection. Now I subconsciously blame condoms for any problems. Using them is too stressful.

Let men get used to them! If you're with a man who has trouble with his erection, just play with him for a while. Don't make a big deal of it. Let him know it's okay. If he can't reach his orgasm inside of you with the condom, bring him to one in other ways. If he gives you a choice between him and the condom, take the condom and say goodnight to him. Don't fall into the guilt trap. You don't need to be with a man with no sense.

It seems impossible to have safe sex and keep my partner happy.

Getting tested with your partner is a great way to safely stop using condoms, if you use the testing properly. Research has shown that HIV will show up on most tests within six months of coming into contact with it. Therefore, if either you or your partner had sex with another partner less than six months before you take the test, you have to take it again in six months or six months after your last sexual experience. The waiting period can be frustrating, but you have to do it! You can call the CDC (Centers for Disease Control) national HIV and AIDS hotline at (800) 342-AIDS or visit *http://hivtest.cdc.gov* for a list of places in your area to get tested. There are even places where you can get tested for free, so there are no excuses.

I was warned by Scott to make sure to go with my partner when he got tested because "men will lie if they can get away with it. They'll say they took the test when they really didn't, to get you to have unprotected sex with them. Some men will say anything to get you into bed without a condom." Or, they may have had a test this year but omit telling you about the five partners they've had since their test. When my ex-jerk went for an HIV test, he admitted to me that he'd lied to his own doctor because he was uncomfortable with his sexual history. I will repeat myself: You cannot take chances!

Enjoying Safe Sex

"All men are jerks until proven otherwise," especially in bed. A majority of men told me they would wear condoms if their partner insisted. But they won't volunteer to do so on their own. Therefore, you must take responsibility for ensuring safe sex. Forget what his responsibility should be. It's your life, so you need to own and protect it. You basically have three choices when it comes to safe sex: you can abstain; you can use condoms; or you can take an HIV test with your partner. There is no fourth option.

People tend to be less careful in a monogamous relationship. The trust issue can become a major source of guilt when insisting on condoms. So many women told me that they used condoms in the beginning with their boyfriends but stopped when it became more serious. Being with someone for a steady period doesn't make them less likely to be infected with something. If you're in a monogamous relationship, the best thing is for both of you to get tested together. Don't let serious intentions get in the way of that ounce of prevention.

So how do you handle safe sex and still have a good sex life? Carrying your own condoms on all dates and keeping some handy by your bed gives you a sense of control. You can't count on guys to have them. I spoke to the manager of a condom shop and he said that about 80 percent of his condom-buying customers are women. Even I was shocked. He explained that the same reasons men have for not opening up to others with their problems probably keep them from being comfortable discussing condoms with a stranger. Women are happy to get answers in a comfortable environment. Men don't care to deal with things that way.

Before you make love to someone for the first time, it's best to have a talk about safe sex. Don't wait until you get aroused. Establish that condoms are a must, before you reach the heat of passion. Be firm about safe sex and don't be coaxed out of it by a sweet-talking jerk. Learn to put the condom on him yourself. It can be done in a very loving, personal, and sensual manner. Practice with a cucumber if necessary. It's not always easy, but can be learned. Stroke him with your tongue or hand to distract him as you slip it on. Then lead him to intercourse. He may not even realize he's been bagged! Putting the condom on him yourself can definitely make him feel better about using one. Turn him on as you cover him up.

Making sure you always have condoms shows that you care about yourself. You can let him use his own, if he has them. When you have a regular lover, you can even have fun choosing condoms together.

Yes, using a condom can at times be irritating and does restrict spontaneity. Try using a good lubricant and get creative when putting it on him. Besides disease and pregnancy control, there are some advantages to using them. Condoms can prolong his erection, since it lessens the sensations. I love that! Also, if he ejaculates into a condom, you don't have to walk around all day feeling messy. If he doesn't like condoms, he'll get over it when he sees it's the only way he'll get to have sex with you!

Keeping Your Own Head Straight

Women are guilty of allowing men to get away with a disregard for safe sex. Men often revert to being irresponsible little boys when it comes to their penises. But playing games with your life isn't worth the usually short-lived gratification of sex. We often forgo the condoms rather than forgo the man. We let our need to be with him override our common sense. We let our fear of losing him allow us to risk our lives.

Don't let the guilt men throw at you weaken your stance. Think enough of yourself to see your life as worth more than your sexuality. It doesn't matter what he thinks: You know what needs to be done. Whenever a man tells me he never uses condoms, I tell him that's the best signal for me to be especially careful with him, maybe even double bag him! Guys who admit to not using condoms are especially dangerous safe-sex jerks.

PART THREE

SURVIVAL TACTICS

Chapter Fourteen

Activating Your Jerk Alert System

"A little while she strove, and much repented,
And whispering 'I will ne'er consent'—consented."

LORD BYRON

So you don't want to be involved with a jerk anymore? Once you know that you've had it with men who aren't healthy for you, create a jerk alert system. There are definite, obvious signs in men that they are or can be jerks. Those who you recognize the patterns in blatantly, who seem to revel in living up to the label, probably aren't worth staying with no matter what. But men who have the potential to make good partners need to be given a message from the get-go. It's up to you to help them understand you have certain standards that are essential in a relationship.

Many women were brought up believing that it's their responsibility to make a relationship work. And work you do, as you ignore or rationalize away signs that should warn you to change your response or leave. Pay attention to the amount of effort you put into maintaining a relationship as compared to how much effort he puts in. You can't have a good relationship if you're working all the time. When trying to fix a relationship becomes a way of life, stop! What's the point of living in a continuous state of depression or disappointment? When you feel you get nowhere after trying hard to meet his needs, communicating with him, and giving support, you're nowhere.

Men give you clues that they are or can be jerks if you don't change your response to them. Yet we often use defenses to justify what bothers us so things remain status quo in an unhealthy relationship. Yes, "All men are jerks until proven otherwise," but a large number of them have the potential to be reasonably good partners, if you set boundaries from the beginning. Using old defenses to ignore what makes you unhappy won't make you happy. Not waiting until a relationship gets intolerable before you consider alternatives can make him "prove otherwise." Toni told me:

> I look back on my relationship with Jim and wonder why I stayed so long. Why did I think I was so happy when I was miserable at least half the time? Yet I didn't want to admit it. I kept thinking he'd change . . . that he'd come around with more consideration for my feelings. I've always been able to create reasons for staying with a guy who brings me pain. I ignored so much . . . excused so much. I need to find a way to look at what I don't like in a man from the beginning and decide rationally if I should stay. Yes, I feel very irrational when I like a guy. That's why I'll do anything to keep myself from seeing that he's no good for me. Maybe if I weren't so afraid of losing him, I could act differently, in a way that told him I wasn't taking all his crap. Can we do that?

Yes, you can!

Creating Your Own Jerk Alert System

My own jerk alert system has built-in warnings from the beginning. After a few dates, I step back and assess:

- How much time and energy does it look like I'll put into complaining about HIM to my friends?
- How much sleep will I lose while dwelling on what's pissing me off about HIM?
- How much distraction will I have trying to figure out what to do about HIM?

I ask these questions periodically because they're really important. Sometimes you don't even realize how little positive stuff you're getting until you balance it against the negative. Wake up and pay attention. When women come to me for support in dealing with a man, my first question is, "Are you happy?" They're usually surprised at the question, but even more surprised to hear themselves say "no." What's the point of being involved with someone who makes you unhappy? Keep asking yourself this as you read the rest of this chapter.

There are things to watch out for as you create a good jerk alert system as a defense against falling for a jerk. Knowing how to recognize clues can help you avoid getting in too deep with one. By setting a slower pace for getting involved, you can see from the beginning if there are things you can do to prevent him from becoming one. Watch for clues. Trust me: If they're there, you can find them!

Stop Making Excuses for Him

There's no excuse for excuses. Many of us are good at finding justification for behavior in men that isn't acceptable. We sometimes let them get away with things that hurt and upset us because we concentrate on what we like about HIM and the crumbs that give us gratification. We use our defenses to deal with the aspects we don't like. The main defense for those aspects is excuses. We use excuses to keep ourselves from facing the reality of why he's not good for us in his present state. Excuses represent our unwillingness to face the truth about him.

Let's be real. You often make excuses for men not treating you the way you know, at least deep down, that you deserve to be treated. Excuses sugarcoat the truth but don't make it go away. Instead, they keep you stuck in a place that's no good for you. You use excuses because you're scared to face the whole truth. It's easier for the moment to avoid having to call HIM on his intolerable behavior or to let him go. Since you don't want to lose what you think of as the good stuff, you rationalize what you don't like and make excuses to yourself and to friends who try to make you see the truth about HIM. You create a web of rationales for staying with a man who you know deep down is a jerk. Kim revealed in a group:

> Bryan is a good guy. He's had a rough time. His mother is sick, and he's having a hard time at work. So he's not as considerate as I'd like him to be. He yells at me too much. But that's because he's got so much stress. He doesn't listen to what I say. But he's got a lot on his mind. He comes over when he pleases, without calling. When I ask him to come over, he often doesn't. I guess I'm not happy most of the time, but I love him. He can't help the way he treats me. He's got problems.

Several members of this group got on Kim's case as she made more excuses for Bryan's behavior. I asked her to keep a record of how she sees Bryan treat other people. Does he lose his temper with friends and family? Does he show up when they want him to? Kim came in the next week very quietly. She told us that Bryan treats everyone else better than he treats her:

Bryan rushed me Saturday because his friend was having a barbecue and he'd promised to get there early to help. I reminded him he'd promised to change the battery on my car a few weeks ago. He muttered excuses and practically pulled me to his car. All the way there he got on my case about things. But with his friends, he was all smiles.

On the way home I asked why he takes his problems out on me, and he jumped down my throat again. I finally realized I'm his scapegoat and he can do the right thing when he wants. Guess I'll have to eventually make the break. I have changed my attitude. He's aware of it because he's been making more of an effort. Maybe he can stop being a jerk. It may be too late because now that I've opened my eyes, I don't like him as a person.

Kim learned that when she dropped the excuses, she could see that Bryan selectively took his problems out on her, because she allowed him to. Excuses prevented her from making him stop handling his problems at her expense. Of course you want to be supportive of a man you're involved with, but it must be in a healthy way. You can't be a victim of his abuse because life's not treating him right. In order to take care of yourself, you must accept that YOU ARE NOT RESPONSIBLE FOR HIS PROBLEMS! Period!

Remember, men can be very spoiled and may be used to people cutting them slack about what they do. I had a similar situation with my last jerk. He was known for making sarcastic, nasty comments periodically to his friends. One day, he did it to me. I mentioned it to a good friend of his and she said that was just his way. Everyone knew he made those types of remarks and ignored them. They all made excuses for him, saying he couldn't help it. I called him and said that although everyone else accepted what was considered "his way," I wouldn't. When I told him I didn't want to see him anymore if he acted that way, he got upset, apologized, and promised never to do it again. He had other problems, but never got sarcastic again. It proved he didn't always have to do it.

You can take risks by looking at a man objectively and stop hanging onto the good things he does as a way of justifying the bad. You can choose to stop making excuses. Make him own his inexcusable behavior instead! You can't let his good qualities cloud your vision and boost your tolerance of what's painful. By letting good memories balance things that bother or hurt, you sell yourself short.

Become vigilant about excuses you make for him. Write them down. Ask yourself if each excuse legitimately justifies the negative emotions brought on by him. If it's a regular pattern, beware. Any time you make the excuses to friends, double beware. Stop the excuses and see him at face value. Only respectful behavior should do! Even if he has a good heart, you shouldn't pay for his problems.

Love Means That Saying You're Sorry Isn't Enough

If you make it easy for men to use excuses to get away with bad behavior, why shouldn't they take advantage? Tim told me:

> I listen to myself when I give a woman I'm dating excuses for something I did wrong. They usually buy them! No matter what I do, I can almost always get over on her with a good story. We all have problems, so I can always think of something to tell her ... work pressure ... my mother needs me ... still haven't gotten over my last painful relationship and need her to bear with me.
>
> Do women really believe these? I'd never let a woman get away with telling me that kind of stuff. A loving apology usually gets me off the hook.

Many men feel they can do anything hurtful, mean, or just downright wrong if they say "I'm sorry" afterward. But saying "I'm sorry" doesn't excuse bad behavior. When someone hurts you, does "I'm sorry" erase the pain? It never did for me. The reality is that most people will be sorry after they hurt you. Your response must make them sorry enough so they know they'd better treat you well or they'll lose you. Period. No more chances. I once had a boyfriend who thought it was my duty to forgive whatever he did, as long as he said "I'm sorry." At first I did forgive him, until I saw that good actions never followed the apology. He'd forget to call. "I'm sorry." He'd lose his temper and jump down my throat for something trivial after a bad day at work. "I'm sorry." He wouldn't come over when he said he would. "I'm sorry." Fortunately I was savvy enough at the time to know this was unacceptable. When I told him not to call anymore, I didn't say "I'm sorry."

Get it through your heads: You're not responsible for men's shortcomings, problems, or the other factors you use in excuses. Stop saying things like "He does things that hurt me, but ..." What can you say to finish the excuse that will make his behavior justified? Perhaps you'll say he means well? Or he can't help being insecure? Those excuses shouldn't cut it! Just because people have problems doesn't mean they have a right to take it out on you. Why should you accept the brunt of their problems?

Men have learned to fall back on their problems as excuses for not doing the right thing. If they took responsibility, they'd have to find more acceptable ways to deal with you. Putting up with his baggage is unacceptable. Let him unpack it and put it away, or take it on a trip with someone else!

"But He's Such a Nice Guy"

I hear women use this phrase all the time. It's a pat excuse for rationalizing negative behavior in an otherwise "nice" guy. Has your mother or an aunt tried to arrange a blind date for you? When you ask "What does he look like?" the answer often is "He's such a nice guy." That usually means he's homely, with no personality, but has manners that please your mother. To the person making the intro, being "nice" is supposed to excuse all shortcomings. Many of you use this rationale for excusing a "nice guy's" un-nice behavior.

"Nice" is one of those catchall words people use to explain a variety of things. A guy labeled "nice" is often given license to get away with behavior that isn't nice. Society teaches us that if someone seems polite and kind on the surface, he must be a "nice" person. My last jerk was very nice, except when he was hurting me. I still don't believe he meant to, but his problems made him do things that weren't right. His intentions were good, but I had to leave him alone with his intentions.

In the past, I've labeled guys nice because they had manners and were considerate when they could be. They talked sweetly and might have been there for me if they could have, but they also did things to me that weren't nice. It's confusing to get treated badly by a "nice guy." Sami explained:

> Keaton is a truly nice guy. I know his heart's in the right place and he means well, but often he does things that hurt me. I know he doesn't mean to . . . he just has problems. But it doesn't feel good. Everyone says I'm lucky to be with such a nice guy. But it's confusing. He's nice, but he sometimes gets nasty . . . then apologizes nicely. He goes hot and cold. His signals are mixed. I feel on edge with him . . . yet guilty doing something about it, since I do know he's basically a nice guy. Sometimes I wonder what that means.

We often label a guy nice because his intentions are honorable. So he didn't call to say he'd be an hour late—he meant to. So he didn't keep his promises to spend a weekend with you—he does want to, but just can't get around to it. So he struck you over and over—he didn't mean to, but has a bad temper. He feels awful afterward. So he sometimes loses his temper in an irrational manner—but most of the time he's incredibly kind. What do these contradictory signals say? You need to re-evaluate what "nice" means so that you don't use the label as an excuse.

Integrate the "nice" side of him with the side that doesn't follow through on his word. See how consistently inconsistent a "nice" guy can be. It's not enough for a man to be nice on some levels (usually by what he says), while causing you pain on others (usually by what he does). Nobody's perfect, but the price of being with a "nice" guy shouldn't be continuous aggravation or worse. That's just not nice!

"He Could Be So Wonderful, If Only . . ."

You meet a cute and witty man, who has many qualities you want in a partner. The best thing is that he's available and likes you. Yes, you think, "There are things about him I don't care for, but just wait. When he falls for me, he'll want to give me what I want." You decide that he's bright, so maybe he'll go back to school and be able to earn a decent living. Or, he likes things his way, so maybe he'll stop living with his mother soon. Or, he may be irresponsible now, but he'll make a great husband and father when he sees how happy you can be together. Rubbish! It doesn't work that way.

I already said you can't fix men, so keep that in perspective. Your desire to develop a relationship with a man should be based on who he is now. Milking the good stuff while mentally drawing a blueprint for renovating him won't work. You must accept men as they are! Sometimes when you effectively change your response to his behavior, you may get what you want. But blinding yourself with visions of his potential can help you ignore the negative signs. These visions can drive you to keep working on your latest HIM, while taking energy away from your own well-being. Jennifer told me:

> Jeff can be lots of fun. We have so much in common that it's a shame to waste the great chemistry between us. He's been in and out of temp jobs since I met him, but I know how smart he is. When he gets it together, I'm sure he'll get a good job. I get a

lot of pressure to leave him because he's so irresponsible. But if my friends could just hear his ideas . . . his dreams, they'd know that there's something more to him. Sometimes he doesn't come around for a while, but I know he needs space to deal with his situation. I always try to help him out by feeding him and sometimes loaning him money. I don't like that part, but I want to trust him. If only he could see the potential I see in him.

If only . . . Dreams and good intentions do not make a good relationship. You can find the strength to step back if you see unacceptable behavior. Choose to be vigilant and not get so carried away that you look beyond what will always make you unhappy. You can't base your relationship on what you hope he'll be. Of course, you don't have to like everything about him. He's human and you can't always have everything your way. But you know what men do (or don't do) that will continue to make you angry and unhappy. If you remove your blinders, you can recognize what's unacceptable. You know what you can't tolerate, what will drive you crazy, what takes too much of your energy trying to change, what wastes your time when you complain about it. Your only choices are to throw away your blueprints and learn to live with a man exactly as he is today, or to leave.

"Do You Know What's Out There?"

Many of you stay in relationships with men who don't quite make you happy because you feel it's better to settle than not to have a man at all. I hear it from women regularly, and in the past I said it myself too many times. I was once dating a much younger, hot, very good-looking guy who was so disturbed that I decided not to continue seeing him. I told a woman I worked with about my decision, and she was horrified, saying, "How could you let go of such a cute guy? See if you can get him back." When I reminded her of all the pain he'd caused me because of his problems, she held her position, saying, "Do you know what's out there? At least he's good-looking. Deal with his problems and keep him. You'd be crazy to give him up, even if he is crazy." She scared me!

Not all the men you settle for are horrible people or genuinely psychotic. When it seems like most available men have too many problems to even consider, the "not-too-bad one" you have may appear worth holding on to. So you settle for crumbs rather than risk having nothing at all. Consider Elizabeth, who was with Leonard for four years. He had a job that took him on the road a lot, often without much prior notice. Elizabeth kept all her time free in case he'd call to come over:

> I'm crazy about Leonard. He's very good-looking . . . in great physical shape, which is important to me. He sees me when he can, which isn't even once a week. Usually we have a great evening, and he leaves in the morning. I'd kill to spend more time with him and love the few times he doesn't rush out the next day. Leonard always has things to do.
>
> After four years, he's still not giving me much of what I want in a relationship, but I can't let go. I try going out to meet men, but it's depressing. No, I'm honestly not happy most of the time. I suppose I keep hoping he'll give me more. But I can't let go. I don't say a word because I'm afraid he'll leave and I'll have nothing. The quality of available men is poor. At least I have someone who looks good. It really is better than nothing, isn't it?

Is it?

"But You Don't Understand"

I hate those four little words that represent denial. When a friend says "But you don't understand" to me when I'm questioning the behavior of a man in her life, I know she can't see HIM for what he is—that she doesn't understand. I used that expression when I was in destructive relationships, and my friends tried to convince me to either change my attitude toward HIM or let go. I never wanted to hear anything negative. I always thought my situation was different and used an assortment of excuses to confirm that.

Have you ever said "But you don't understand" when a friend tried to point out defects in your relationship? When you're immersed in HIM, it's hard to face the truth. Since you need HIM, you want to see him as good and caring. You delude yourself that he has good reasons for hurting you. "He doesn't mean to talk down to me. He can't help it. You don't understand. When we're alone he's very sweet." Denial. Excuses. Marci explained her relationship to a coed group:

> Pat changes moods a lot. I never know what to expect. My friends don't understand. I'm the first woman he's trusted. He had a rough upbringing, with alcoholic parents who were very abusive. Sometimes he's very warm and loving. Sometimes he's cold. Sometimes he yells at me. I feel bad when he does. The hard part is never knowing what to expect. He puts me on edge all the time. He can change in the middle of an evening.
>
> But he does love me . . . needs me. If he's in a good mood he's loving . . . he even clings to me sometimes. I wish my friends understood why I stay with him. I just wish I could be happier more often. If only I could keep him from going into those moods, it would be perfect.

The men in the group were stupefied. One asked Marci if she'd ever listened to herself. She told him, "You just don't understand." Gray told Marci:

> I've dated women like you before. You always think you know it all . . . analyzing and judging me to find reasons why I can get away with stuff that even I know I shouldn't do. I don't

respect women like you . . . who allow us to use manipulation by giving just enough attention and romance so you're placated. More often we abuse your tolerance, secure knowing you won't leave us no matter what we do, as long as we give loving in between.

I once heard a woman arguing on the phone to her best friend, who was obviously telling her to leave me. She kept telling her friend that she didn't understand how it was between us . . . that we loved each other and I couldn't help doing things that hurt her. Well, you know what? I could have. It was she who didn't understand. I wasn't a good boy because I didn't have to be. I was a total jerk in those days. If a guy really likes someone and she won't accept bad behavior, he'll at least make an effort to be good.

If you find yourself defending why you stay with a man by saying "But you don't understand," see if you can actually write down what it is they don't understand. Try putting it on paper. You might find out that you don't really understand it yourself. Then you may have to force yourself to understand that it's time to stop accepting unacceptable behavior.

"I Didn't Think It Was a Big Deal"

Men like to use this line when you call them on something. Nothing is a big deal if it doesn't affect them. They often act like you blow everything out of proportion. My ears perk up when I hear this line from a man when he's defending something I've brought to his attention. Women tell me that men have used it to explain why they didn't tell them that they had a disease, had a girlfriend, lost their job, or any other "insignificant" factor they didn't want to share with them. Josette had been away for ten days when she made plans with Richie for the next day. He was supposed to get in touch to arrange a time to see her. She continued:

> He called and said he had to go somewhere for a while, act-ing like it was something he didn't want to do but had no choice. I felt bad that he wasn't in a hurry to see me. Up until now he had been romantic, attentive, reassuring—saying he'd work hard on our relationship. He said he'd be back between 3:00 and 4:00 but didn't call till 5:30. I told him it was late and I had work the next day, but he played on me, saying "Aren't I worth it?" I told him I'd come over.
>
> When I got there he tried to have sex right away but got a phone call. I overheard him whispering about a great restau-rant he'd been to earlier that day. That made me say to myself, "Girlfriend, you're keeping your legs closed tonight." He said he was with a female friend who'd bugged him to get together. When I asked why he hadn't told me he was having lunch with another woman on my first day back, he said he didn't think it was a big deal. I left and never heard from him again.

Men have their own definition of a big deal. It's almost as if they see nothing as a big deal if it doesn't hurt or hamper them. If they hurt or bother others, "no big deal." I've found this line is often a coverup for something that women see as a big deal. To be fair, I'll acknowl-edge that we often do blow things out of proportion. We sometimes do get on his case for things that really aren't a big deal. Men com-plain about this regularly and contend that their "no big deal" atti-tude is a defense to our constantly fussing about everything. Dean admitted to a class:

> I've had women make a big deal out of everything. We'd get delayed and arrive a little late . . . I had to work late when she

was expecting to see me . . . I forgot to tell her I bumped into her sister at the park. They'd get upset over these unimportant things. I began to automatically say "It's no big deal" to everything when I heard their voices go up a pitch and their tone get agitated or stressed.

I guess I do use it at inappropriate times. But women go off for almost any reason. If they wouldn't make a big deal out of everything, we wouldn't say that most things were "no big deal." I can't get out of the habit.

Okay, guilty as charged. We do often take things too seriously. But that still doesn't give men the right to minimize things that are important. If men continually fall back on this reasoning for things that mean something to you, beware. Usually the things they label as "no big deal" are things that may hurt you. Jill told me:

Charles, who I'd been seeing for two years, told me he'd see me one Saturday. I didn't hear from him all day and hung around waiting to hear from him. My roommate came home upset. She said she'd seen Charles walking in the park holding hands with a man! When Charles came over, I told him what Cheryl had seen, and instead of apologizing or giving me an explanation, he said it was no big deal. He then explained he was bicurious and had accepted a date with a man. Charles said it had nothing to do with his feelings for me. When I asked how he could stand me up for a man, and possibly put me at risk for HIV, he kept telling me it was no big deal.

"It's no big deal" as a pat answer on a regular basis is something to watch out for. Men should be made to change their tune or you can show them it's no big deal to walk out and not come back. Staying with a man like that *is* a big deal.

"What I Really Meant to Say Was . . ."

Men know how to use words to confuse or appease you for a while. They have their own lingo, and you don't always know what they really mean. It's important to read between the lines when some men speak to avoid setting yourself up to be let down. Pay attention to what a man is really telling you. Don't overanalyze and get carried away by what you think he means or by what you want his words to be saying. Watch out for more subtle messages he gives you, sometimes expressed through his actions. Listen to his more blatant messages, such as when he tells you jokingly that he's not good at relationships.

Pay attention and you'll hear what you don't want to know but need to. Here are a few examples of expressions that women have told me were used on them.

- **"You're so easy to talk to"** often means that he needed someone to dump his problems on. But since he opened up so much, he'll probably be uncomfortable dating you.
- **"I could fall in love with you in a minute"**—but he doesn't have a minute for you.
- **"If I was ready to get married, you'd certainly be the one."** But that's easy to say because he has no intention of getting married, so give it up.
- **"That was fun. We should do this again sometime."** I've yet to hear a woman say she heard from a man who said goodnight with that phrase.
- **"I really like you, but think we should see other people."** This cushions the blow before he tells you he already is seeing someone else or has lost interest.
- **"Everything is fine. Why are you looking for trouble?"** means denial; that he doesn't want to deal with an issue. It's commonly used in response to questions about changes in his behavior. For

example, he comes over and seems distant, so you ask, "What's wrong?" He may get very annoyed and sarcastically respond, "Everything is fine. Why are you looking for trouble?" I've had men scream it at me. If he doesn't want to face reality, you'll have to live with it or leave. You can try explaining over and over to him that he's acting different. But when he responds like this, he doesn't want to acknowledge a problem. It may have nothing to do with you. But do you want to be with a guy who goes into moods that put you on edge and who refuses to let you in?

Stop believing everything they say. Remember: "All men are jerks until proven otherwise." Men can be great storytellers. The best way to interpret their words is to ignore them and pay closer attention to their actions.

Don't Let Him Talk You Out of It

We have moments of lucidity when we're hooked on a jerk. These come when you get burned and pay some attention. He may do something painful that wakes you up temporarily. You see clearly he's no good for you and resolve to change. Determination takes hold of you to either stay away from him or set stricter boundaries for acceptable behavior. But when he comes over acting apologetic and sweet, playing on your romantic needs, resolve goes down the toilet. No! You can force your eyes to stay open and keep your resolve strong by remembering "All men are jerks until proven otherwise" if he's using his charm to make you forget. Phil revealed:

> I know when I've gone too far with my woman I have to make a magnanimous comeback. She'll let me get away with a lot, but when I do a major dirty, I work hard to fix it. Loretta can be tough, but I attack from all sides with romance and guilt.

First, a good excuse. Then I tell her my plans to take her out. By the time I finish, she's apologizing to me!

Men sometimes defend their bad behavior by counterattacking and trying to make you feel guilty about something you did. This puts you on the defensive and breaks your resolve. They label you as insecure, jealous, and other monikers to control you. These words sometimes make you feel guilty enough to drop your resolve in favor of reassuring them. He can turn the tables on you, making you fearful of losing him when you were ready to break up. The game I hate the most is when a man retaliates to my questioning his behavior or challenging what he does by declaring that something's wrong with me. I have to keep reminding myself that the only thing wrong with me is him! Monique told a class:

> Jimmy's slick. I knew it but got suckered in over and over. I can tell you stories about his being a jerk. I'd be ready to kick him out because I caught him with another woman, and he'd have me defending myself for spying on him. He promised to take me to a movie on Friday night and didn't show or call all weekend. I'd be determined to not let him in when he shows up with a big bouquet of flowers and a devilish smile . . . starts talking me up until he gets me into bed, where he knows I can't resist him.
>
> So many times I've decided no more, but he knows how to play me. Last week he disrespected me so much that I threw him out. I wrote on big pieces of paper what he'd done and hung them up around my apartment. So far it's working. The signs are the constant reminder I need.

Don't let him sidetrack you. It's not worth it. You can choose not to forget what opened your eyes. If necessary, write it down. You can't let HIM wheedle his way back into your good graces if he doesn't deserve it. You can be strong and not let him manipulate you. Clearly defining what the problem is can help you stick to your guns. The best thing you can do (which I know is very hard because it actually works) is to call a trusted friend or two and tell them why you're leaving him, and ask for reminders of these reasons if you weaken.

"But the Chemistry Is Perfect"

I hear many women thrill over having great chemistry with men they've just met. Or, they admit to blowing off an otherwise great guy because the chemistry wasn't there immediately. Nothing can be lovelier than meeting a delicious man who turns you on like crazy and your feelings are reciprocated 1,000 percent. You spend time together in a romantic bubble. The attraction is intense. You're always tingling. Sounds perfect, huh? It would be great if it could sustain itself, but it usually doesn't. Instead of it ending up as a forever kind of love, you often find out he's a jerk.

Sex is sex and love is love. It's lovely when chemistry can hold its own with other facets of a good relationship. If you're too quick to judge a man by his chemistry, you might give up a chance to get to know one who could make you very happy in a long-term relationship. When you get to know a man well, he can start to look more attractive. That chemistry you crave is usually a sexual attraction, which doesn't mean he's right for you anywhere else but in bed. I've had many women tell me that when they first went to bed with a man they didn't expect much from, he turned out to be an intense lover and ignited the chemistry. Be careful when that chemistry hits. It can addle your good judgment. Give yourself time to know a man before getting sucked into something not good for you.

Men without good longevity potential are more inclined to rush into the intense aspects of a relationship when chemistry hits. But they bolt quickly too. Don't sell yourself short by waiting for the chemistry to hit you. And hold off when it does. When you meet a good guy, work on the friendship aspects. You may be pleasantly surprised at how delicious creating your own chemistry can be.

Don't Wait

After breaking up with a guy you liked a lot, how many times have you told friends that it was probably for the best? Why do you acknowledge negatives only after you break up? It's time to start seeing clearly at the beginning. There'll always be something that's a problem in a relationship, but you need to set limits on what's acceptable. To what degree does his behavior bother you or cause pain? Pay attention to how frequently it troubles you. Once in a while is normal. Regularly isn't. Watch for the signs in this chapter. They'll keep your jerk alert system on guard.

Chapter Fifteen

The Jerk-Lover's Tool Kit for Change

"A good marriage would be between a blind wife and a deaf husband."

MONTAIGNE

Controlling Your Need for HIM

Awareness is an essential tool for growth and change. Developing an awareness of specific times when you're most vulnerable to jerks can prepare you for them. Certain occasions, such as a friend's wedding or a baby's birth, may trigger a stronger need to be with a man. It's normal. You see your friend happily in love or bearing the fruit of love. If you want those things, sharing in these types of events can heighten your need for a man. You're more tempted to let your guard down and jump into something too quickly or call an ex-jerk. If you're seeing someone, you might need more from him. If you're not seeing anyone, you might feel down. Preparing yourself before the events and acknowledging your vulnerability softens the blow.

Affirmations can keep you stronger. Speaking with a trusted friend about your fear beforehand helps. If you plan to do something fun, don't think too much about it beforehand. Arlene put this into action before a friend's wedding:

> My friends are getting married, one by one. Each time I went to a wedding, I'd be depressed. I'm supposed to be happy, and I'm wanting to cry. Number one I went to with Chris. I'd been getting stronger with him. He was good-looking and sexy but had a bad attitude . . . very controlling. He'd been improving as I kept a distance . . . then at this wedding I get weak. I just wanted Chris to love me and let him know . . . giving him his way. And did he take advantage! Number two . . . I go alone . . . get all sentimental and go home and call . . . I'm ashamed to say, Chris. Well, I let him abuse me again until my weakness passed. Number three . . . I meet the best man during wedding weakness . . . slept with him that day and never heard from him again. Number four . . . I talked with my minister and admitted feeling weak at weddings. Made an excuse and left the wedding early to go with friends to hear some live music. They kept my spirits up, and I survived this one.

I can get cravings for a guy on gorgeous days. Clear blue skies can do it. A jerk looks great under radiant sunshine. Temperatures in the 60s and low 70s with low humidity can be an aphrodisiac for me. I have to keep myself in check during these times. Other women have told me certain seasons make their need for romance higher. Sultry summer nights or crisp winter days can make jerks appealing. Beware of these times. When you're vulnerable, it's safer to avoid places that attract couples holding hands, and so on, such as parks and beaches.

Why do we set ourselves up to be vulnerable? My friend Ellen visited me when she was trying to be stronger with a jerk who'd let her down. I was seeing one who usually made me miserable. He'd just let me down again. There we were—consoling each other as we nurtured strength to end these relationships for good. So what did we two brilliants do to take our minds off them? We watched a rerun of the romantic and sexy movie *Dirty Dancing*. We cried and both moaned, "I want HIM!" After we licked our wounds, we acknowledged that these types of movies should be off-limits during vulnerable times. Seeing all that perfectly scripted Hollywood romance can make you yearn. It's better to avoid movies at all costs when you're lonely, vulnerable, and horny—and when you're trying to distance yourself from or leave a jerk.

Write It Down

Writing lists and journals are great self-defense weapons against jerks, keeping you resolute about caring for yourself. That can be a great tool for developing and maintaining awareness. Putting your thoughts and feelings on paper make them more concrete. I highly recommend keeping a journal to record feelings and growth. I love them as a barometer of progress. Often you don't realize you've changed much until you read earlier journal entries. Then it hits you.

It doesn't have to be a formal journal, nor must you write every day. This is your personal tool, do what you choose. Journals can be kept in notebooks or your computer (if no one else can access it). I like starting off with details of my current status and feelings. Then I record events, feelings, pain, anger, growth, joy, and whatever else comes up. It's very enlightening to read later on. I used to save e-mails I wrote to friends in my computer. A few years ago I reread old ones. It was the best reminder of how far I'd come. Reading them was painful. I wanted to tell the person writing them, "Read my book!" but it was me. Recognizing the extent of my growth was exhilarating.

Write—write—write! It's a terrific way to get things off your chest. Often you're driven by anger, which causes headaches and stomach problems. Spiritually, I believe that many physical ailments are caused by holding anger, guilt, frustration, disappointment, etc., inside.

Putting your emotions on paper can relieve the pains of the stomach and head. I've gone many nights without sleep because of anger toward a jerk. I'd lay awake and dwell on what I'd like to tell him, which I hated. With my last jerk, I decided to write my feelings down, as if I were writing him a letter. I kept a list of things I wanted him to understand on a big pad, leaving space between thoughts to add more specifics. I believe we hold onto things, mulling and mulling, so that we don't forget them by the time we speak to him. Writing things down gives you choices. Everything you need to say is on record. You needn't rush into anything. Your notes are always handy if he calls.

Writing down your anger toward anyone is very therapeutic. Keep a pen and pad around, even by your bed, to record things that trouble you. That's what I do. Whenever I find myself unable to sleep due to anger, I write it down on my pad. I may turn the light back on once or twice when I think of something else. Then I can go to sleep. With my last jerk, writing kept me sane. When I read back what I'd written, I realized how much of a jerk he was. I sometimes used my notes when we spoke. Often I didn't even want to get into it after writing it down because he wasn't worth the energy.

Writing lists has worked very well for my clients too, so give it a try. Write a separate list of what makes you angry, what scares you, what makes you feel guilty, or what you'd like to change in others. Pick and choose which of these lists would help you, or try them all. Keep adding to each list as you think of more things. You can learn a lot by reading them later, but use them any way you want. It's your list.

Don't Take It So Personally

A man's world may not revolve around you the way your world may revolve around him. Yet you might assume that you're the cause of all his bad moods, his need for space, his every action. Hey, you shouldn't give that so much importance—he doesn't. Don't personalize his every move or feel responsible, because most of the time you're not. Men get funny sometimes, just as we do.

It's important to stop putting your insecurities on him. We personalize because we're afraid of doing something wrong. Don't panic when he shuts down for a while. Men often need space because they need space, not because you've messed up; not because he doesn't love you; not because he doesn't want to be with you. He needs time on his own for its own sake. You can't assume responsibility for his bad moods. It's not your fault he has things on his mind. Don't you have your moods? Moodiness is part of being human. That's reality. Men react differently but do get moody too. Women tend to snap at someone or need comfort. Men need to get away. Ashley was upset with this in a class:

> Tony wants to be with me a lot. But sometimes he just doesn't. I ask why, and he says he has things to do at home. "Things?" I ask if he's tired of me. He gets annoyed. I don't mind if he comes over when I have work. I love being with him and get nervous when he stays away. If he'd explain, I'd feel better. But he says nothing's wrong. He just needs space. I try harder, but he still stays away at times. I wish he'd tell me what's wrong.

Paranoia is too common among women. But your reaction to it can cause someone who's not a jerk to get fed up. I experienced it for many years. If I smiled and he didn't smile back, I'd ask what was wrong. If he decided not to come over, I wondered if he was getting tired of me. If he didn't call on time, I worried he was angry with me. Now I realize how silly this was. That was living on the edge. Even when everything turned out to be okay, it didn't prepare me for the next time. I figured this time was the big one! George complained about this situation:

> I can't change my behavior an ounce or Sheila gets scared . . . always worried she's done something wrong. It's too much pressure. I can't change my mind without her going nuts. Last week

I was supposed to see her, but my friend offered me a ticket to a big football game. Of course I wanted to go. I was just supposed to hang with Sheila, so I postponed it.

She kept asking was I angry at her. She couldn't understand it had nothing to do with her. It was a ballgame. She's done that many other times . . . like when I was in a bad mood from work and stayed home. She made a big deal over me wanting to be alone. I can't begin to understand what she thinks I think she's done wrong. Now I am getting angry. I care about her but don't know how to explain these things.

Just as men take your moods in stride, you have to take theirs. Control your fears. Get into the habit of stopping yourself before you lose it. If you look for blame within yourself when he steps back, remember that you've done nothing wrong and everything will be fine. Stop it immediately. If you know you've done nothing wrong, you've done nothing wrong. Affirm that to yourself. If he needs breathing room, give it to him with a smile. Develop your own activities! (More on that topic in Chapter Eighteen.) If you allow men their space, it can make a relationship stronger. Most will be grateful. Then they might not seem like jerks. You shouldn't be so dependent on him that you get crazy when he has a change in plans. Surprise him sometimes and change yours!

Stop Overanalyzing

I said earlier that men take things more at face value while women delve deeply into everything. Analyzing men is counterproductive. Yet I did it regularly. In retrospect, it was mostly wishful thinking. Analyzing situations gets you nowhere but disappointed. After a date, I'd call everyone and recall the positives until at least one said, "I'm sure he'll call." Nineteen friends could say, "forget it," but I'd listen to the one who gave me hope and then got let down. You shouldn't continually read things into his words. It's too much energy wasted on setting up disappointment.

I've accepted that it's healthier to think as little as possible until he does something to let me know he's interested. I try not to talk about him to friends until that happens. It's frustrating to remember how much time I wasted going into long details about men I didn't hear from again. Don't tell friends too much, since they can incite problems that you should deal with on your own. Now when my friends ask about a date, I force myself to say that he's not worth the energy of an explanation yet. It does keep me saner.

Now that I've stopped analyzing as much (I confess, I still do it sometimes but never to the same degree as before), my intuition has become much more reliable. You can't use your intuition if you don't take things at face value. Someone advised me of that years ago when she saw me trying to figure out what my intuition was telling me. Since I stopped analyzing, I've been able to trust my instincts 100 percent more. Now intuition is my power tool! You all have it, but should use it without overanalyzing the initial indications you get.

Stop Talking and Start Communicating

You know good communication is key to keeping a relationship solid. Yet it can be hard to establish. You may wonder why men have so much trouble with it. But the desire to communicate doesn't always help you get your point across without men getting an attitude. Why is this?

Many men have developed selective hearing. Certain signals cue the low/off volume control on what they hear. Let's take at least some responsibility for this. Bad experiences have conditioned men to tune out from specific triggers, like the attitude in your voice. If you tell him something bothers you in a tone that reminds him of his childhood, he won't want to hear it. Mommy scolded him enough, and he learned to tune her out so he does the same with you. He certainly doesn't want to hear that tone from a woman he's sleeping with. Men state their point and move on. We state and state and beat the point senseless. Men know when we approach them in a certain way that the ax is going to fall. Instead of paying attention, they duck. Greg told a class:

> I know when she's got that "you've done something wrong and I'm going to call you on it" in her voice, I want to bolt. Often it's something trivial, but she puts me through a guilt thing every time. She does things that annoy me . . . I just mention most annoyances. But she makes everything a big deal. If she saved that routine for serious stuff, maybe I'd listen more. But she uses it whenever she has even a small complaint. I feel my back going against a wall when she corners me with that tone, and my head starts singing "la la la, I'm not gonna listen." I really do hear, but I won't give her the satisfaction of reacting.

I tell women in my classes that if they want to quickly shut down many a man's hearing system, say those four little words: "We need to talk." When he hears them, he expects something unpleasant, so why should he listen objectively? His guard goes up while you tell him how you feel, and he's thinking ahead to his next defense. Men admit this is often the case. When he's told what he's done wrong or could do better, his sense of self is attacked. As you talk, he's either trying to protect himself by thinking of what to say in defense or tuning out in an effort to not deal with it. If he knows that he's really wrong, he'll often try harder not to face it. Guilt can distort hearing.

My Ten Commandments of Good Communication

Developing effective methods of communication takes work. But it's worth the effort when you get the responses you want—finally! I've put together my own Ten Commandments of Good Communication. If you follow them, your communication should get better results.

1. **Find a peaceful time to talk.** Wait until neither of you is in a bad or angry mood, or else one of you might say something you'll regret when you calm down. Sometimes you may have to wait for a conducive time to spell out problems. The best opportunity for objective listening is when he's in a good mood.

2. **Decide what's most important to say.** Be concise. Use as few words as possible. Women are great talkers, but communication is more than throwing words at someone. We tend to say too much, explaining and explaining—communication overkill—until the desired response comes or he gets alienated. My rule is the less said, the more you get across. Don't get carried away with every little thing that annoys you. Be specific and choose your battles well. You can't have everything your way. Too often when you get his attention, you try to include as many complaints as possible. Try to stick with one train of thought. Men can't work on too many things at one time.

3. **Speak with the same respect and tone you'd want for yourself.** Put yourself in his place and think about how you'd like to receive the message you're about to give. Listen to yourself when speaking. Be objective about how you'd like this method of communication directed at you. Becoming aware of how you present your thoughts can get them across more clearly. Simply paying more attention to yourself (see later in this chapter) can help.

When I got in the habit of listening to my tone of voice when I communicated, I didn't like what I heard. Now I actually get nauseous if I hear myself fall into old patterns. Girls whine and nag to get heard and often get their way until they become adults. Boys break that habit early when they're taught to keep emotions to themselves. It's hard for us to break the habit, but you must. It gets you little as adults.

4. Start and end with a positive statement. Remember, men raise their guard when expecting a negative. So fool them. Start by saying something nice first, such as "You know, I'm lucky to have you" or "You've been great about . . ." or "It feels good being comfortable speaking to you." Base your opening on what's appropriate with him. Starting with a positive statement can lower his resistance and make his ears more receptive. Then you can segue into the problem. End with a good feeling. Thank him for being such a sweetheart about listening. Leave him with good vibes.

5. Explain. Don't complain. This is my #1 motto for getting a man to listen without an attitude. Don't nag, lecture, demean, blame, criticize, or talk down to him. Explaining means just stating the facts without letting emotions get into play. Presenting your problem without threats, accusations, or demands might motivate him to pay more attention. Explain why a situation bothers you, without any annoyance in your voice. Choose your words tactfully.

6. Use positive words instead of negative ones to say the same thing. Softer words can take the sting out of a message. For example, instead of saying "You're wrong," say "There might be a more effective way to . . ." A tactful choice of words can mean the difference between his hearing you with understanding or with hostility.

7. Ask for more sensitivity to your needs and feelings. Don't ask him to change—he won't. Asking for more awareness of and sensitivity to your needs is the fairest request. For example, if he forgets to call when he knows he'll be late, explain briefly how you worry. Perhaps he can be a bit more sensitive about letting you know next time. Tell him you don't expect perfection but that you'd just like some sensitivity for specific things that don't make you feel good.

8. Say it just once. Give him credit for not being stupid. He understood you the first time, even if he acts like he didn't. Frustration over not getting a reaction from a man makes you repeat what he's already heard. Even though he's silent, he probably knows what you said. Be patient. Don't expect an immediate response. Often you want instant gratification and repeat what bothers you over and over if you don't get a satisfactory response right after you've communicated. He may need time to absorb what's been said, so leave it alone after saying what's necessary. Looking expectantly for an answer will put him on the spot, making him defensive.

9. Listen as much as you speak. We often forget to develop listening skills when we're trying to communicate. Communication is a two-way street, an interaction between two people. A good communicator is also a good listener. That means hearing what he's saying, as well as relaying your own message. If you're so absorbed in your mission to get the point across that you can't listen objectively to him, you're not communicating. You're attacking him with words.

10. Let him know you appreciate his efforts to communicate. Since women think we make the rules, we often have expectations about how men should communicate. As I told you, they don't open up as we do. If a man makes an attempt to communicate, however feeble it may seem, tell him you've noticed. Men often complain that even when they do try, women aren't satisfied. You may want him to share the way you do, and he may never be able to do so. But if he's giving it a shot, thank him. He may try harder.

Communicating with Actions

Sometimes words just don't work. When I was dating a jerk, I'd explain my feelings to him . . . and explain my feelings to him . . . and explain my feelings to him. I kept trying to make him understand why his attitude/behavior/words bothered me so much. I nagged, and I spoke nicely. I tried it all but rarely got through. My inability to find the right words to get him to stop doing things that hurt me was thoroughly frustrating.

I eventually learned that if men don't want to understand, they won't, no matter what words or techniques you use. I'd try harder to hang in with a man, hoping he'd give me what I wanted. Forget it! I eventually learned that when my words and efforts didn't get him to change, I had to change my own way of responding to him.

Years ago, my friend Mary would listen sympathetically as I groaned about my latest jerk and my attempts to get HIM to understand how he was hurting me. I used all the excuses in Chapter Fourteen to stay with HIM. I wrote long letters trying to invoke sympathy over the pain he caused, while assuring him I knew he didn't mean it. I talked on the phone, and in person to him. No light went on in his head. Mary pointed out that talking wasn't getting me anywhere and that perhaps I should start acting on what I felt. If I'd respond differently to his behavior and keep my mouth shut, either he'd get the message or he wouldn't.

Since then I've followed Mary's advice. Too much energy is wasted when you explain without results. You can't communicate if he doesn't want to understand. If you keep complaining but go along with his behaviors, why should he listen? Changing your response to him is a more effective form of communication. It says you mean business. It's healthier for you. Even if he proves to be a jerk and moves on, you're more in control. As you stop encouraging unacceptable actions by staying, you slowly detach yourself. As you stop making yourself available for his every whim, he takes you more seriously. Remember, actions do speak louder than words!

When you're talking to a brick wall, having a life (more in Chapter Eighteen) bolsters you, making it easier to take control. There are ways to send a message loud and clear. Start with having the strength to accept you may see him less, or live without him. If you have a life, you can be strong. If he's taking you for granted by calling at the last minute, don't say you're busy—be busy! It's much more fun. Make plans if he doesn't contact you. Don't cancel plans when he does. If your relationship is meant to be, it'll survive. We discussed this in a coed group, and Claire said weeks later:

> Cary did as he pleased, knowing I was hooked on him. I kept telling him off, and he kept doing his thing. You all said I should claim my life, so I tried making plans with friends. Cary got mad when he couldn't find me home. I told him I'd love to see him but wouldn't wait around if he didn't call. I still see him but feel in control now, so I don't need him as much. It's a wonderful feeling to be able to put myself first. Now he's doing more for me.

Patrick added, "If a girlfriend complains, I prefer to ignore her. If she cools off and I like her, I try harder. We do listen to that." I communicate a problem once, so that the guy knows what bothers me. Then I force my mouth shut. Men often respond to changes in behavior. If I'm troubled by how a man acts, I don't feel as friendly, and I slowly pull back. I get cooler but not cool. A subtle change can be more effective than a drastic one. Let him wonder if he's imagining it. Work on your own happiness and let him play second fiddle, but be friendly when you feel in control. It may confuse the heck out of him, but maybe he'll get the message that something's wrong, and he needs to change.

If he comes around, don't play what I call romantic Ping-Pong with him. Often when a man gives in, you may go back to your old ways. You can never do that, or he'll eventually return to his. Then you'll have to pull back again (hence, Ping-Pong). By maintaining your control so he's never 100 percent sure of you, he's less likely to take you for granted. If he's not a jerk, less attention from you can motivate him to give more care to the relationship. Shelley told me:

Jared came on strong. He couldn't do enough for me, and I worked my schedule around his more rigid job. It was perfect, until out of the blue he got distant. I asked what was up, and he denied it. He called less and our weekends together became a few hours. After talking to no avail, I thought it was over.

I've read about men coming on strong and exiting quick. You suggested I give him lots of room and go about my life. I stopped complaining. I went out with friends and wasn't free to respond to texts or calls. I was friendly but distant. I stopped making myself available.

Jared was stunned. Here he was pulling away, and I was cheerfully going on with my life. I still enjoyed seeing him, when it worked for me. It took time, but he got closer. I think he trusted me, since I didn't make a fuss. Now we're solid again. He recently told me he'd gotten scared and was grateful I'd left him alone.

When a man withdraws, follow his lead. Don't try to get him to talk or pressure him. Men retreat for a reason. Have the courage to turn the tables around. Remain friendly and get on with your life. What can you lose? Chase a man and he'll back off more. Pressure him and he'll use it as justification for why he needs to step away. Leaving him alone provides the best shot of his coming around. He'll see that he can't take your being there for granted. If he doesn't want to lose you, he'll make the right move.

Speaking with actions is my favorite tool for feeling in control. I wasted energy trying to explain feelings HE didn't want to understand. Now I go on with my life. My favorite power moment was when a guy started taking me for granted. It wasn't serious, but I had to let him know. He left a voicemail one night. When I called him back the next night, he joked that I must have been out late with a hot date—ha ha— since I didn't get back to him back that night. Normally I'd have told him where I'd been, but I didn't that time. He finally asked where I was when he called. I just said "out." I could swear I heard him gasp at the other end, but he asked no more questions. He did get more attentive.

Should You Call or Text Him?

Another technique for staying in control is to be the one who ends phone calls and dates first. Does this sound silly? Women tend to try to drag out time spent in person or on the phone. I used to talk for as long as he'd let me. When I finally began to take my leave first, I truly felt in control. Being practical, men often initiate a goodbye first. Being romantic, women often want to linger, milking any interaction with a guy we're into. The first time I told a guy I liked that it was time for me to go home, he was caught off guard, perhaps not used to women ending an evening first. The control felt marvelous. Now when I talk to a guy on the phone, especially before he's "proven otherwise," I try to be first to say I have to hang up, at least half the time. Control over these situations has been a high. I either get some of what I want or know quickly he has to go.

Should you call or text him after a date? Do what feels comfortable. When I'm seeing someone I'm comfortable with, I have no problem reaching out some of the time. But we often do for the wrong reasons—because we haven't heard from him and want to know how he feels. When a man says he'll call and doesn't, do you look for any reason to contact him? Perhaps you'll send a text to remind him you're there. Waiting is hard. Sometimes I call right after a date, preferably when I can leave a voicemail message or send a short text. I thank him for dinner or whatever and say I had a nice time. Now the ball's in his court and I don't have to go through "Should I call or wait?" It honestly doesn't matter. If he likes you, you'll hear from him. Contacting him and feeling rejected because you can sense he doesn't want to communicate can damage your self-esteem more than just not hearing from him. That's why I prefer to leave it alone.

I learned a valuable lesson from Pete. He called two weeks after our first date, leaving a message saying that he wanted to see me again. It was a Thursday, and I was out for the next two days. Saturday night I was with another guy when I listened to a second message from Pete:

> I called you, and you didn't call back. I thought you were interested. I had a good time when we went out. Well, I called again because I realized I hadn't left my phone number last time and thought maybe you lost it, so here it is. I do hope to hear from you soon.

There was an attitude in his voice. Pete had waited two weeks to call me but was annoyed that I hadn't called back in two days. He used one of my old excuses for calling: "Maybe he lost my number." Admit it: You've used it too. Or you've called to see if something happened to him. "Maybe he had an accident and that's why I haven't heard from him." Etc., etc., etc. Trust me: When he doesn't call, there was no accident. He isn't dead. The only thing that's ready to be buried is that excuse. Pete turned my stomach with his message. I couldn't figure out what it was that got to me until the guy I was with said, "That sounds like the messages women leave." Guilty as charged. I swore I'd never leave another one of those messages. Be in control and call him only for the right reasons.

See the Real You

One technique I use for self-awareness involves trying to step outside myself and observe my interaction with others. Often you're not aware of how you come across. In order to change how people treat you, cue them by changing your own behavior. But how can you know what to work on if you're not aware of your responses to others?

You often take yourself for granted, assuming you're handling things as well as possible. You need to pay serious attention to yourself in situations where you don't get a response you like. Listen to yourself carefully. Becoming aware of what you do enables you to see what doesn't work. When I first heard my whine, I wondered why I'd never noticed it before. I paid more attention to other people's communication than my own. Now I listen to me, and watch my movements. Sometimes I feel like a detective looking for clues. The only way to change is to know how you act. Remember: Self-awareness is a first step toward self-improvement!

What can you watch for? Do you complain with a whine or an air of superiority like a know-it-all? How many times do you get apologetic, saying "I'm sorry" when you've done nothing wrong? Saying "I'm sorry" regularly puts you on the defensive and affects your self-esteem. Does your demeanor or tone of voice say more than your words? How does that tone make you feel? How would you like someone to speak to you like that? Be objective. Maybe it's time for a different intonation, volume level, or attitude. Be honest about how you'd respond if you were the other person.

Become aware of your body language. Do you look impatient, frustrated, or angry? Are you positive or negative? Do you appear confident or insecure? Men pick up on these things, and it affects their response. Are your hands clenched on your hips? That may put him on the defensive. Do you look relaxed about what you do or say? Are you smiling? These appearances affect how others perceive you. How often do you get emotional when you know you should be in control? What situations change your balance from being in control to letting your emotions take over? Become aware of yourself and your interaction with your partner. Identifying the signs allows you to find more empowering ways of interacting with men.

Learning from Others

Observing how others handle situations helps identify what might work for you. Seeing your traits in others can make you more objective about them. I'm not saying you should imitate people, but it's easier to see personality styles in others. Become a people-watcher. After being one way all my life, I didn't know how to change. So I took bits and pieces I liked in others and incorporated them into my own style. I recommend choosing designated role models. Find women who get what they want or whose persona you wish you had, and study them. Ramona told a support group:

> There's a woman I work with who I admire. She has everyone's respect. No one gossips about her. She always has a boyfriend who's not a jerk. I've always wished to be more like her. I took the suggestion to observe qualities about this woman's behavior and personality and have been able to pinpoint specific ways she handles people. I'm learning from her. I've seen several ways she's spoken to men that I'll try. She exudes confidence in everything she does. I hope to emulate her enough to develop my own confidence.

How do you respond to the tone of other people's voices? Are there things in their behavior that make you respond positively? What puts you off? Use these factors as a barometer for yourself. I was able to hear the whine in my own voice more objectively after I heard it in other women. Yuck! Hearing their whines turned me off so much that I made a concerted effort to lose mine.

Become a couple-watcher. Watch how other women interact with men. Observing them showed me what I didn't want. Is she fawning all over him? Is there a balance between them? Is she giving more affection, holding on, and in general putting out more energy? You may notice more women clinging to men, while the men give little reciprocation. I personally no longer want to be like the women holding on to a man tightly, caressing his butt, kissing him periodically, and so on, while he struts beside her with a look of indifference. Been there, done that. Having seen this behavior in others, it won't work for me anymore. Julie told my class:

> I listen in on the conversations of couples near me—in restaurants, in lines, in the park. Women complain a lot. They get that naggy sound when they do. Or, they let a guy run all over them while they show love. Since I've been snooping, I've recognized my own patterns in women and don't like it. It was quite an awakening to discover this. I used to wonder why men don't take me as seriously as I'd like. Now I know one reason. I consider my snooping an education in personal growth. You can really learn from others.

Do you see patterns in other couples reminiscent of the interaction in your past or present relationship? How does it look to you on someone else? I've watched couples interact and thought, "Nope, I never again want that to be me."

Chapter Sixteen

Accepting the Differences Between Men and Women

"Men are taught to apologize for their weaknesses, women for their strengths."

LOIS WYSE

In my classes, I encourage people to have a more realistic view of their relationships. The philosophy behind it is that if you ever want to be happy, you must accept people as they are. Your only healthy choices are to find ways to deal with them as they are or choose not to deal with them at all. That includes men! You don't have to like the way they are, but you must accept it. Men won't change because you don't agree with their ways. The only person you can change is yourself. The good news: You *can* change your responses to things you don't like, which may ultimately get you what you want.

One of the first realities you can choose to accept if you want to get along with men is that they're raised differently from women. Their communication techniques, levels of intimacy, need for space, etc., might not be the same as yours. And they have a right to these differences, whether they suit your needs or not! This is a reality that most women don't want to accept but accept you must if you want the best chance of having a good relationship.

Think about how many times you've stewed because a man in your life hasn't done what you thought he should. I've been very guilty of this myself. I thought I knew how a relationship "should" be and how my partner "should" act or respond in various scenarios. Women set their own timetables and agendas and then see them as rules. I believe the biggest frustration that women experience with men is our inability to get them to do what we think they're "supposed" to do. We use "should's" and "supposed to's" as if we're the supreme beings in a relationship. The key to getting along well with men in general is to accept the answer to a question I finally asked myself: "Who the hell gave women the right to set the rules, to make their needs more important, and to decide how men should act or are supposed to respond in a relationship?" We gave it to ourselves. Is that fair? No.

Let Men Be Men

I addressed this earlier, but it needs to be repeated. Men have a right to be themselves. They have a right to their differences. They have a right to expect to get some of their needs met, whether you agree with them or not. Be fair. I've talked about how men can be manipulative. Well, so can we. Men consistently say that one reason they hesitate to get involved in a long-term relationship is that they're loathe to deal with the rules SHE sets. You can learn to distinguish between things about a man that are intolerable/wrong and those just not to your liking.

It's funny how when you first fall for a guy, you accept many of those things that you later find intolerable. At the beginning of a relationship, you may make yourself very "user-friendly," going along with what he wants and viewing some of his faults as endearing little annoyances. Later, you try to change those faults. Dave told me, "If she finds a lot of things about me objectionable and complains all the time, I wonder why she's with me." By accepting his quirks and flaws as part of the total package, you'll have a more realistic relationship. By allowing him more freedom to be himself, you can get along much better with him. In the long run, this might include getting more of *your* needs met. Michael related his experience:

> When I start dating someone, I'm on edge, waiting to see if and when she'll dictate what she wants. Women can be so sweet in the beginning. But often when we start sleeping together . . . sometimes before . . . they change . . . all those damn rules. Why do so many women think they're the more important one in a relationship? Sure, plenty of men are pigs. I don't blame women for having standards. But I'm a good guy and don't like being treated like I'm regularly wrong. "I want this." "I want that." I'm not just in a relationship to get laid, but that's how a lot of women act . . . like my needs don't go beyond bed. A lot of women don't seem to care what men need. When I meet one who just flows with it . . . who doesn't criticize or complain much, I try harder to make her happy.

He doesn't have to be romantic all the time. There's no law saying he has to communicate on your level. Try to see those annoying differences as his lovable quirks, the way you did when you first met. If you can use your energy to work on yourself and stop concentrating on him so much, he may relax. It's fine to let him know *once*, in a nice way, what you have a hard time with. If he doesn't get it, alter your own behavior. Trust me: If he's not a jerk, he'll appreciate your efforts and may try harder to give you more of what you want if you're not hassling him regularly. Save your energy for things that cause you legitimate pain.

You've seen that trying to change men often means losing them in the long run. It's more effective to find ways to respond to his differences that you feel more comfortable with. By lessening his importance, his differences can seem less irritating. After all, your happiness shouldn't be too dependent on what you get from him. That doesn't mean you should sell yourself short, but it's time for you to accept that men don't have to change because you have a specific image of what you want. Men don't deserve to be labeled as jerks because they don't do things the way you want them to.

Choose Your Battles

Men are people, not clay. If you don't wise up and face the reality of men, you'll spend your life complaining about and/or fighting with them. Getting angry, nagging, or dumping them won't change things. Showing respect for who they are is a healthier direction. Focusing on making yourself healthier and happier in your own right is more practical than always struggling against reality. Speak up for the important stuff, but choose your battles wisely instead of making a big deal out of everything. You can get more that way.

Since I've adopted this attitude, I've had men treat me better out of appreciation for my accepting them. The bottom line is, if he's not a jerk and does care about you, he'll want to please you. As Lyle said:

> I used to be on the defensive at first when a woman tried to change me. It didn't seem fair that women knew what they wanted in a man when it's often what most men aren't. So when a woman tried to make me someone I'm not, I'd get an attitude. Even the smallest complaint made me bristle. When I finally

met someone who accepted me as me, I married her. Sometimes my wife lets me know what bothers her. If it's reasonable, I'll make an effort. My friends agree with me that if a woman is reasonable, there's more incentive to pay attention to things that do bother her.

Understanding why men have different needs and ways of responding to situations can help you accept reality. If you're open-minded, you might actually learn something from men. I have. It's funny because since I've developed more autonomy, I'm often told that I think more like a man. Maybe they are doing something right!

Whose Fault Is It, Anyway?

Is it men or women who are at fault in what has become known as the battle of the sexes? Neither is. Just as women might be victims of our upbringing, men also carry the burden of theirs. Believe me, not all men like having to be "the stronger sex." Many told me that they hate having to achieve or feel restricted in showing their feelings about people or situations. They wish they could share their fears and shortcomings with their friends but have been taught not to. Stereotypes taught in childhood affect both sexes. Boys and girls are brought up differently, and there's no right or wrong. Most of the stereotypical qualities that annoy you about men were conditioned in their childhood, just as you were conditioned to be more emotional and needy and not to live an autonomous life.

Showing respect for those differences can go a long way. Developing the patience to find ways of compromising instead of always trying to have things on your terms is more realistic. All men are not jerks because they don't live up to your expectations. They may just not be right for you. If you keep looking for perfection, you won't find it. Too many good men are written off as jerks because they don't fit your mold.

By putting your energy into making yourself happy, you may not need a man to be a certain way. If you develop a sense of self, of autonomy, your world won't revolve around him. When I'm seeing someone, he may be the sweetest, most delicious piece of my life. But he isn't my entire life—I am. Now I can live with many differences that I never could before.

Why Can't Men Think Like Women?

Of course life would be easier if men had the same mentality as women. But they don't. That's reality. And this disparity in the way men and women think isn't something either sex can help. You've heard it before: Men have been brought up to be goal-oriented. They see their worth in terms of their accomplishments. Women are brought up to please. We see our worth in terms of who likes us. The ultimate form of validation for an average man is to succeed in a goal. The ultimate form of validation for an average woman is to have a man want her.

Average men define themselves by less personal factors than women do: by how much money they make; how important their job is; being able to repair their car or install something in their house; how much power they believe they have; how much danger they can conquer; how safe and protected a woman feels with them; how many positive results they see from something they've done. Average women define themselves by more personal factors: Do I have a man in my life? Do people like me? Am I pretty enough? Is my body thin enough? Then man meets woman, looking to achieve, and woman meets man, looking to be loved and romanced. And the clash begins.

While both sexes have lots in common, our responses may be different. We all want to be liked and appreciated. Men aren't the heartless creatures we like to make them out to be. They just aren't equipped to handle their feelings like we are. They haven't learned to share and communicate emotions the way we've been allowed to. Men are more subtle. Too often you want the overt reaction so badly that you miss the low-key expression of feelings he gives. Men feel everything you do but don't show it the same way. That doesn't make them wrong. For example, Joan complained to my class:

> Wayne never tells me how he feels about anything. Well, maybe he does try, but it's so little. I keep asking him to open up more, and he insists he is. But he doesn't tell me what I want to hear. He does say that he cares more often, and I guess he calls more regularly too. But he doesn't share that much. He says he does, but he doesn't. Maybe a little, but it's not very deep. Why can't men open up?

Forget the "but's"! Joan had a "but" for everything that wasn't exactly as she wanted it. I told Joan that Wayne sounded like he was trying. She wanted him to communicate the way she did. That's not fair! When a man makes an effort to open up, even if it's not on your level, you should show appreciation and not keep trying to get him to do it your way. Let him get comfortable with his progress before pushing him further. Men can learn to trust you enough to let you in, as long as they can do it on their own terms. Making demands will put them on the defensive and they'll be less willing to give you what they think you want.

From Heart to Heartless

One complaint often lodged against females is that we're more emotional than men. Although there's a difference in the genetic makeup of males and females, I believe women exhibit more emotional behavior because we're allowed and often encouraged to show our feelings as children. Crying is completely accepted in girls. Boys are discouraged from showing tears, often being ridiculed or even punished for shedding them. They may be told it's unmanly or just plain unacceptable to cry. Boys showing tears in front of other children may be labeled a wimp, or even (heaven forbid the insult!) a girl! Memories of these stereotypes stay with guys into adulthood. They still hold back because they don't know how to let go or they're scared of being judged.

You know what? No matter how much they said they wanted a man who can express his emotions, most of the women I interviewed found it unmanly when their partner showed a lot of sensitivity and expressed himself. We're just not used to it. Men are supposed to be the stronger sex. It's harder to feel safe with someone who seems vulnerable. I once dated a guy who said he was in touch with his feelings. Whenever he felt an emotion, he'd get teary-eyed. I'd get nauseous. He took showing emotions to the extreme. Having never experienced this reaction in a guy, it was a turn-off. Surprisingly, men crying or showing a lot of vulnerability is unattractive to many of you when you finally get what you think you want. And men know it. As Jim revealed:

"Don't cry. Don't let people know how you feel." My father and older brother drummed that into my head my whole life. I still felt fear and hurt and disappointment but never let anyone know. My friends were more or less the same way. I actually got up the nerve to go for therapy and tried to let my feelings out more, but it didn't work. It wasn't me that had a problem. I still couldn't let my friends see the feeling side of me. They made fun of other guys who showed their emotions, calling them gay. I tried letting my walls down with several women I was involved with, but they didn't like it much either. At first they liked having a guy who could cry a little and express feelings. But when the novelty wore off, I could feel that they preferred me to keep it to myself. One told me I wasn't sexy anymore when I opened up. Another said it made me seem weak. So what's the answer?

Men believe getting in touch with their emotions carries a stigma. We're on the other end of the spectrum. I believe that young girls are conditioned to use emotions to get gratification. If we cry when we fall down, we may get a hug and a fun Band-Aid to cheer us up. Boys often get told to take it like a man. Girls learn that if they whine and cry enough, daddy may give them their way. It doesn't work for boys nearly as often. We also learn that "no" can turn into "yes" if we relentlessly prod adults to change their minds. Hence we get trained in nagging. We learn to use our emotions to manipulate, whereas boys learn that hiding theirs gets more approval. As we grow from little girls into grown women, we continue these patterns, often using tears and nagging to get what we want, which isn't effective or healthy as adults. Boys grow into men who continue stifling emotions to gain respect, which is unhealthy to the degree many do it. These habits are so ingrained that they're hard to break, even when we want to. When neither partner can relate to the other's emotional direction, a clash is unavoidable.

Communicate Your Needs

A common frustration between the sexes is a man's inability to understand what a woman wants from him. When they're upset or not in a good mood, men tend to crave space and women want comfort. Since their needs are so opposite, it's hard for each sex to accept what the other wants. You may talk to a man about something that bothers you and he says nothing. It can get frustrating when you want some consoling words and he seems not to be listening to you. He may hear every word, but if he has no solution to your problem, he'll remain silent as you wait for empathy. Brad told me:

> Susan sometimes comes home complaining about something that happened at work. She gets very worked up. I'm very tired after work and can't do any heavy thinking then. I wish I knew what to advise her to do. She gets very upset if I don't

respond. But I'm no good at that. She seems to get good answers from her friends. If I knew what she wanted, I'd try harder. When I ask what she wants from me, she often cries or tells me she wants me to listen. I do listen! She makes no sense to me at these times.

Men are so practical that it can be hard for them to understand the dynamics of our complicated emotional needs. A man hears a problem and feels obligated to fix it. If he has no solution, he backs off. We, on the other hand, may just need to vent and crave a sympathetic ear to hear our woes. We don't want to be told what to do and just need to get our feelings out. A man doesn't know that. He gets frustrated because he doesn't know what we want. We get frustrated because of that. We don't know how to tell him what we want because we think he should understand. What a mess—out of something so simple on the surface!

Men need it spelled out to them. They aren't intuitive like we are. They often can't understand your needs because they don't have the same ones. Nor do they read minds. A man needs to be told that you just need an ear to talk to and that if he'd just listen, you'd be grateful. He needs to be reassured that if you're not asking him for answers, it doesn't mean that you don't trust him. He needs to understand that when you say, "I want you to listen to me," you mean "This means looking at me when I speak and giving me your undivided attention." You must be very clear about what you want and explain why it's important to you. He may very well be listening as he cleans his boots. Then he gets annoyed when you accuse him of not listening. And to you that reaffirms he's a jerk. But he's not.

When experiencing stress or going through a rough time, women tend to need more personal contact and men tend to need more distance. How confusing to both sexes! Those little girls who got cuddled and pampered when they were upset still want that kind of attention during rough times as adults. Those little boys who were encouraged to handle their problems more stoically still need to sulk in private. So while you reach out to be touched, a man tries to get away. Learn to respect his need for space. When you do, he may listen more when you explain what you need when something bothers you. It can be a two-way street. If you stop fighting his needs, he may stop fighting some of yours. Compromise is possible. Lori related her story:

Bill and I had serious rough spots. When he'd come home after a bad day, I'd try to hug and kiss him. He'd push me off. I'd get upset, and he'd ignore me. At times I'd have given anything for some soothing. We'd fight about it regularly.

One day his sister told me that when he was young and had a problem, he was made to go to his room to sort it out alone. I asked Bill about it, and he said it was the only way he knew to deal with problems. He didn't know how to handle me being all over him when he had things on his mind. He couldn't understand why I'd want that.

For the first time I explained how I was used to being comforted. We finally understood each other's needs. Now we respect each other more. I still want to throw my arms around him when he's unhappy, but I hold back. When I'm upset, he tries to be more consoling, even though he feels awkward. I wish we'd had this conversation sooner. We've been talking out more of our differences when we're not upset. It's great.

The Differences in Communication Styles

One area of communication in which men and women go awry is expressing their feelings. A common complaint from women is, "I know he loves me, but I need to hear the words regularly and he won't say them." Men don't feel the same, so they don't understand. We need reassurance, and they think we're nuts. Remember, men are much more practical than we are. They don't understand why certain things are so important to you. If they don't understand the reason for something, they have a hard time accepting it. If it doesn't make sense in their way of thinking, they may not take it seriously. Then we may get frustrated and demanding in our desire to get verbal reinforcement from him. Don said:

> I honestly don't understand why women need to be told I like them, I care, I find them attractive, and everything else they need to hear all the time. I'm not used to those words. I feel them but don't want to say too much. I try to be good to a woman I'm seeing. Isn't that enough? Why would I take her out if I didn't like her and find her attractive?

I had a boyfriend who gave no compliments or caring words. It drove me crazy. He treated me well and there was little doubt that he cared, but I wanted words. When he picked me up, I needed to hear that I looked nice. I'd see it in his eyes, but words never came. Sometimes I'd complain, "You never tell me I look good." He'd answer that since on our first date he said I was pretty, why must he repeat himself? I was exasperated. It proved how ingrained our needs are, as it continued to bug me. Yet logically, he made sense. Although he never said the words, he told me with actions. A large part of me was grateful to be with a man who "proved otherwise." But I still craved words, and he never gave in. I didn't know whether to be mad at him or myself.

Men don't need as much verbal reassurance as we do. They probably don't spend nearly as much time getting ready for a date, so they don't need their appearance to be acknowledged. They're more practical about needing to hear you express feelings to them. Many actually prefer not to hear them, knowing our expectations might increase. So they can't put themselves in our shoes to understand why we need their compliments so badly.

Since men are practical, communicating to them on a less emotional, more concrete level can help get your message across. Rather than wasting energy whining about what you need from him, you may get through better by clearly explaining how you feel, what you'd like, and why. Men need to understand before they can relate. And they need to be able to relate before they can take your needs seriously. If they can't relate to them, they may see your demands/requests/needs as unimportant and label them as "women stuff," treat them as trivial nonsense, or just ignore them.

When you learn to accept others—including men—as they are, it may help you accept yourself more as you are. Actions really are more significant than words. Jerks throw the right words at you freely, and you lap them up. It's doing the right thing that they fall short on.

Chapter Seventeen

Building a Relationship with Yourself

"To love oneself is the beginning of a life-long romance."

OSCAR WILDE

This chapter isn't about having a relationship with a man. It's about having one with yourself. You can jump from one man to another, but until you find peace within yourself, you won't easily be able to find and sustain a healthy relationship with someone else. The next two chapters focus on YOU instead of HIM. Please read them with an open mind. By embracing a sense of faith and trust in yourself, you can turn HIM into him. It can be the beginning of a happier, complete life on its own terms, if you choose to make it so.

Getting Rid of Old Messages

When I was fifteen, a friend's boyfriend told me, "With your shape and face, you'd be a knockout IF you'd lose some weight." Those words haunt my life for years, making me feel not good enough. They crumbled the fragile foundation of my self-esteem and continued to shatter my sense of self as I grew up thinking that my weight would always hold me back. This one guy's words set a tone for my life: I needed to know my place; that gorgeous guys would find me fat, so I should settle for anyone who liked me; that women who seemed very put-together and fit wouldn't want to be friends with someone who wasn't thin. In retrospect, I get annoyed remembering that this guy was a slovenly pig who was more overweight than I ever was. How dare he say that to me! And I was never fat. I just wasn't perfectly slim.

Your growth can be curtailed by worrying about what others think. I learned at a young age to please others and judge myself by their opinions. I wanted everyone to like me, and they liked me more when I worried more about them than about myself. This mentality influenced my relationships. Insecurity about my appearance drove me to please men so that they wouldn't notice my cellulite or that my hair wasn't always perfect. I figured they'd tolerate my faults if I compensated by being a good girl. When I finally began working on my self-esteem, the "security" I got from men was no longer worth the price of giving myself away. I was brought up to please and finally turned that instinct onto myself!

I've learned through experience that I'm the only one who can get me what I want in life. The strength and power to attain happiness and control must come from inside me. It's not easy to do, but it's important to realize that you all have the power to create a wonderful life for yourselves. The keys for getting there are a strong sense of self-esteem, building your self-love and creating a belief system based on your individual spirituality. Years ago I'd have laughed at the thought of ever saying that, because I hated myself and had no faith. Today I set myself up as an example of how powerful it is to love yourself and have trust in a higher being.

How many hours and days and years and decades have you spent reading books and taking classes, trying to find answers about how to get what you want? How much energy have you put into the others you looked to for your happiness? It's taken almost a lifetime to discover that my happiness can only come from me—that I've always had the answers but just never knew where to look.

Building Your Self-Esteem

Self-esteem or a lack of it is the reason why you get/don't get what you want in life. In her book *Revolution from Within*, Gloria Steinem says that "self-esteem isn't everything, it's just that there's nothing without it." So what's self-esteem, and how can you all get some?

I've always thought of self-esteem as simply unconditional self-approval. But good self-esteem doesn't mean being perfect. Having it requires accepting yourself in your imperfect, human state. You don't need to get rid of what you see as your faults. Instead, you can begin to accept yourself as you are, imperfections and all, even if there are things you'd like to change. I'd love to lose ten (okay, twenty) pounds, but I'm still happy with myself and feel strong self-love. If you set standards that are impossible to attain, you'll always fall short. By accepting yourself as is, warts and all, you can stop judging yourself by your shortcomings. My personal definition of self-esteem is feeling comfortable in your own skin.

Self-esteem refers to what you think of yourself. Since you may have been brought up to judge your worth by how others see you, how can you easily develop a positive self-image? Developing good self-esteem begins with redefining what you've been taught. It requires you to understand that having a good-looking boyfriend with lots of money doesn't make you who you are, though it may feed into old messages. Does having a man always make you sincerely happy? Developing the power to take control of my life has been key for increasing my joy. As your self-esteem develops, the power to control your life increases. The more control you take, the greater your self-esteem becomes. What a nice vicious cycle! It's a beautiful process that's available to everyone.

Self-esteem motivates you to take good care of yourself. It gives you confidence to go for what you want. Self-esteem enables you to stand up to people and helps you take responsibility for what happens in your life. Instead of blaming a man for your unhappiness and just calling him a jerk, self-esteem can motivate you to take responsibility for being in the relationship in the first place. It enables you to see that it's your choice to stay or go. And if you choose to stay, self-esteem helps you change your response to him in ways that might get you more of what you want. It gives you confidence to do what you have to do, even if you risk losing HIM. As Cynthia said:

> I've been working on myself for years. What I've noticed the most is my standards are higher than ever. Sometimes I don't realize I'm expecting more until I look back and see how fast I called someone on something I didn't like. I used to go out with any guy I was remotely attracted to. When they did things that today I wouldn't take, I gave them every chance. Today I've little patience. I think well of myself . . . can't be bothered with a guy who doesn't show he knows my worth. The ones I date know if they play games, I'm history. I get fussier and fussier as I feel better and better about myself. It's nice.

Get to Know Yourself

To develop self-esteem, you must accept yourself in your imperfect state. How do you do that? One baby step at a time. Start on the ground and work your way up. If you've hated yourself all your life, you won't just wake up tomorrow filled with self-appreciation. Developing self-esteem is a process that begins with the first step. Start by saying the affirmation "I approve of myself as I am" many times a day. It will eventually sink in!

Self-awareness helps develop self-esteem. How do you treat yourself? Get to know yourself—I mean really pay attention. What do you think when you make mistakes? Do you treat yourself with kindness? Do you make an effort to take care of yourself? Treating yourself more lovingly is a catalyst for building self-esteem. You can choose to make a concerted effort to do things for your own well-being. By paying more attention to what you do, you learn what to work on and develop more appreciation for your good qualities.

As I said earlier, writing things down increases consciousness. Start with a list of things you like about yourself. Add to it daily as you think of more. Include anything you like about yourself, no matter how trivial it may seem. Also include compliments people give you, however silly they seem. If you stop focusing on big qualities and start appreciating less obvious ones, you may start to see that there's more to appreciate than you thought.

Keep the list in a convenient spot where you can see it and read it regularly. Allow yourself to feel good about things you never considered special before. Continue saying "I approve of myself" on a regular basis.

Learn to Accept Yourself

Having good self-esteem enables you to cut yourself slack. You're often harder on yourself than on others. When you goof up next time, think about how you'd reassure a friend who's done what you did. You'd be kind, wouldn't you? Well do that for you, too! Be reassuring instead of tearing yourself apart. Don't get angry at yourself for being human! Find positives in what doesn't go right. For example, you may have been nervous and not given your best presentation, but the information was well documented. Feel pride for that. Just because you're not perfect, you're not a failure. Mistakes don't make you a loser. Get out of the habit of all-or-nothing thinking. That's not being fair to you! You wouldn't call a friend a loser if she makes a mistake. Learn to cut yourself the same slack. Practice being your own best friend and forgive yourself.

How many times do you get angry with yourself for doing something dumb/wrong/stupid/idiotic and other adjectives you use when you're not perfect? I did this until I started doing something that's had a profound effect on my outlook. In the past, I'd spill a glass of milk and say, "That was stupid." Or, I'd lament something inappropriate like, "What an idiot I am." When I realized I wasn't treating myself fairly and needed a way to show myself forgiveness, I got in the habit of replacing negative words with "silly." "Silly" takes the bite out of "stupid." I laugh when I use it instead of calling myself unkind names. If I use a harsher word, I quickly replace it with "silly." I equate "silly" with self-forgiveness and a desire to be kind to me. Every time I call myself "silly," it reinforces my self-acceptance.

Do you have trouble accepting compliments like I used to? I see self-esteem growing by learning to say "thank you," and then quickly shut your mouth. For most of my life, I was very uncomfortable when something nice was said to me. I'd always diminish the positives. If someone complimented my shoes, I'd immediately say that I'd bought them cheap in a flea market, even if I didn't! When asked if I'd lost weight, I'd say "no," even when I had. I'd make excuses for why I might look thinner. I denied every compliment in some way. Subconsciously, I played the old message that people wouldn't like me if I thought too much of myself. One day I caught myself and forced my mouth to just say "thanks" to compliments and then shut up. It still feels a bit funny, but it's also empowering in a weird way. For the first time in my life, I'm conscious that I deserve the compliments.

Be very patient with yourself. You've spent a lifetime developing bad habits. It'll take time to change them. Be gentle with yourself but persevere. If you get extremely silly at times, forgive yourself and start again. It's okay to goof up (another less harsh term). Remember that you're still wonderful!

Affirm a Great Life

What's an affirmation? I define it as something you say aloud or to yourself, as if you believe it to be true. By saying it regularly, it can become a reality. How many times have you said "Bad things always happens to me!" And then bad things do indeed keep happening? That's because you're making a negative affirmation. People unfamiliar with affirmations often start off not believing that they work, which is okay. But if you keep saying them, they eventually sink in and make you a believer. Esther, a sixty-seven-year-old woman recommended to my group by her therapist, told us:

> People have treated me like a doormat all my life. I have grown children who treat me with disrespect. Recently my daughter Jean asked to move in with me when her lease expires, and I begrudgingly agreed. She knows I'm looking for a tenant. I know I'll be miserable but couldn't say "no." I've agonized about how awful it will be but don't know how to get out of it. I feel supported when this group insists I do what's best for me. But I don't have strength at home.

I told Esther to say "My daughter will not move in with me" to herself on the way home, and aloud in private as much as she could. The next week, her therapist called and asked what I'd done to Esther. At a session with her daughter, he was thrilled that she was firm about Jean not moving in. Esther then arrived for our group all excited:

> I used affirmations to convince myself my daughter will not move in with me. I said it over and over and was surprised when I actually felt determined! I shocked Jean when I said I'd changed my mind. I repeated affirmations that she wouldn't live with me above her cries. I deserve to live peacefully, and my

daughter would prevent that from happening. For the first time in my life I feel in some control. I smile more and feel much more positive. And my daughter will live elsewhere.

Affirmations work. If you don't get instant gratification, it's not the right time. Often you're not ready for what you think you need and lose faith when you don't get what you ask for. You don't always get what you want, but you do get what you need. Learn to trust that it will come when you're ready for it. Understanding this power enables you to flow with life's ups and downs.

I use affirmations for confidence. Whereas I used to write notes before making an important phone call, saying "I trust myself to say the right thing" now enables me to speak with confidence. I use affirmations to break obsessions, including a need for a man when only jerks are in sight. "I have control over my choices." "I attract only healthy men into my world." I do believe it. It's the most secure feeling one can ever wish for.

I also use affirmations to calm myself down during moments of stress. My favorite one, "Everything will work out fine. Whatever's meant to be will be," is my mantra for staying grounded. When I'm in a situation that makes me nervous, I repeat my mantra and know it will be fine. Remember: You can't always have it your way, but it will work out. The stronger your belief, the more you can use this power.

Count Your Blessings

We often complain that life isn't doing right by us, or we resort to thoughts like "Why does this always happen to me?" These thoughts can keep you negative. Since your thought patterns affect your life, giving out positive, happy, and benevolent vibes will eventually attract positive, happy, and benevolent situations and people into your life. A good place to focus on the positives is to count your blessings. You may have wonderful things happening in your life, but focus more on the negative circumstances. Stop that now!

Make a list of all the good things you have to be grateful for. I'm not just talking about a large pay raise or a very special person. I also mean the little things, like having sunlight in your apartment, friendly service people, your freedom, healthy parents, good eyesight—I could go on and on. List anything that gives you pleasure, satisfaction, relief from problems, etc. I always assign this as homework to my support groups. Then the participants read their lists of blessings. Often they're surprised to realize how much they have to be thankful for. Pat told a group when she read her list:

> I never thought about all the good things in my life . . . the ones I should be grateful for but never think about. Guess I'm too busy complaining about what I don't have. Men take up too much of my time. I worry so much about where to find one and then how to keep him happy. Men have become so important to me that the rest just falls by the wayside. I'm so glad we did this exercise. It made me remember how blessed I am. There are a lot of good things in my life. It's funny, because I haven't dated a guy in a long time who I'd consider a blessing. Now that tells me a lot about my priorities. I'm much happier now.

Become aware of the small things in your life that you may take for granted. Add to your list. Next time you're saying "Oh, woe is me!" take out your list of blessings and remind yourself of the good in your life! We all have blessings. You just have to look for them.

Tap Into the Power of Spirituality

I believe with all my heart that the best support you have for finding and keeping happiness is a sense of spirituality. It still amazes me that

I'm writing this because I had no true sense of God for most of my life. I scoffed everything spiritual. Now I live by faith.

What is spirituality? It's hard to describe, since it really is an individual definition. For me, becoming spiritual meant developing faith in a higher power that supports every aspect of my life. I developed trust in what I referred to as the Universe and worked my way up to believing in God. Creating spiritual support can be easier if you already believe in God, which I didn't. I tried to believe out of desperation when I felt low about my life. When I started trusting that I'd be taken care of and that the Universe worked with me, it did.

If you look to your higher power for support, you get it. As you relax into faith, life works with you. People who doubt the power of faith often ask how I can believe in a higher power that allows people to suffer or have tragedies. They tell me they've prayed to no avail. My answer is that you get support in what you expect, I mean seriously expect with faith, and for actions to get it. If you sit home and pray, you'll get support sitting and praying. If you get off your butt and work toward getting what you need with the expectation of receiving, you get support working with you toward that end. Worrying endlessly expresses doubt that you'll be taken care of, which defeats you by projecting a lack of trust. Trusting that you'll get what you need invites support.

I truly believe it's nearly impossible to develop good self-esteem or to take control of your life without a belief in something. You need faith and support. So the first step toward finding answers inside of you is trying to develop faith in whatever feels comfortable to you. When you see that it works, your trust will intensify. Faith keeps me whole, happy, and secure. I'm not religious, but my faith is pure and solid.

Being very spiritual has helped me relax about most issues in my life, including men. I know I'll meet someone healthy for me when the time is right. Faith allowed me to understand when I wasn't ready for a relationship yet. I had to get myself in order first. When I reach that point, I'll put out a message that I'm in the right place to meet a healthy man. For the first time in my life, I believe I'm close. Faith helps me trust that there's a reason for everything that happens. When things don't go well, I know that something good will come of it and affirm that, "everything happens for a reason." It keeps my sanity and helps me get through situations I don't care for. Life can't go my way all the time, but my trust is strong enough to flow with almost anything. Each time something I don't like is going on, I look back later to find the reason. I always discover it!

In life, you get back what you put out. If I give out good, my life attracts good. Grasping this concept and making it part of your life can provide the most powerful tool you can have for taking control. It doesn't require practicing a formal religion or going to a place of worship. And it's free, easy, requires no installation, and can last forever. The only hard part is being patient enough to allow yourself to believe and to give up some control to God, the Universe, the source energy, or whatever you believe in.

Fall in Love with Yourself

I love myself. I have awful flabby thighs and would like to be thinner. But I love myself. I talk too much. But I love myself. I don't have a man in my life at the moment. But I love myself. Even with my shortcomings, I still love and approve of me, imperfections and all! That's what self-esteem is all about.

Self-esteem begins with self-love. When you love yourself, good self-esteem is a natural result. Say "I love you" regularly to yourself. Say it to a mirror even if you don't feel comfortable about it. If it's difficult, see if you can figure out what's making it tough, but keep trying. It may take awhile. Try to say it every day without a mirror, until you can look yourself straight in the eye. I still do it every day, often many times . . . when I brush my teeth, comb my hair, walk by a mirror. Self-love is the purest because it's not destructive. It's the most bountiful love affair you'll ever have. Alice admitted to her group:

Looking in the mirror was one of the hardest things I've ever done. I didn't like looking at myself. All I saw were my faults. I hated my hair . . . the lines on my face . . . my body. But I did it. At least I tried for weeks to do it. But my eyes couldn't look. I did say "I love you" to myself, with disgust. I only did it because the group encouraged me. But one day I took a peek as I said it. It wasn't that terrible. I peeked again later. Slowly I was able to look at myself. Now I say it all the time. It's such a big deal for me. It's changed my whole life. I'm actually starting to believe it. It's a source of peace now. I'm starting to look better.

Getting love from others starts with loving yourself. If you don't love and think well of yourself, why should someone healthy love you? If you don't love yourself, what will motivate you to set high standards about how men treat you? If you don't like yourself on your own terms, you'll never approve of yourself beyond the approval you get from a man. Then your validation as a woman will disappear when he does, which can keep you clinging to a man at any cost. Holding on to a man for the wrong reasons batters your self-esteem.

Listen, I've been there, and spent many good years of my life thinking that I was nothing without a man—that I only looked good if HE told me so—that I had very little worth as a person beyond what I could do for HIM; that nobody would want me unless I made HIS needs a priority. I've spent years looking in the mirror and seeing only what HIS eyes saw. I've hated myself for having cellulite. But baby step by baby step, I walked away from my need for a man as day by day I worked on being more loving to me.

As I loved myself more, I stayed with each jerk for shorter periods of time. I started standing up for myself instead of always leaning down to kiss their butts. It wasn't easy, yet once I started building my self-esteem, I loved myself more. Getting control over myself and my needs was the most exhilarating feeling I've ever experienced—better than great sex! Now I'm someone who thanks God every day for helping me to find and love myself unconditionally.

Ask yourself: Besides sex, what need does a man fill? Does he give you validation? Make you feel wanted? Give you security? Make you feel normal? Give you someone to care for? I used to need a man for all those reasons. Good friends I've attracted now fill in some of the holes. And I fill them myself! Self-love helps me do that. Keep remembering that a man can be the most delicious part of your life, but he shouldn't *be* your life! After years of struggle and pain and work and opening my eyes, I finally know that the only one who can give me a happy life is me.

Take Care of Yourself

Show yourself love by making a concerted effort to treat yourself well. I do something for myself at least once a day. It can be a simple act like giving myself a fifteen-minute break on a work-intensive day to go for a walk, even though I can't spare the time. It's nice to treat yourself to something special occasionally, like a massage, a good haircut, or that sweater you don't need but love. I'm not saying you should break the bank, but sometimes you say you can't afford things because you're being practical. You'd buy HIM a sweater if he wanted it. You spend money on others sooner than on yourself. Yes, sometimes what you want would be a hardship to pay for. More often, though, you're just being cheap with yourself. You're worth a splurge once in a while.

I once went shopping with my friend Ellen. Everything she tried on looked great, so I told her to buy it all, since there was a sale. She hesitated, saying she shouldn't spend the money. She admitted her husband wanted her to splurge on herself, but she felt she should wait. Finally Ellen agreed to take all but an expensive shirt that looked divine on her. I asked her if she deserved it. She made excuses. I told her that if she knew she deserved it, the Universe would help her pay for it. I put her in front of the mirror and made her look at herself and say "I deserve to buy nice clothes." After saying it a few times, Ellen yelled, "I do deserve it!" When we got to the register, we discovered that everything was 30 percent off the sale price. Ellen saved more money than the expensive shirt cost. She just looked at me and asked, "How'd you do that?"

I did nothing but show her how to use her spiritual power, fueled by self-love. You can show yourself love in a variety of ways, such as making time for the gym. Fitness is always a loving priority. Some show love by playing hooky from work, wearing silky lingerie without a man around because it feels good, getting a facial, canceling a lunch date you didn't want, and so on. People in my groups report what they do for themselves. Val told us:

> I made time for a bath last night. I told my roommate the bathroom would be occupied for an hour, so cope . . . hold the phone calls. I lit a candle, played music, had some wine, and read a book. It was very nice. My roommate thinks I've lost my mind. She saw the facial mask I bought too. I'm usually so practical. But I followed directions to make time for me, and I plan to do it regularly. It does make me feel better about myself when I do these things.

I love pampering my body. I get my legs waxed and take very good care of my skin with good creams. When a friend stayed with me overnight, he laughed when he saw me putting on my face creams. He said I don't just put it on but lovingly smooth it over my skin. It's true. I think of it as being good to myself, and love doing it. He was amazed at how I glowed while applying it. I buy good cream and enjoy feeling it go on. Do something special for yourself regularly. It keeps you conscious of being good to you, and you deserve it. Try it—you'll love it—and yourself!

Redefining What's Attractive

There's a lot of emphasis these days on how beauty has become too important. Obsessions with looking gorgeous, being thin, maintaining youth, etc., can diminish your self-esteem. Who you are inside is definitely more important. But there's nothing wrong with making a healthy effort to maintain your appearance. There's a big difference between linking how you feel about yourself to your looks and keeping yourself fit, healthy, and well groomed. Taking care of your body can play a large part in building confidence.

I enjoy keeping up my appearance as a personal choice but don't go overboard trying to lose weight. I do try my best to stay as fit as possible. I don't strive to be perfect. Instead, I work on staying healthy, which translates into a more realistic beauty. If I gain too much weight and my clothes get tight, then I don't feel good. Eating healthy foods reflects self-love and respect for my body, not a need to take off five pounds. A focus on living a healthy lifestyle ultimately looks good on everyone.

People prefer to deal with individuals who have a nice appearance. It's human nature. Taking pride in yourself helps build your self-esteem. What you do to look good is an individual thing. For you it can mean being well groomed, which radiates confidence. It can mean being feminine or finding an individual sense of style and flair and working it to the max. Whether you're thin or overweight, young or older, gorgeous or average, you can find a style that works for you. Clothing that fits you well, colors that give you some life or set a mood, a radiant smile, and good posture are examples of things that every woman can integrate into her own personal style.

It's nice to have a presence when you enter a room. John agreed:

> Millie isn't the most gorgeous woman I've gone out with. If someone sees her walk into a room, they might not think her special. But she knows who she is . . . she's comfortable being herself. I've gone out with too many women who need to be reassured all the time. I'm attracted to the front they put up at first. But once we get involved, I see how insecure they are. "Am I too fat?" they ask, when they have a great body. "Do you see my wrinkle?" when there's none.

Millie doesn't worry. She's confident even when we're alone. She does take good care of herself because she likes being in shape. But she doesn't go crazy. She loves to eat, which I find sexy! So many women just pick. Millie's whole look and attitude says that she feels good about who she is, and I find that incredibly attractive.

Redefine Yourself on Your Own Terms

Once your self-esteem kicks in, look at yourself again and take inventory. Slowly change your perception of who you are. Clean out old messages. The one my friend's boyfriend gave me about losing weight has turned into wisdom. I'm sure many people think I should lose weight, but I don't see that in the mirror anymore. I know I'd look better if I weighed less, but I think I'm a hot babe anyway! If a man passes me up because of my body, it's his loss. I won't obsess over my weight or allow it to distort the overall picture. Today I know who I am and walk with pride. I see extra pounds as more softness, more delicious, feminine curves. I still watch my weight but for health reasons. I exercise because it's great to take care of myself. I like my clothes to fit properly.

You can define yourself and choose to work on your appearance to make YOU feel good, not to please HIM. A fitness program can increase confidence. I recently told Tracy, who hates exercise and is overweight, to just walk to the corner and back every day. Making an effort to do something healthy is a start. She called two weeks later and said:

I did it. At first I felt silly. But I kept remembering I was doing something healthy for me. So I continued. I enjoyed knowing that. After a few days I walked around the block. Now I look forward to it. Even when it rained, I got out my raincoat and umbrella and walked.

I feel more in control of myself than I have in ages. For some reason, I've been more careful about what I eat. I've even started praising myself in the mirror. Who knows, maybe someday I'll join a gym. For now, I'm happy to be changing even in a small way.

One baby step at a time can build good self-esteem. Working on your health and fitness is a great step. Consciousness about food and physical activities say, "I love me." Caring about your health and taking vitamins and whatever is good for you are self-loving acts. I've no patience for doing cardio in gyms but I speed walk and run regularly and feel very fit. It gives me confidence. Although cellulite is still there, I feel great knowing my body is healthy. Exercise helps you control yourself. It's certainly more productive than sitting home and waiting for HIM to call. How you appear to others is influenced by your own perception. People who feel fat act fat. Those who feel insecure act insecure. Women who feel beautiful come across as beautiful. Lovingly developing self-esteem helps you feel in control. Faith wrote after attending a group:

I have always been my worst critic. I used to have low self-esteem...never good enough, pretty enough. My opinions weren't worth that much. I always felt I wasn't strong and capable. I put up with a lot of criticism, mainly in relationships. When men put me down, I always thought they were right. I was submissive, "as good girls should be," and could never question criticism.

As I worked on my self-esteem, I finally stopped listening. I now know they were wrong. It's been a long process of growing, and I'm far from done, but today I'd never put up with any of what I accepted years ago. Now I like myself, know I can do anything I choose, and feel totally confident that I'll succeed—quite a change from years ago. I've learned when you love yourself, anything's possible.

Amen!

Chapter Eighteen

You Want a Man? Get a Life!

"So live that you can look any man in the eye and tell him to go to hell."

ANONYMOUS

Looking Out for Number One

Before you worry any more about men, before you read more books or take classes on how to find and keep a man, before you go into plan Z for luring a man into your life, spend some time with yourself. In order to be more attractive, open, and ready for a healthy man, concentrate on developing a fulfilling life based around YOU, not HIM. For a large number of healthy men, the most attractive woman is one who doesn't need him but chooses to be with him.

You want a healthy man? Get a life! Focusing on yourself makes you attractive to many men who aren't jerks. It's crucial for a healthy relationship. Women often put their lives aside after meeting a man. Men don't devote their entire being to you. They have outside interests and their friendships might not be as intimate as ours, but men have fun!

They still see friends when they're in a relationship. Too many women are content merely to talk with friends on the phone and keep themselves available for their man.

Many women still think they need a man to feel complete. That's nonsense! It's what Mom told you all those years ago. Since when do you always listen to her? Men love being involved with a woman, but don't necessarily feel incomplete alone. Many might be dirtier or live on junk food without you, but a majority would still have a life and sense of self. Men are encouraged to find satisfying careers. My generation of women was told to work until we bagged a husband. Forget that! You can absolutely be complete and happy without one and provide your own validation.

We want to be loved, and to give love. What is love? Is it an excuse for giving yourself away to men? Do you fall in love with the man or with the idea of being in love? Think about it. Many of you need to have a man by your side in order to feel whole, whether you actually love him or not. You use men to fill what you perceive as an otherwise empty life. Are you with HIM because it's better than being alone?

Well, you know what? Living without a man can be the best experience you may ever have. It can attract the most healthy people into your life, including men who can prove they're not jerks. Laura shared her experience with my group:

> I used to want to fall in love. It seemed special. I fell in love with most boyfriends. Lately I see how much work falling in love can be . . . destructive. I used to try to keep him happy so he'd love me. I didn't worry what I got from him . . . I thought love was enough.
>
> Now I've had enough of love for a while. It's not the lovely, romantic thing I thought it would be. It's mostly painful. Now there's time to do what I like or wanted to try but never had time for. I'm taking a break. My next boyfriend will be good for me, or I'll wait.

Take Control of Your Life

If you want a life, first take control of your life. Letting others dictate what you do relinquishes control. Letting your need for a man guide you leaves you powerless. Once you have control over your life, the world can be yours. It allows you to direct where your happiness comes from!

One of my favorite affirmations comes from Louise L. Hay: "I take responsibility for what happens in my life. I know that responsibility is a gift because it gives me the power to make changes." This hit home, reminding me that you can't blame others for what goes on in your life. Men took me for granted because I let them. Men verbally abused me because I stayed with them. They led me on with sweet words because I wanted to believe them and let me down many times because I went along with them. I now take responsibility by saying "no more." By taking responsibility, I'm no longer a victim. I can accept or reject whatever comes into my life. You all can! That's your power.

After giving others responsibility/blame for your life—your happiness, security, and choices—it's hard to own it. Trust me, owning it is worth the effort. Control enables you to cut loose a man who makes you unhappy and keeps you from getting involved with men you know are jerks. Good self-esteem and controlling your life work together. The more you value yourself, the more good you'll expect. The more you love yourself, the less garbage you'll take. The more you respect yourself, the more conscious you'll be about who you let into your life. The more you own your power to make choices, the more choices you'll have.

Thinking in terms of "I choose to" instead of "I have to" opens up choices. You all possess the ability to control every aspect of your life. That power is amazing! Susan told me:

> I've spent my life following rules . . . took a traditional teaching job I hated . . . married a man my mother thought was right . . . kept my mouth shut if I was unhappy—good girls don't complain. I got divorced five years ago and continued listening to

other voices. "I had to find another man. I was worthless on my own." Don't know if I was more miserable married or single.

Last year I broke free after therapy. Otherwise, what was the point of my existence? To pass time until another unsatisfying relationship? I kissed teaching and my safe pension goodbye ... took a low-paying but stimulating job. I waited to make decent money. Now I do what I want ... trying everything I thought would shock people. My mother still disapproves, but I'm happy. I found many possibilities once I listened to my own voice. Oh yeah, I'm seeing a great guy. Just when I didn't care!

Work on Yourself

A great way to build self-esteem and your life simultaneously is to take control of what you see as bad habits or shortcomings. Working on yourself is therapeutic. Make a list of what you'd like to change about you. Include anything: being late, talking too much, losing weight, being messy, overextending yourself, etc. Choose one problem to tackle at a time. It's easier to start with a not-too-serious bad habit. Try to figure out what causes you to do each thing. Do you overeat while upset? What need does that satisfy? What do you get out of talking so much? When you give in to people, is it out of fear of not being liked? After getting clues about where your habit comes from, try to take control. That's what it's all about. When I'd like to lose a few pounds, I don't call it dieting. I call it trying to control my eating.

Baby step your way to control. Let's say you tend to be late and want to be on time for work. Don't try being prompt every day—it's too much at first. Instead, choose one day a week to work on punctuality. For example, make a concerted effort to be on time on Tuesdays. Control that one day. Baby step your way and enjoy each little step. Being on time will make you feel great! As Tuesdays get solid, add another day. Now you're in control on Tuesday and Friday. You may not do it every day, but the great feeling that it brings might motivate you. Taking control of what's always bothered you absolutely builds self-esteem. I feel so positive about myself when I get at least some control. Meg shared her story:

> I was an overweight kid and overcompensated by being loud and boisterous. I couldn't break the habit when I grew up. Sometimes people would ask me to speak softer, and it was embarrassing. I'd listen to myself talking loud—too much—very fast, and hate myself, but felt out of control.
>
> This year my New Year's resolution was to get my talking under control. It's taken almost the entire year, but I've done it. It's affected my whole personality . . . probably because I like myself so much more. I'm proud that I did it.

As you control one habit, work on another. Try cleaning, which is great therapy. Getting rid of clutter in your home is like cleaning out your life. I'm a natural clutterbug, a slob conditioned over years. I always hated when people visited and saw stuff all over the place, but accepted this as just my way. After deciding to control this bad habit, I started with my bathroom, the easiest room because it had the least amount of clutter. The rest of my apartment was a mess, but I made a concerted effort to keep my bathroom spotless. I took serious pride in my gleaming example of control. After many months I made the same effort with my kitchen. A friend commented on how sparkling my kitchen was, which motivated me further. I smile as I clean because I know how many years it took just to get into the habit of washing the dishes promptly.

The rest of my apartment was harder to tidy up because of all my stuff. One day while feeling down I overhauled my home office and bedroom. It was great to see my apartment look neat! I felt terrific about myself! I still have slob tendencies but periodically take time to clean up and love it. Every year my apartment stays neat longer, making me feel more powerful. My standards are higher too. Getting a handle on my bad habits improved how I saw myself. When I'm feeling out of control, I get my office neat and organized. When I need a jump start for my self-esteem, I clean. When I'm feeling down, I get rid of lots of things. It always makes me feel better.

Practicing moderation when trying to improve yourself increases your control. Often things don't work out because of an all-or-nothing focus. Finding a middle ground is more relaxing and easier to achieve than perfection. When you work on yourself, it's healthier and more effective over the long term to do it slowly. That way, realistic goals are easier to reach. Similarly, losing weight slowly is more effective, and gives you a better chance of maintaining the loss. It's harder to keep up an intense exercise program than to find a moderate workout you can do regularly.

Your Most Important Relationship

If you want a healthy relationship with a man, start by having one with yourself, the only person you'll be with forever. Find out who you are. Many of you are clueless about yourselves. You can lose your identity as an individual as you go from one relationship to another. When I left my marriage, I had no sense of self. After spending most of my adult years being a good daughter, wife, and then mother, I was all of these things and nothing. It took time to develop an individual identity. When I encouraged Ellie to leave her abusive husband, I related when she said:

> How can I leave? I wouldn't know what to do on my own. I'm not anyone away from the people who are close to me. I'm a wife and mother at home, a nurse at work. There is no Ellie outside of other people. I'm a shell of a person without being something to someone. I have no idea who I am on my own and don't know how to find out. It's too scary.

I gave Ellie many of the exercises in this book. By writing things down she was able to find her way. It took years, but she's now happily remarried to a man who treats her very well. She has a strong sense of who she is. There's someone inside all of you. Sometimes you have to look to find the special treasure you are.

It's amazing how concerned you can be with what HE wants and what makes HIM happy, while not even considering what you'd like outside the realm of HIM. When you don't have HIM, you may feel lost. Forget men for a moment. What would you like to try? Painting? Canoeing? Theater? Travel? Writing? Create your own reality instead of developing a fantasy with a man. Try doing one thing that interests you by yourself. Take a class, join a club, etc. Do this with no thought of meeting a man. Enjoy activities for the sake of doing them, not because of what men might be there. Make new friends that share your interests. See a life beyond HIM.

You can't share your life with a man if you have no life. By not giving men your all, you can create a satisfying life. By putting energy into a fulfilling life on its own terms, you'll get a life. Once you have one, it's easier to keep your need for a man in perspective. When you have a life, you control your happiness and are more content. When you have a life, you're more attractive to people. So, you want a good man? Get a life! You have freedom to be picky when you have one. That's much better than settling for a jerk so he can give it to you.

Why You Need to Get a Life

Once I was invited on a live TV news show to talk about a "girl's night out." The producer planned to interview women on the street about what they do when they go out with friends and have me comment on their activities. She was excited, thinking she'd get some great responses. I warned her that it would probably be a boring segment. It was.

When your partner wants a night out with the boys, why do you often feel lost? Why do many you say, "What will I do?" in response to his wanting to spend time with friends? Why do so many of you have no life when your world isn't revolving around a man? One reason is because, as girls, we never learned to have fun like boys did. We didn't have activities encouraging us to bond with other girls. Boys played more team sports. They didn't have to stay clean and quiet, so they had more fun together. Though we have closer intimate friendships than men, they have a male bonding for which there's little female equivalent. Men's camaraderie often has a stronger and healthier foundation.

On the TV show about a "girl's night out," most women said they went out for dinner with friends. Some went to the theater, a lecture, or concert; some had drinks. What did they talk about? Many discussed work, but a big topic was men: their current partner, where to find men, anger toward them, frustration without them. Women often get together to commiserate about men on some level. Talking out problems with friends is fine. It can be good for you. But when do you just have fun? When do you carouse, get silly, or totally let your hair down? We often don't.

In contrast, men do. As boys, they shared sports and activities, while we played with dolls—often with only one friend. So, as those boys were having mindless fun, we practiced being mothers. Guys continued bonding through sports, drinking, doing crazy stunts together, etc., as we spent time with friends trying to look good and find a boyfriend. Men still have fun with their friends as adults. You don't necessarily have a foundation for having a great time with yours. Your upbringing might not have offered appropriate or acceptable avenues for fun with other females. Many of you never learned to have a "girl's night out" that's nearly as much fun as being with a man, or to have interests beyond HIM.

Women often complain that friends disappear when they have a man. When you're happily in a relationship, you may not need a friend, except as a sounding board. When men are in a relationship, they often don't want to give up going out with their friends, to let their hair down and go back to childhood. Guys still share activities with no female equivalent. Women get judged for the behavior men enjoy. Men get drunk together. If we do, there may be a stigma attached. Men carouse and get stupid. That's not considered ladylike. Men play sports. We play too, but not with the same intensity as they do. Many men are so into bonding that they often don't care about meeting women on nights out with friends.

In one of my men's classes the guys couldn't figure why many women would rather be with a man all the time and not see her friends. Jerry said:

> I still get together with my buddies from school. We try to hang a few times a month. We play basketball in nice weather and go watch games in bars. My wife always gets mad. She tells me to grow up and stay with her. What's her problem? My friends have the same problem. Leigh occasionally has dinner with a friend after work. She goes shopping with one when I play ball. It's funny, 'cause she has more friends than me, but she's happy to just yak to them on the phone. I ask why she doesn't go out with a bunch like we do, and she says one of us is grown up. I don't get it. I have a blast with my friends.

Adam chimed in, "Women should learn from us. They stick their noses up at what we do, but all they do is complain. At least we have fun."

We meet with friends for dinner or drinks to talk about men. We go to various functions looking for men. We shop for clothes to attract men. Boring! I know too many women who won't go anywhere with no potential to meet men. Many of you don't share interests that you truly enjoy with friends. It's not your fault. Girls aren't encouraged to enjoy each other's company like guys are. Men may go back to being frolicking little boys for a few hours with their friends. When we're with ours, it's not enthralling to relive being good little girls who sat quietly doing a task or raising our dolls. We weren't taught to have a life.

But you can change that by developing interests that can consume you with pleasure. You can put the thought of men aside as you explore adding interesting facets to your life. You can learn to have fun without a man. Big, smiling fun!

Developing New Interests

So how do you build a life? Think of yourself as an adult on your own and check out all opportunities available that can lead to more fulfillment. Get involved in organizations that relate to something you do on a professional level, or that cater to people with a hobby or interest that appeals to you. There are groups for almost everything. It's a great way to meet people. Don't worry about meeting men. Just allow new and interesting people into your world.

Earlier I suggested making new friends. I'm serious. If your friends are boring, try making new ones who are more fun. Joining clubs and going to events that interest you provides an opportunity for this. Leave your shyness at home. As you feel better about yourself, make an effort to meet fun people and develop friendships. There are loads of potential friends around. Getting out more gives you the best chance of increasing your social circle. When you start having fun, you'll attract more good energy and healthier men and women.

Play *Fantasy Island* with yourself. What would you love to do if there was nothing in the way? Forget about doing it with a man. The activity is what's important. What if money or time were no object? What if you had no responsibility? Let your wishes flow. Write them down and be creative. Learn from your wish list what might make you happy. Choose something on it, preferably the most realistic choice, and work toward making it a reality. Often you make excuses for not doing what you'd truly like—"I shouldn't spend the money"; "I haven't the time";

"What would people say?"; "It isn't me"—and you defeat yourself. Ginger related her wish:

> I always wanted to go to Africa. That was first on my wish list. When I wrote it down, my fascination with Africa wouldn't go away. I can't afford to go now, but I bought a book about Africa. For the first time, my dream seems possible in the future. I've made a separate savings account for this. I called a museum and found a group to join. Now I know people who'll go with me to hear world music. Maybe I'll even travel with them someday. I've met people who offered a place I can stay in some of the countries I want to visit.

There's a world of possibilities if you open yourself up to them. For example, if going to London is your dream, start saving now. Even if saving takes a year or more, you can look forward to the trip. If you aren't ready to go alone, check travel groups or tours. Get prices. Create a travel fund and a specific plan for doing what you want. Squash the excuses. You can find ways to afford the time and money to do special things for yourself no matter how long it might take, if you want it badly enough. You'd be surprised how easily it can be done once you decide you deserve it. If you have faith that it will work out, it usually does.

Many of you are in ruts from childhood and can see in only one direction. That old upbringing can limit your horizons. Trash "should's" and "can'ts." You want to be happy, don't you? Are you happy now? Try a new direction. The old one may have discouraged spending money on something frivolous, like a trip to Hawaii, a day in a fancy spa, or helicopter hiking. Listen carefully: There's nothing wrong with doing what makes you happy, even if it's not your style or it costs more than you usually spend on yourself. When was the last time you experienced pure joy? Make it a regular habit. Remember, it's YOUR life and can be what YOU make it. Have fun, as long as it doesn't hurt anyone.

Get a Life of Your Own

What does it actually mean to get a life? It means developing a living situation that you're comfortable and happy in. You can't control everything, but can choose what's most important, such as pleasant surroundings. For example, by taking the apartment I live in, I had to modify other spending. For me, it's worth it because living in a place I love makes coming home a joy. Instead of feeling lonely like I used to, I'm content and cozy. It's a constant reminder that I'm worth a nice home. You can make your space a warm haven instead of a constant reminder of loneliness. Play music you love. Light candles when you feel on edge. A living space can be made more pleasant by adding nice touches to the décor or keeping it tidy. Jan told my class:

> I used to hate being in my small studio. It reminded me I didn't have a boyfriend. I'd get restless and lonely. I saw a painting with a relaxing pastoral scene at an art fair. I thought about it until I knew I had to have it. On impulse I found an ATM and bought the painting. I almost danced home.
>
> When I hung it, my apartment changed. I had hand-me-down furniture. The painting made the apartment MINE. Whenever I see it, I feel peaceful. Now I enjoy my place more. I can relax because I splurged on a painting. I guess it reminds me that I have to do things for myself.

Getting a life means doing what you can to create a lifestyle that provides support and satisfaction. It means letting go of negative friends. It means not always feeling obligated to do what you don't want to do and having or working toward a job that satisfies you. It isn't always easy, but you can put out feelers and send resumes. It is possible to create a life you'd love if you use your energy to do it. Getting a life means that almost everything is your own choice.

When Stacy began attending a support group, she was unhappy. The group encouraged her to change jobs and create a life, but she felt stuck. At our last session she said:

> My job was boring, but I stayed for the benefits. I was restless—determined to find a man to make my life interesting at any cost. My passion is helping people use social media, and I wanted to do it for a living but was scared. I thought I was too old . . . seems like kids have all those jobs.
>
> When you pushed me to look for one, I reluctantly got a resume together. Through your encouragement, I worked on becoming more spiritual and put out that I was looking for a job in social media. Last week I was looking over my resume on the subway and struck up a conversation with a woman sitting next to me. She asked what I was looking for . . . then gave me the number of a friend who was looking to hire someone with my skills, and I got the job! I'm so happy that I can't even think about men. I plan to change other parts of my life now that I see I can.

Getting a life means keeping men in perspective by changing the direction of your energy toward yourself. If you can't be happy without men, they can become an addiction. I was addicted for years, obsessing over my latest HIM. When I had no man, I'd obsess about meeting one, feeling anxious and almost itchy on my own. I repeat: A man can be the most delicious, sweetest, most enjoyable part of your life, BUT HE CANNOT BE YOUR LIFE. I am my life. You must be your life. HE can be the treat, if he proves he's not a jerk. When you have a life, you can be fussier about men because without them, you still have a life.

Develop Your Autonomy

Having a life means being whole on your own, being comfortable with yourself and your own company, something many of you have never experienced. As your self-esteem grows, so does your confidence to do things on your own. Getting a life and self-esteem go hand in hand. Working on one develops the other, so the effort can be a two-for-one deal! As you do more on your own, you'll feel better about yourself. As your self-esteem gets stronger, so does your appreciation of who you are and the desire to do things on your own. Good deal!

Being on your own takes courage. When you've spent your life needing someone to do activities with, trying them alone can be scary. The advantages of being in your own company are worth overcoming your fears! You can do what you want, when you want, how you want—a nice, greedy benefit. You can do more without having to wait for someone to go with you. Start with small stuff. Go walking or to the movies. Eat alone at a restaurant that's not intimidating. Bring something to read for company. Go at an off-hour the first time if you're self-conscious. Gradually try bigger things. Susan told me:

> I always needed someone along. When I'd go shopping, I couldn't buy anything without a friend's approval. If I had no one to eat with, I'd get take-out. As I worked on myself, I saw I usually let friends pick where to go and I'd follow. I wanted a choice. A few of us decided to order theater tickets. I was dying to see *Jersey Boys*, but they wanted a play that didn't appeal. I started going along with them but decided to see my choice, even if it meant going alone.
>
> When I got on the train to the city for a matinee, I felt like a little girl trying to be grown up. It started to feel like an adventure, and I ended up loving every second. After the show I even went for a bite. Now I plan other adventures alone: I go to muse-

ums, concerts, or just to walk around in the city and shop. I trust my own judgment more.

You have to start somewhere. Try the list of things you'd like to do. Throw out the excuses. In a class, Carol said she envied me for doing fun things. She explained, "I work long hours, and after work I'm too tired to go out. Weekends all I do is clean and do laundry. I've no time for a life." Carol complained she was unhappy, but still chose to spend weekends on chores. I suggested getting someone to come in and clean, but she balked. I suggested planning a vacation, and she complained about money. I suggested spending a half hour each night working on her apartment. She said she preferred doing it on the weekend. There it was—her choice to occupy all her spare time so she couldn't do something fun, yet she continued complaining. Remember, you all have choices.

Enjoy time alone by making dates with yourself! I love planning a whole day out, walking for miles and going to outdoor cafés where I read or people-watch. I look forward to choosing where to eat and where to go for coffee after. The freedom of not having to rush because I have to meet someone is wonderful. I leave when I'm ready and love doing everything my way. Solo activities are my choice, not my problem. Some of my best time is spent in my own company. The more comfortable you get with yourself, the more you may choose to spend time on your own. Cheryl revealed:

My friends actually get angry at me when I want to spend a weekend alone. Or, they feel sorry for me that I have no plans. Me? I'm thrilled to have a weekend on my own: no pressure, no routines, no timetable. Sometimes I stay in bed till 3:00. I do everything spontaneously and change my mind a million times. No one cares! If I stay in, I may not shower till Sunday. These weekends with myself are my most relaxing times. I always go to work on Monday smiling. Those who don't know me well think I have a secret lover.

You can do nice little things for yourself as a regular routine, and treat yourself to something special occasionally. Get a facial or massage. Pamper yourself. Plan ahead for things to look forward to—a vacation, tickets to a special event, a visit from a good friend—that can keep your spirits up during a cold winter, a tough period at work, or while longing for a man. Love yourself a little more each day as you own your life. It's not too late to change. Learning to enjoy things on your own is empowering. I'm thrilled to have time alone to read, write, or just do silly things. It's nice to make all the decisions and not have to compromise. Appreciate your space. It's your own!

Taking More Risks

Taking risks increases your self-esteem. As you trust yourself, trying new things becomes more comfortable. Many women narrow their lives out of fear of leaving their safe havens to try something new. Taking a risk increases confidence. Even if what you do doesn't work out, it's powerful to know that you didn't let fear control you. It's better than sitting home feeling powerless. Take a risk: Go for a job you want but worry it will be too difficult. Take a risk: Walk up to someone at a party and start a conversation. Most people don't bite. Take a risk: Ask for something you've been intimidated to ask for. Do something you were too scared to do. What could happen? At worst you still won't have what you didn't have before.

Expand your horizons. Often we box ourselves into a small world by limiting the type of people we let in. Try being friendly with people of all religions, nationalities, ages, and educational backgrounds who you meet in your activities. You don't have to be best buddies with people you're not used to, but you can at least take the time to be friendly. It's amazing what you can learn by getting to know those who are different from you, even if only during an activity. The more folks you meet on every level, the more you increase your possibilities. The more you get comfortable with others, the more you'll be comfortable with yourself.

Most healthy men are attracted to a woman who's comfortable with herself, which translates into confidence. Confidence is powerful and attractive to everyone. I'm much more drawn to friends who feel good about themselves than those who don't. The more you get to know and trust yourself, the greater your confidence. Working on your self-esteem and faith in yourself instills confidence without even trying. Taking risks helps you conquer fears, which increases confidence tremendously. As yours grows, so will the life you begin to create. Developing strong confidence in yourself isn't achieved by being in a relationship, unless it's a relationship with you!

Men Are Attracted to Women with Lives of Their Own

Many men feel safer with women who keep their distance and can take care of themselves. They're attracted to ones who don't seem too fragile. Independent women feel less of a burden and men like the challenge of getting a woman to make time for them in her busy schedule. That's more appealing to an achievement-oriented man than someone whose life revolves around him. Nobody wants to feel responsible for someone else's happiness and vulnerability. Wallace explained:

> I like a woman who can handle herself. It's sexier. I don't want one I have to handle with kid gloves. You know what I mean? Women who get hurt easily or who need me all the time are what I run from these days. The ones seen as bitches to some have more qualities I'm attracted to. Women need to get their lives together and stop depending on us so much.

When I was once a guest expert on a TV talk show, a couple, Barb and Chris, had been invited to speak about the problems in their relationship. Barb wanted marriage. She went on about how good she was to Chris and how difficult it was that he wouldn't give her the security she needed. Chris insisted that since his last relationship ended painfully, he wanted to wait until he was sure. The audience berated him for not appreciating a good woman who loved him and for not giving her the security she deserved. Barb went on about how she wanted to know that Chris would be there to pick her up if she fell down.

When it was my turn to speak, I told her to get a life—make herself happy—get a job that satisfied her—and learn to pick *herself* up if she fell. Barb and Chris both applauded me. Barb acknowledged she had been dependent on Chris for her happiness. She didn't like her job and had lost touch with her friends. I gave her some advice about fixing those situations. Plus, by constantly pressuring Chris to get married, she put him on the defensive, always having to say "no." That made it hard for him to assess objectively if marriage was in his cards. He agreed that it was hard to think about marriage when he was always dodging bullets. After the show, they both thanked me.

A few months later I spoke to Barb. She had gotten a good job, was going out regularly with friends, and in general had created a satisfying life. She told me:

> Getting a life can be better than getting a man. I was always a doormat, more to myself, but it set the tone for others to stomp on me too. After the show I did more for myself. I got a job that I love and am doing things I've never done on my own. I've never been so happy. I think about what you said about taking care of your own needs every day. It does work.
>
> Chris has never wanted me more. But now that I have a life, I don't need him. We're still friends and who knows what the future holds, but for now I love my new life on my own. Thanks so much! It's nice not to be a victim of my needs anymore.

Once Barb got a life and off Chris' back he proposed. At that point she decided she didn't need him for the things she thought she did and said "no." She needed time to decide if he was right for her and her new life and changed their relationship to friendship. A woman with a life is more attractive. You usually meet the best people when you're not looking for them. So, get a life. It's more pleasurable, with or without a man! Getting a life means that even if Mr. Right isn't in your life yet, you can still be Ms. Right for yourself. If you develop a sense of spirituality, focus on creating a life that's not based on someone else, work on building your self-esteem, you'll learn as I did that the greatest gift to yourself is yourself.

Chapter Nineteen

How to Get Over a Jerk

"Those things that hurt, instruct."

BENJAMIN FRANKLIN

The number one reason given in my classes for not taking more steps to leave a jerk is fear. Often, women stay in relationships that they know aren't good for them because they're scared to leave and be alone. Fear keeps you from telling someone how you feel; from letting go of a man who isn't good for you; from many other things that in the long run would be healthier for you. So what is fear, and why does it keep you in bad relationships?

Leaving HIM usually requires having to face fears. That in itself can make you stay. I place fear in two categories. The first type is facing situations that could legitimately have a bad outcome, such as fear of jumping off a cliff, driving in snow, undergoing surgery, etc. The other type is irrational, based on speculation of the unknown. The anxiety of "what-ifs" is scary. Expectations of what might happen can create a foreboding that you want to avoid at all costs. You don't know what will happen but imagine the worst scenario, which affects your decisions. Fear keeps you from moving on, from calling him on his behavior, from leaving him. When you assume something awful and build it up in your mind, anticipation becomes your expectation. You may do nothing if you're too afraid to find out what will really happen. Roseann confided:

> My husband's never laid a hand on me, but his mouth is painful. Everyone tells me to leave, and I know I should. But I'm scared. Of what? I'm trying to figure that out. I have a job and can support myself. I have no kids. The truth is, I'm scared he'll get mad at me. Why should I care? I don't know. In my mind, I know it's silly because if I leave, I won't be around him when he's mad. But I'm so scared of him getting mad at me that I stay. It makes no sense, but the thought of leaving him scares me so much I stop thinking about it.

It's normal to be afraid of change. It makes you think before you act so you don't make snap decisions. But a consuming, irrational fear keeps you stuck in one place, preventing you from doing what's necessary to leave a bad relationship. It keeps the "what-if" tapes replaying in your head. Letting fear control you takes away all your power and prevents you from being happy.

Get Your Fears under Control

So how do you overcome fear of fear? By doing what you're afraid of. When you see you can handle it, your confidence builds for next time. That doesn't mean you won't be scared again, but it gets easier. It's natural to be apprehensive about change, but living with a bad situation can be worse than doing what scares you. Facing fears makes them go away.

"What-if's" can be scarier than reality. Facing fears is often better than imagining the worst. Try this: When you're scared, ask yourself, "What's the worst that can happen? Can I cope with that outcome?"

Be honest about whether you can cope. You don't have to like it, but will it stop your life? Can you survive? If you're honest, the answer will probably be "yes." You may find you can handle almost anything. If you don't do what scares you, you'll get nowhere. By anticipating what could realistically happen, you can find a way through it.

Build a support system around your fears. Talk to friends and family about possible outcomes. Discuss your options. If your fear of leaving a man holds you back, plan with your support team for all possible repercussions. To control your fear of leaving him, go slowly but go. Here are some tips for getting ready. Let his unacceptable behavior motivate you. You can do it!

- **Accept that fear is a natural response.** Don't get angry with yourself for being afraid. As long as you choose to live fully, there will always be things that scare you. If you wait to take action for a time when you're not afraid, you may always be waiting. It's natural to be scared of making new moves but the fear usually won't go away on its own.
- **Identify what you're afraid to do.** What are you specifically afraid of? Leaving him is too general. Is it telling him you're leaving? Making a life without him? Dealing with loneliness? Having him hassle you? Pinpoint what part scares you.
- **Identify the worst thing that could initially happen in that situation.** What's the worst that can happen if you tell him how you feel? Your guy loses his temper and leaves? He cries? He tries to convince you to come back? He gets violent? You're lonely? Identifying what could be a problem can help you to find a remedy before it happens.
- **Decide how the results will affect you and how you'll handle it.** Can you handle what might happen? If he gets angry, what do you lose by leaving him? Will you die of loneliness? Who can help you? You'll probably find that you can handle it all if you plan for it.

- **Learn to see all situations as offering you a choice.** It's your choice to stay or leave. It's your choice to let the result get to you. There are always options if you look for them. Prepare contingencies before taking action. Have some fun things planned in case your relationship is over. Have a self to fall back on. Find a support group. Build your life as discussed in Chapter Eighteen.
- **Find something positive in the result.** "Well, at least _____." Fill in the blank. In most cases, you'll find something positive. You still have friends and will see who your real ones are. You've learned. You're free of a jerk. You took control and overcame your fear! What a powerful thing! Revel in it! When you successfully face your first fear, write it on paper: "I [say what you did]. I can do anything I choose." Let it empower you!

Remember: You Don't Have to Fix Things

Women often feel responsible for making a relationship work. You take classes and read books on how to handle a man and work things out. Often it's you doing the work of two. You're not encouraged to let go and leave HIM if he's not good for you and you feel like a failure if you don't give HIM every benefit of the doubt.

Stop! You can't take his shortcomings personally. You're not a failure if you don't try to make a bad relationship work. That takes two people. How much energy do you put into figuring him out? Now weigh that against the amount of energy you give yourself. You should be getting the majority. And how much energy does he give you? Don't make excuses for him. Either it's a fair balance or not. If he's getting the majority of energy from both of you and tells you not to expect him to change, pay attention. He's telling you it's going to be his way or nothing. If he isn't being fair, you have to accept that letting go is a healthy choice.

Don't Grab Another Man ASAP

Don't wait to find another jerk before leaving the one you're with. Many women jump from one bad relationship to another because they can't leave a man without a replacement. Don't put one foot out his door and into someone else's. It's hard to be objective about a new guy when you're leaving another. Develop your autonomy instead of taking care of someone else. Build your own life! If you have a life of your own to fall back on, leaving him is easier. No matter why you break up, it's healthy to give yourself time alone to develop closure and heal wounds. You can live without a man for a while. The victim mentality is outdated. You always have choices. You're only a victim if you choose to be. It's nicer to choose to be a happy, healthy woman!

Stick to Your Decisions

There's no good time to break up with someone you think you can't live without. You can make a zillion excuses for waiting a bit longer, but that can last indefinitely. Decide to end the relationship and just do it. You can't wait until after vacations, birthdays, holidays, or promotions. You'll never get out if you keep putting it off.

Don't let good memories blind you. Of course there are wonderful things in a bad relationship, such as hot sex. You tend to cling to these as life preservers for staying afloat when it's not working. Are you really in love with him, or are you just staying to avoid being lonely without a man? Be honest. Why love a man who doesn't love you enough to treat you properly? Once you practiced loving yourself, that love will give you strength to follow through on your decision to leave him.

Write, write, write. Here we go again, the old writing tool. Well, it's effective. If you're struggling to take that final step out the door, that last roll out of his bed, that decisive move to reclaim your life, get out your pad and pen. Jerks leave clues all over the place that they're jerks, but you brush them off. Stop brushing and pay attention. Get a letter-size notepad. List EVERYTHING he's done to hurt you, let you down, etc. Don't justify some of the painful stuff and leave it off your list. If there are things you feel guilty/hesitant/blind about including, put them on the list with an asterisk. Make a note on another page about it if you must, but include them. Add to the list as you think of more.

When you've been honest and put your main pain down, allow it to have an impact on you. This list can be your best tool for leaving and staying strong afterward. It's proof of why he's not worth staying with. Do the self-esteem exercises in Chapter Seventeen with the list in front of you. Don't you deserve a better man than one who treats you like that? A list of what he's done to hurt you is a power tool.

That power tool saved me when I was in a relationship with a jerk. I was crazy about him—I thought I couldn't live without him. He stood me up on New Year's Eve. Can you imagine that pain? I wrote a list of all he'd done to hurt me and wrote NEVER AGAIN! in red marker on top. When he called days later with excuses, I put him off. Two months later, we tried again. He stood me up again, coming over the next day full of stories. He had an appointment, but I wanted him to come back after. He insisted on talking the next day. I excused myself to use the bathroom, grabbing my list on the way. I read it: NEVER AGAIN! I returned and said I was tired of doing everything his way. I told him that I needed to see him that night and if he didn't come back, it was over. I stuck to it when he didn't return. The list made my resolution strong enough to end it for good.

The night I set boundaries and stuck to them marked the beginning of my sense of self. I finally learned how to set limits and knew I'd always follow through on them in the future. Decide when you've reached your limit, take control, and cut him loose. Love yourself enough to do it.

Getting Over Him

Here you are on your own. You left him, or he walked on you. Either way, it's not easy. But you can accept that it's over. You *can't* live on the hope that one day he'll wake up to realize how much he's lost, hop on his white horse and ride to your house. You *can* find ways to stop dwelling on him. Otherwise, missing him will consume you, and you deserve better. You lose part of yourself in a relationship, and your energy is best spent working on getting that part back. Reclaiming, or maybe first discovering, who you are on your own can be a constructive remedy.

After breaking up, you need time to accept it's over for good. It's okay to incorporate good memories about the relationship into your thoughts about him, as long as you don't lose your perspective. Becoming bitter or angry isn't necessary. While you think fondly about some of the good you got from him, remind yourself why it ended. Go slowly, one day at a time. By coping with today, you gain a touch more strength to cope with tomorrow.

It's constructive to have a mourning period before moving on. When you've been in a relationship that wasn't right for you, look back at the unhappiness during the relationship as part of that mourning. You shouldn't, however, allow yourself to get so absorbed in mourning that you can't get over him. When people die, we grieve for a time and then move on. It's the same with the death of a relationship. Maryann explained her mourning in my class:

> When Jeff and I broke up, I built a wall around me. I tried being strong, stoic and refused to cry. He didn't deserve tears. But I was in pain . . . angry with myself that it hurt not having him in my life. I knew I was better off, so I sucked it in and kept it inside but felt lousy. I got desperate to get rid of the awful feelings and finally allowed myself a good cry. For two weeks I cried every night before bed. It felt good to let it out, to express my loss. Then I buried him in a way that felt better, instead of burying my pain.

If the breakup is painful, allow yourself time each day to actively grieve. Choose a specific time and allow five, ten, fifteen minutes—whatever suits you—of time alone to get rid of some of the pain, anger, and frustration. Cry. Scream. Punch pillows. Curse. Do what's necessary to get it out. This is your mourning time.

It's good to have support during these times. Rather than always mourning alone, a good cry on someone's shoulder occasionally or talking with a friend afterward is therapeutic. Then the rest of the day should be earmarked for getting on with your life. Knowing that you have grieving time set aside can help you get through the day. When grieving time is over, take deep breaths to calm yourself down, force a smile, and pat yourself on the back for taking care of YOU.

Clearing Him Out of Your Life

Ah, so many memories. Everything reminds you of him at the beginning: the bathroom where you'd watch him shave, the rug you snuggled on together, the cologne he left, his Twinkies still in your cabinet. Keep the reason you broke up with him in perspective. Remind yourself by looking at the list I recommended you make earlier in this chapter. Absorb it to reinforce why you can't stay with him. Though you know what's written down, reading it helps to reinforce it. Ask yourself what you've lost besides a warm body.

- **Make a ritual of getting rid of all memories of him.** I've broken up with jerks in the past who stayed in my head for months because I let them. I'd play painful music, either "our" songs or soupy, romantic love songs that talked about missing someone. Cut out music that reminds you of him or the romance you don't have. Change your radio station for a while if necessary. I used to play songs in my car that would bring me to tears. I'd sing along with them and get more depressed. I finally grasped for control by forbidding those songs for a while. I got rid of anything I could that reminded me of him. Romi told me:

> When I broke up with Jack, I was devastated. I guess I felt if I couldn't be with him, I'd at least keep his memory alive. I played a CD over and over that we used to make love to. I kept his photo by my bed. I fantasized about making love to him. I couldn't let go. I went to all "our" restaurants and got depressed.
>
> A friend noticed and yelled at me, asking what good I was getting out of it. I realized I was almost trying to keep him alive in case he came back. It was like rituals to his memory. After a strong pep talk, I threw the CD in the garbage. That was a big thing for me. It made me feel a shred of control. I slowly cleared all the memories away. It was hard, but I felt better after, ready to move on.

- **Take HIM breaks.** Set boundaries for when you can't talk about him, to give yourself a healthy respite from constant reminders to clear your mind for a while. For example, you can set Sundays aside as a day you aren't allowed to bring his name up. Let your friends know. It's healthy to immerse yourself in other thoughts and take a break from the mourning. Your friends will probably be relieved, and you'll probably get more calls on Sundays. Eventually increase the days for HIM breaks until you don't want to ever mention his name.

  You might also schedule HIM breaks for times when talking about him is most distracting. Perhaps work can be neutral territory. Or it might be more fun if you didn't talk about him during dinner with friends. That will certainly help your digestion. If you can't resist, wait until you have dessert before his name comes up.

- **Avoid HIM obsessing.** Find ways to break that habit. He shouldn't be in your life all the time if you've broken up. What's the point otherwise? You might as well go back with him if he's always with you, putting a damper on everything. Get in the habit of exercising when you start obsessing. Getting into shape while getting over him is a great double benefit. If necessary, go for counseling. Have someone professional on your support team. I highly recommend joining or forming a support group. Friends are great, but a support group can be more objective because those people are separate from your real life. It's wonderful to share your joy and sorrow with people who you're not personally attached to. It's also helpful to hear that others feel the same pain, joy, and fear. As Olivia said:

> I wallowed in Bert when we broke up. Don't know how my friends tolerated me. All I did was talk about HIM, HIM, HIM. When my friends couldn't listen, I joined a support group. Joyce had gone through it a year before and knew what I was feeling. She encouraged me to force myself not to talk about him to friends . . . I'd save it for the group. When I felt an urge to call someone to whine, I'd go for a walk with music playing to distract me. Each week my group encouraged me more, giving me strength to move on.

- **Create a HIM box.** Gather all memories you can't bring yourself to throw out: cards and letters; photos; stuffed animals; the scarf you adopted from his wardrobe; a dried rose, etc. Get a box or a big carton, if you've been together for a while. When you're alone, go through each item, one by one, as you retire them to the box. Read the cards. Hold each item to your chest. Cry. Mourn him. Keep loading the box. After a good cry, close the box and put it in the back of a closet, under your bed, or anywhere not easily visible. When you need to grieve, take out the box, go through it, put all the items back, close the box, and retire it to its place. Get in the habit of moving away from your grief as the box closes. This has worked for me. It set limits on the times I felt haunted and provided control over memories and grief. And someday, throw it out.

Leave Him Alone

Anger often prevents you from letting go of him completely. Dwelling on him affects your life. Whether you ended it or he did, you'll probably be angry about something. Anger usually creates more problems for you than for the one you're angry with. While he's off doing his own thing, you may be stewing, working yourself up into an unproductive rage. Anger makes you unhappy and frustrated. It serves no good purpose. So vent yours and let it go. Writing him letters that you'll never send is a good way to get it out.

The first direction in which anger may send you after you've first broken up is a desire to tell him how you feel. DON'T! I can't begin to describe how many women said that after a breakup they've called him, left voice messages, and written e-mails or letters—all to tell him how they felt. Been there, done that too. I wrote l-o-n-g letters, pouring out my feelings, saying how much he hurt me. What did that tell him? That I still cared. That I couldn't get over him. What an ego boost! "Look how much energy she put into that letter, all because of me!" Richard told me:

> I can't help laughing when I get a letter from an ex-girlfriend to tell me off. Like I didn't get enough of that when we were together! What do women feel they'll accomplish by once again laying out how I hurt them? I've been a jerk many times but always knew it. I wasn't proud, but I accepted it. These letters. Does she think I'm going to walk around feeling guilty and down? Does she think it will get me back? No way. When we break up, I move on. They actually make it worse—I lose respect for that ex. Doesn't she have better things to do than dwell on me? I've heard many guys say they've received a letter from hell from their ex. We just make fun of them. Tell women, when it's over, it's over.

I've finally accepted that men aren't stupid. They know what they've done, without you telling them. And if they acted like they didn't know it during the relationship, why should they acknowledge your pain now? We all think our case is different, special. Everyone gives me that "But you don't understand" line, which I also gave to friends when I convinced myself I had to let him know how I felt. Trust me: He knows. Jerks know when they've been jerks. While they often don't act like it, they do understand the difference between right and wrong. And if a man doesn't understand, he still won't after you communicate with him. I don't know of one woman who has ever sent one of those letters or made one of those calls who received a satisfactory response. Not one.

My need to communicate was a way of not letting go. Deep down I hoped that if I let him know how he hurt me and how much I loved him, he'd wake up, get the white horse, and come back. But it doesn't happen that way. If you need to tell him how you feel, ask yourself why. Be honest about what your real agenda is. Why is it so important for him to understand? If you're letting go, it shouldn't matter what he thinks. I've gotten an occasional response from my communication, but it's always a hostile one, making me feel worse. If you have a need to get it off your chest to achieve the closure to move on, do it with that agenda only. Make it clear that it's over and leave out emotional stuff. Don't leave yourself on edge, hoping he'll see the light and come back or respond positively. He probably won't.

Don't Try to Get Even

He cheated. He hurt you. He dumped you. He has a new girlfriend and you're angry. Now you want to hurt him the way he hurt you. Maybe you could speak to his new girlfriend or harass him. I know women who erased important things on a man's computer or cut his clothes. That's mean. Remember: "What goes around comes around." It's tempting to hurt the jerk who hurt you, but it honestly won't make you feel better. You may make him mad, but he'll never give you the reaction you want. Why give him the satisfaction of knowing that he's still important enough for you to go out of your way to get even? Every time you do something to him, even something negative, he gets that little ego boost. Jerks love attention.

Trust me: He's not worth the energy. There's nothing positive to be gained from getting even with a jerk, even if he does deserve it. Danielle admitted:

> The first six months after Clark and I broke up was a negative nightmare. I wanted to hurt him, and my friends encouraged me. I'd call him and hang up. I wrote him nasty texts and e-mails. I stalked him to see who he was with. I'd get in his face when he was with another woman. I thought about him all the time. I think I still needed attention from him, even if it was to hate me. Thank God I was able to see that none of it helped me get over him. Working on my self-esteem helped me let go. Getting even hurt me more than it did him.

Until you cut him off from your energy supply, there will always be a painful tie to him. If you don't cut him off, it never ends. There's always one more phone call or way to get even. Anger at a jerk is hard to satisfy. There's always a friend who'll egg you on to do something else. Rather than making you feel better, though, trying to get even with a man who hurt you prevents getting over him and moving on. The best kind of revenge is positive. Write down what you'd like to do to him. Throw it out or put it in a drawer. Then work on getting your life together so that when you bump into him, you can honestly say you're doing great. My favorite way to get even with an ex-jerk is to be able to smile broadly or downright laugh at him. Jerks hate that because it lets them know that they mean so little to you that you can laugh about it. That's the best revenge!

Keep Him Out of Your Life

Put up an invisible wall between you and him, and keep both feet on your side. If you both want to stay friends, make sure you can handle it. If even a teeny piece of you wants him back, leave him in the past. Tell him you'll call when you can handle it. Don't continue doing things for him. He can get his hair trimmed elsewhere or hire a secretary. Don't let him use your things, even if he needs them and you don't. Cut all ties if you have any desire to be back with him! Don't make up excuses to talk to him. If he left a file on your computer, too bad. You owe him nothing! Lisa told a class:

> When Paul and I broke up, I still saw him. He liked my TV, so I let him come over and watch. He'd call to talk about his problems at work. I still ironed his shirts and sent him home with cooked meals. I was always there for him, hoping I'd get him back. I wasn't prepared when he came over to talk about problems with his new girlfriend, who loved my meatloaf, who he wore the ironed shirts with. He never told me he was seeing someone. I had even had sex with him occasionally.

Above all else, don't sleep with him, even if it's tempting. That's too much intimacy, especially if it keeps you hoping to get back together. Intimacy makes it harder to move on. You keep these ties open when you still want him in your life. You keep these ties open because you hope he'll wake up one day and realize how much he needs you. You keep these ties open because it's too painful to completely let go. But if you don't break these ties, you'll never be free. You can't break up and let him keep one foot in your door. You deserve better. Make a clean break. Do affirmations about moving on. Have a wonderful life without him. You can!

Keep Loving Yourself!

Continue loving yourself. Don't take the blame for a relationship not working! Affirm to yourself that even though he dumped you, or you had to give up on him, there's nothing wrong with you. You're still a lovable and desirable woman. Think of it as his loss. If necessary, write down the things he's missing because you're not with him anymore. *His loss.* It's not your fault that he's a jerk. Lovingly pamper yourself. Treat yourself as the loving person you are. *His loss.* Too much food isn't the best direction if it makes you gain weight, but working on a healthy lifestyle is. *His loss.* You have a great life ahead of you. *His loss!*

Continue writing. If nothing else, it'll give you something to do. If you miss him, use your list of what he did that hurt you to stay strong about not going back. Write down what you've learned that will help you in your next relationship and everything you want in your next one. Don't sell yourself short. Then think, really think, about what you'd like to do now that you have your freedom. Since the past is set on paper, look toward the future.

When missing him is hard to endure, clean your home. Wash your floors. Do laundry. Clean out your closets. Keep cleaning out your life. Exorcise him by doing exercise. Getting into shape during this time will boost your self-esteem and help you to feel better. Walk. Ride a bike. Take up karate—it's great for keeping control. Learn to box or something else that may seem goofy to you, just for fun. Try something new. Keep loving yourself enough to stay away from him. It doesn't just get better, it gets great!

Chapter Twenty

If You Keep Him . . .

"If I have freedom in my love,

And in my soul am free,

Angels alone that soar above

Enjoy such liberty."

RICHARD LOVELACE

Really Get to Know Him

We show our best side at the beginning. "All men are jerks until proven otherwise." I say this to ground myself, to remind me to go beyond the initial rush of being with him before he can "prove otherwise." That "honeymoon stage" at the beginning of the relationship can cloud reality. When Jenny McCarthy was on *Chelsea Lately* once, Chelsea Handler asked what happened to the guy she recently announced that she loved and would marry. Jenny sheepishly said she thinks she's addicted to dopamine in the beginning of a relationship. She admitted, "I get so high off of the beginning of a relationship. I love it!" Chelsea asked what happens? Jenny answered, "It becomes reality."

Many of you do that. That delicious romance, hot sex and every-thing being perfect can suck you in. Then reality hits and the fairy tale is over. If you get to know each other at a slow pace and still like each other in real life, you may really have grounds for a healthy relation-ship. That's why you should always keep some distance from a man by not allowing your life to revolve around him. He should never be 100 percent sure of you, unless you like being taken for granted. Show by your actions that you have a life with or without him. Remember, he's a treat, not your whole life. Keep your distance, and maintain outside interests and low expectations. Don't lie about being busy. Be busy! "All men are jerks until proven otherwise." As you get to know him, lower your guard slowly but never all the way. When you have a life, you con-trol your choices.

Control Your Sexuality

If you see long-term potential, I highly recommend waiting as long as possible to sleep with him. This isn't about playing games or worrying about what he thinks of you. Things change when you sleep together. Sex creates intimacy that neither of you may be ready for. It speeds the pace of a relationship, making it harder to get to know each other on all levels. Once you cross that line, you can't go back. Bridget told my class:

> Jess and I were good together. The chemistry got to us on the third date—we made love. It was great till then. The next day he said he wished we'd waited. It made me feel crappy. We dated for several months, but I felt sex came between us. Jess sometimes said he wished we'd waited. It didn't give us a chance to become friends. It got heavy too fast.
>
> I never understood clearly till I met Gary. I liked him right away but waited months. He tried many times but respected my

wishes. He was my best friend when we finally slept together, and it was intense. We've been together for three years, and I hope it never ends.

Vernon heard that and explained to the women in the class:

> Women don't understand. When we're attracted to you, it's instinctive to try to get you in the sack. Right then, it's all we want. We come on strong saying whatever to get it. BUT, we don't want sex with someone we like too soon, even if we say we do. Does it make sense? Our brain wants to wait, but "the stick" has its own mind. You need to keep us in check. Make it easy— no challenge. We get scared you'll make demands. No, when I like you I don't want to cross the line too soon. I enjoy getting to know each other in the beginning. After sex, that's over. I love sexual tension, teasing, fantasizing the first time. It's better to wait until you know what's between you. But "the stick" will keep trying.

Isn't it nicer to be certain he's not a jerk before sharing intimacy? Sex can enhance a good bond but can't be the bond. As old-fashioned as it sounds, the fun of courtship is often forgotten. It's a wonderful time to get to know each other in sweet ways: a time of tenderness and teasing; of learning about each other; of pure, unadulterated romance; of taking your time; of cold showers. Sex after courtship can be very deep. Waiting can make sex sweeter. It creates more desire. The thought of sleeping with you becomes more appealing as you postpone the pleasure. Janice related her experience:

> I waited a long, I mean long time, before sleeping with the last three guys I was involved with. I know I drove them crazy by letting them stay over without going all the way. Yes, we fooled around. But I always stopped before going too far. It was hard

for me to resist but worth it. All three proposed marriage to me. I'm happily married to the third one, who waited the longest. When you give it away too easily, it doesn't have as much value.

Control means not letting your genitals rule you. It's your choice to get laid if you're horny (be careful about safe sex!), and know you can handle not seeing the guy again. Losing control isn't a choice. Controlling your sexuality is a powerful feeling! Take care of your own needs until you truly feel he's proven otherwise, with actions over time.

Getting a Commitment

Are you ready for a serious commitment? Make sure you know him well on all levels. If marriage is your goal, ask yourself why. Is it because you want him for a husband or that you need to be married? The latter is not a healthy reason. Try soul-searching before approaching him and be prepared to lose him in the process.

When he's in a good mood, explain what marrying him means to you. Listen carefully to his response. Don't get an attitude if it isn't what you want. Respect his feelings. If he's not sure what he wants, ask how long he needs. If marriage is very important to you, agree to wait for a specific period of time with no pressure—six months to a year. Set a date for a decision, making sure he understands the time limit. Circle the date on your calendar in red. Then DO NOT BRING IT UP again!

Pressuring him won't help. Allowing him space to make a decision works best, no matter how much you want to convince him or know what he's thinking. Convince him by working on making the relationship good and enjoying it without the pressure of marriage. Let him see what he'd be missing if it ended. Have lots of fun, intimacy, and great sex without mentioning marriage. Become more independent so he sees you have a life on your own. Leaving him alone during that time allows him the greatest opportunity to make a rational decision.

Without pressure he can think most objectively. It will also make a good impression on him.

If he's not ready for a decision at the deadline, end on pleasant terms. Don't tell him off or throw emotional garbage at him. End it in bed if you may regret not having made love once more. Leave him with the sweetness of you. Be friendly, loving, and say goodbye. Tell him you're sorry it turned out this way, without tears if possible. Don't leave one foot in the door or agree to see him occasionally to give him little fixes of you. If he loves you, he may return when he misses you enough. If he doesn't love you, remind yourself that it's better you found out now. Some men can't commit. If that's what you want, move on.

Work at Fixing Your Problems

A relationship takes work on both sides. You can't keep score, but shouldn't do most of the work. A relationship starts with acceptance of each other. Learn to differentiate between who he is and how he treats you. Choose not to accept any unacceptable behavior, even if you continue to accept him on the whole. For example, you can't work on his cool nature, but rude or irresponsible behavior shouldn't be tolerated.

Conflicts are healthy in relationships, as long as they're not abusive. When a woman says she and her partner never argue, I wonder what issues they're avoiding. Couples tiptoe for years and decades around many things for fear of hurting/losing/angering their partner. If issues aren't dealt with as they come up, resentment can destroy a relationship.

Like the people in them, relationships aren't perfect. It's important to acknowledge that something isn't working properly so that you can try to fix it. This may require several frank discussions. Couples' counseling is an option. A trained, impartial professional can put problems into a more workable perspective. I know, it's hard to get self-sufficient men into counseling. If problems get intolerable and his only choices are counseling or a breakup, he may begrudgingly agree.

Don't try to fix it all yourself. That's usually done at your expense. Get over the fear of losing him if you speak up or don't go along with him. Make it clear in a loving way that he has to want the relationship to work as much as you do, or it might not work. Don't make threats. In a good relationship, two partners work as a team, not as competitors. Always remember you're both on the same side. Your approach to problems will get his cooperation—or put him off.

Many of you get angry when you feel that you're working harder to please him than he's working to please you. Get over it! It's YOUR CHOICE to do things for him. There are no laws about your having to be the one who cooks and cleans or gives support and nurturing, etc. Learn to give only what you want to give, with no expectations. There's nothing wrong with trying to do things to make your partner happy. But if you get angry because it's not reciprocated, you may be giving for the wrong reasons. If you get angry about giving so much, don't give so much. He doesn't have to do things for you just because you do things for him! Instead of getting on his case, get on your own. Practice communicating with actions, or lack of them. Just slowly slack off . . . no huff or telling him off. Then you don't have to get angry that you're doing so much for him. He might get the message, and if he questions it, just give a nice neutral reply such as "I've been busy. I'm sure you understand, since you've been too busy to do things too." Smile! You'll have more time for yourself.

Couples have told me that women are more sensitive to problems. "Why do you look for trouble when there's none?" I've heard that line more than once from a man when something was wrong and he didn't want to deal with it. Men can be simpler. A man can be content keeping life on an even keel with a woman when he's home, eating and having sex regularly. Simple. Women are more alert to problems and know the importance of working on them while they're small. Complex. When there's simple versus complex, it takes gentle maneuvers to keep the team on the same side.

Work at Communication

Communicate gently, letting him know what things are hard for you to deal with. Instead of saying "You have to do this," ask him to work with you to find solutions for situations that cause potential problems. Don't make it personal or take it personally. Focus on specific causes of irritation, such as tone of voice, burping at dinner, lack of attention, and so on, rather than on the person. I may hate when he leaves dirty dishes around, but don't hate him. Keep the act separate from the person so that neither of you feels personally attacked. Ask him for suggestions on how you can deal with behavior you don't like, and return the favor. Sometimes it's easier to come up with a rational plan when the annoyance isn't present.

Cissy and Doug came to me for techniques to deal with their blow-ups. Cissy said, "We love each other but do things that annoy the heck out of each other. We'd keep it in most of the time, but if one of us lost it, it all came out . . . like an explosion between us." Doug was uncomfortable about counseling but came with Cissy out of guilt about the "obnoxious streak" he developed as a defense against women from his past who he perceived as hurting him. He couldn't stop it with Cissy, though he knew it drove her crazy. I recommended that they take a week to write down what they had a problem with and how it made them feel. Then they should put aside an evening to exchange lists and discuss solutions. Four weeks later Cissy reported:

We liked getting everything on paper. It sorted bigger problems from small annoyances. After working together, some don't matter anymore. We worked on serious ones and finally grasped how each other felt. Before, our response was to attack. When attacked, we defend instead of trying to understand. I never thought how Doug felt when I talked to him like a child. Now I try harder not to. He feels the same. As you suggested, we made a mutual decision that when Doug gets obnoxious, I can say, "You're getting obnoxious. I'm leaving the room." And I do. He does the same. We've hung up when we do it on the phone. We've become very aware, and this week there was less need for either of us to leave the room. We talk more.

Some couples choose a regular time to sit down in a relaxed setting and take turns sharing their perspective on the relationship, both positive and troubling. Each listens to the other. Then they discuss how to keep the good stuff strong and work on rough spots, together. By focusing on the annoying act rather than on the person, you limit anger by making it less personal. A bad habit or action doesn't necessarily make someone a bad person. By taking your anger off the person, neither partner feels attacked. You can say, "I love you but dislike the times you insist on telling me what to do."

The tone in your partner's voice can set you off. For example, he's annoyed and automatically gets sarcastic, which you hate and he knows it. In your defense you whine, which he hates and you know it. Tone can blow a problem out of proportion. What can stop it in its tracks? When I counsel couples and each points a finger at the other as the one who started an argument or issue, I recommend a technique I call "Meatballs." "Your sarcasm gets me angry!" "Your whining sets me off!" What can one of you say when you see it coming but can't say "Shut up before there's a problem"? Say "Meatballs" or a similar innocuous expression that tells him or you that trouble's brewing and you need to stop and talk rationally.

"Meatballs." It doesn't reprimand and can take the edge off an argument. Many laugh when it's said. You often say things out of habit, not meaning to irritate your partner. The annoyance, sarcasm, whining, bossiness, arrogance, and other responses to frustration or anger come into your voice automatically. Often you're not even aware of how annoying you sound. Saying "Meatballs" lets him/you know without being critical that the tone is coming into his/your voice. Then you can deal with the real issue.

Practice Forgiveness

Forgiveness is essential in a relationship. When you don't forgive, you hold on to anger that leads to ingrained resentment down the road. Forgiving doesn't mean continually excusing unacceptable behavior. But if he acknowledges he's wrong and tries to rectify it, you should forgive an occasional mistake or comment and move on. You may be partly responsible for his action, such as when he lies to avoid your overreacting to the truth. By accepting responsibility for how men treat you, you can forgive without anger or bitterness. It's your choice to change your response. Of course, you must also be vigilant that the unacceptable behavior isn't a pattern.

Practicing forgiveness means resolving a problem and moving on. It acknowledges faith in the relationship. Forgiving allows you to let go of anger, resentment, and bitterness. Living in the past isn't healthy. If he does something unacceptable, you should talk it out, see if his response is acceptable, and forgive him. Forgiveness eventually becomes synonymous with trust. When he hasn't "proven otherwise," forgive and keep your eyes open for a pattern. Once you trust him to keep his word about trying harder, you can forgive him more easily. If you can't trust him, you shouldn't be with him.

Keep the "I" in Your Relationship

If you want a healthy man, get a life. If you want a healthy relationship, keep your life. A key to a successful relationship is autonomy. As I've said, women have a habit of losing themselves in a man and men keep some of their life, often to our chagrin. Learn from men. Even in marriage, you're healthier and happier with a life beyond your husband.

"We," "we," "we." Break the habit of speaking as a "we" all the time. "We" want this. "We" think that. Often "we" means going along with him. A couple is two separate people, not one unit. Why share everything?

It's best to nurture your own friends and interests. When I was in a relationship with Jim, we spent weekends together. I had a group of friends I saw Sunday evenings. They invited Jim, but I left him home and enjoyed my friends. Part of me missed snuggling with Jim, but I left him for a few hours each Sunday. It was fun when I came home. When we broke up, these friends were my biggest supporters. They respected me for not changing the nature of our group by bringing him. I was grateful to have kept part of my life separate from him.

Think in terms of "I" a good part of the time. Relationships shouldn't be claustrophobic. Making a man your whole life constrains him. Men get tired of clingy women quickly. One term that men use for women they avoid is "Barnacle Babe." That's a woman who grabs on and attaches herself to a guy. I don't recommend going to the other extreme either, though. Total independence prevents a team effort. As the relationship grows and he begins to "prove otherwise," you can count on him more for some of your needs. Men like feeling needed, and it's good to let him know he has importance in your life. Most of you like feeling needed. Find a balance between making him your life and allowing him responsibility for some of your needs, as long as you don't give up your self-control.

Learn from men about the importance of space in a relationship. After spending time with friends or on your own, you appreciate the time together with your partner more. When you have a life, he's less likely to take you for granted. Having your own friends is healthy. Taking time for you breathes life into a relationship. Some couples say that occasional separate vacations make them closer or they tend to melt into one entity. The "we" thing can breed monotony. Doing things apart brings fresh energy into the relationship. You're more interesting when you have a life. As Karen told a group:

> I finally see how good solo time is for couples. I thought love was being together all the time and got depressed if a boyfriend had plans without me. Before meeting Hal, I got involved in

organizations that I loved. With Hal in the picture, I assumed I'd give it up. He encouraged my meetings and dinners with friends, wanting me to have my life. I accepted his interests. We don't see each other all the time, but our time together is spectacular. We find time to see each other when it's convenient for both of us. I love my life, and Hal!

"My life." His opinions and taste don't have to be yours. I'm not crazy about spicy food but used to feel funny saying so if a date suggested a Mexican dinner. The freedom I've given myself to express likes and dislikes, without being apologetic, is cathartic. I no longer say, "Whatever you like." I'm comfortable being true to my desires. A good relationship supports compromise. Recently a date commented on how refreshing it was to be with someone who didn't just go along with him. He was glad I told him what I'd like to do. Men don't always like taking responsibility. A woman with a mind of her own can be very attractive to men, especially the ones who aren't jerks.

Allow a man privacy, and make sure to get yours. If you live together, create a time or place for some space. Monday evenings you can take two hours alone in bed with a book; Saturday morning, a long private bath. He can choose his times and places also. Respect each other's right not to be disturbed. Privacy also applies to one's thoughts. You don't always have to know what he's thinking. Asking is a sign of insecurity and gets annoying. He doesn't have to tell you everything, and vice versa. Being a totally open book can lead to your partner taking you for granted, even if he isn't a jerk. When you make your relationship as easy and secure as possible, it's human nature for him to assume you'll always be there for him, no matter what. Then he might feel that he doesn't have to put work into the relationship.

You can't continuously tell him what to do and how to do it. Okay, often you do know better, but that's not the point! Trust him to do it his way. Take deep breaths and shut your mouth if he's lost but determined to find his own way. He'll love you for it! Bite your tongue and don't mention the gadget in the drawer to open a jar. Men hate being told how to do things better. Respect that. It's a very little concession if he's a good guy in most ways. Learn to laugh at it, but without him seeing! Cody revealed to a group:

> Women always pick my brain. If I look pensive she asks what I'm thinking. I say it's gas, she goes nuts. Why can't they leave us alone? I'm self-conscious if she has to know everything. And what they don't know they tell. I tried to fix a lock, and Judy kept asking if she should Google how to do it for me. She even coached me cutting my toenails. I'd never live with these ladies because I'd have no space—not to think in, not to work in, not to pick my toes in. Whoever said "A penny for your thoughts" really underestimated the value!

It's best to take care of each other. It doesn't have to be equal, but shouldn't be one-sided, with you doing it all. Resist cooking and cleaning for him all the time. Encourage taking turns. My boyfriends have loved cooking for me, because I praise and thank them, making them feel useful. They eat it up! Tell him he does it better than you and you may never have to cook another dinner, wash another dish, or clean another toilet! Enjoy being taken care of. I love being pampered by a man. Why not? You don't have to be independent all the time. It's great to feel you deserve having someone do chores for you. Of course, you need to keep him happy too.

Keep Your Relationship Fresh

After being with someone for years, you can fall into deeply rutted routines if you're not careful. Relationships don't have to get boring. You can stay out of ruts and allow romance and sweetness to grow, not dwindle. Your direction may veer from the "honeymoon phase," but your relationship can be better in a more comfortable, loving way. When partners want to keep the sparks lively, it's not hard.

Time can make partners take each other for granted. You eventually anticipate each other's every move. Making sure not to forget good manners helps prevent taking each other for granted. Saying "please" and "thank you" shows respect for each other. Express all the appreciation you feel, and let him know you love it when he expresses his. Men love flattery and don't get as much as we do. They rarely compliment each other, except on their achievements. When you show appreciation for personal attributes, men enjoy it. Don't lie, but let him know what you find attractive about him. Show gratitude and admiration if he's done something well. Compliment him with hearty enthusiasm. Tell him he's sexy or makes you feel safe. Men love coming home to a woman who takes more time appreciating him than giving criticism.

Make special dates. Dress as you would for a first date that you want to impress. He can leave the house and come back to formally pick you up. Take turns planning a surprise evening monthly. It doesn't have to be elaborate, but the person planning it should consider what his or her partner enjoys. Be adventurous—try something neither of you has done. Setting aside quality time together is most important. Sharon related her story:

> Billy and I are married for ten years. We both have frantic careers, but Wednesday night we have a ritual. We're home by 7, order pizza and a movie, light candles, and drink wine. Our friends know and wouldn't dare expect to see us Wednesdays. We're together weekends too, but there's always something to do. Wednesday's our night, and we look forward to it. It helps us keep the romance . . . a night just for us . . . usually a night of great sex too.

Good relationships require nurturing. Go to places that sparked passion in the past. Try a restaurant where you first declared your love, a park where you first kissed, or a country inn where you had a special weekend. Surprise him periodically with new lingerie. Recreate passionate memories of your relationship. Go for a romantic brunch regularly. Have breakfast in bed on the weekend. My last boyfriend went for fresh bagels and a paper every Sunday. I'd have coffee ready, and we'd get back into bed with the paper. We looked forward to that time. Don't expect romance all the time, but make time for it. Joni told me:

> Reggie and I fell into bad habits. We had dinner with friends on certain nights . . . did our own thing on others. We forgot about just us. Even sex fell into a pattern. One weekend I made reservations at a hotel without telling him. He was skeptical when I told him I was taking him somewhere. When we got to the hotel, he wasn't into it. But when I stripped for him and he saw my garters and stockings, he came around fast. I didn't wear panties to dinner. It drove him crazy. He couldn't wait to get back to our room. I'd planned to put a spark into our relationship, but I ignited fireworks! Now we do something like this every month.

Do things together. Take dance lessons or a home repair class. Volunteer for a charity. Shower together regularly. Wash each other's hair. Make up signals that say "I love you" or "I'd love to rip your clothes off" for when you're in public. Use expressions or looks to create excitement when you're out together. Don't let kissing goodbye or saying "I love you" become a habit. Responding "Me too" can eventually mean nothing. Leave love notes or sometimes erotic suggestions in unexpected places. Do this all in moderation so it doesn't become stale. And make sure he's making an effort too. It's fun!

Spice Up Your Sex Life

Some partners find themselves in a rut in bed. To keep your sexual relationship fresh and exciting, consciously work on it. Sex is an intimate, emotional connection that can strengthen and improve in a monogamous relationship. Sex between two people in love can be the best and get better with time, even if the "honeymoon phase" ends. The key is not to take sex for granted.

Make time for sex. Don't postpone or rush it. Create ambiance with candles, music, and sexy lingerie. Try different rooms and positions. Laugh together if something doesn't work. Read books on sexuality. Be confident, and communicate with actions. If he doesn't understand what you want, be gentle but talk. Don't just go along with him if you want more. Ask what he likes. Have him show you how he likes to be touched. If he loses interest, ask why. He may be tired and scared of not getting an erection. Never pressure him to perform. Offer reassurance that it's okay to just enjoy caressing if he's too tired. Sometimes when the fear's been acknowledged and the pressure goes down, he goes up!

Confidence inspires great heights in bed. Walk around naked with pride. Men don't notice what you're self-conscious of. The attitude behind naked pride is incredibly attractive. Be seductive. It can be subtle, such as lightly rubbing his neck or nibbling his finger. Be spontaneous. Turn him on in the kitchen. Read sexy books together. Keep things exciting. Making love can reflect love. You can learn every inch of each other's bodies, and how to arouse each part. Ursula said:

> I was very shy at first with Corey. I loved him a lot and opened up. Corey loves sex. I was uncomfortable initiating . . . he encouraged me. When we moved in together, I thought if I wanted to spend my life with him, I should make our sex life more interesting. I read books and got more forward in bed. My

lingerie got sexier. I'm most turned on these days when I initiate sex. Corey says he never knows what I'll do and loves it. He's surprising me more too. Our friendship is very consistent. Our sex life is filled with excitement.

The greatest gift you can give a man during sex is enthusiasm. Men complain about women who act like they're doing them a favor. Try to get comfortable with oral sex. A man's penis is an extension of himself, and he loves having it loved. You don't have to love doing it, but you can act like you do. Let him know how much you love making love to him. If you want to give him the ultimate gift, tell him you love his penis!

A relationship shouldn't lead to boredom. If I love a man, I enjoy thinking of creative ways to interact with him. To me, it's a testimony of my wanting to stay with him. Never take a man for granted or allow him to take you for granted. Appreciate him every day. Keep your life. If you have a life, being in a relationship is a win/win situation: you enjoy your time being with him; you enjoy your time on your own.

Chapter Twenty-One

The Pleasure of Your Own Company

"Today is the first day of the rest of your life."

ANONYMOUS

It's Great to Be on Your Own

Has this book gotten through to you, or are you still dreading the thought of facing life without a man, at least for the time it may take to meet one who's not a jerk? Instead of jumping into the arms of anyone available, why not find out how satisfying it can be to be on your own until a worthy guy comes along? Why tie yourself to a jerk when you can be enjoying life solo?

I'm not advocating celibacy or not being in a relationship. I am encouraging you to find pleasure in being on your own until meeting a man who's worthy of you. Why spend all your free time hunting down men? Why give men the power to control your happiness? Being on your own is a great experience. You have the power to make yourself happy every day. When you accept that, the power to have a wonderful life is yours. People ask me why I smile all the time, and I know it's because I've learned to love my own company.

If you still think being in a relationship is the end-all/cure-all, pay attention to your married friends and those in relationships. Do they often complain? Do they really seem happy? Sadly, I know more unhappy women in relationships than women who are sincerely content. "Resigned" is a word that applies to many of these women. They take aggravation as a trade-off for not being alone. Bah humbug! What's the point of being with a jerk if you regularly feel dissatisfied? Think about what you can do on your own if you're not tied down to one. Think about your last few relationships: what hurt you, angered you, infringed on your time, hampered your career, left you frustrated or with other less than positive feelings you may have experienced. Let unhappy memories temper the importance of having a man all the time.

There are terrific things about not being in a relationship that you never take the time to notice if you're intent on being with a man. Sometimes the little things make a difference. When I'm not in a relationship, I don't have to shave my legs in the winter as often. That's a relief! I can wear old underwear, the stuff that goes in the washing machine instead of being handwashed. I never have to worry about the toilet seat being up during the night. Most HIMs just don't understand that one. Those of you smiling know what I mean!

Here's a sampling of what women told me they've found positive about being on their own. Learn to appreciate these things, because they can be fun and satisfying.

LENA: You learn to be independent.

PAULA: To me, the best thing about not having a man around is freedom from professional sports. Your TV room isn't occupied every weekend by beer-swilling, junk-food-munching yahoos watching overpaid Neanderthals inflict injuries on one another. You can listen to music in the car instead of a background chorus of "Pop fly to left field." And if your local newspaper prints the comics on the back of the sports section, you don't have to fight anyone to read the comics.

ALISSA: I get to read more books, which I've always loved but never had time for with him around so much.

CONNIE: Changing my mind whenever I want!

RITA: I love feeling my apartment is mine again. My boyfriend had practically moved in with me and had his stuff around. He made me rearrange things. We brought the TV from the living room into the bedroom. He moved my big easy chair from the window to a corner, to make room for his bike. Now everything is back in its place, and I'm appreciating it. It's nicer to come home now than when he was here.

HELENE: Doing everything your way all the time. Not bothering to shave the "usually hidden" areas.

GIZELLE: I don't have to worry about the other person having a good time when we go out. I can see movies I want to see. I can do what I want to do without discussing it with someone else.

DOT: Sweatpants!

LINDA: When you're not in a relationship, you can't be cheated on. I am no longer the stressed-out rope in the tug-of-war between my 10-year-old child and my mother-in-law's 38-year-old one. No more toenails, cigarette butts, or boogers on the couch. No more grudge matches over the toilet paper—or light bulb—changing duty.

HARRIET: Being able to do things for myself, and not being judged continually or criticized.

WENDY: I love eating when I want, without a schedule. I don't have to wait for him to come home and be ready to eat.

OLGA: The only thing I need from a man . . . that I can't do for myself these days is sexual intercourse, and I've worked on ways to take care of that too. I have so much more energy since leaving my last relationship. I can give my career more attention, and it's growing. I have more time for a myriad of people. I do more for me. Why didn't I find this life sooner?

JULIA: I love taking off and going somewhere without having to tell him or call him regularly. My time is definitely my own.

PATTI: It's nice not worrying what I look like in the morning. When I'm involved with someone who stays over, I usually go to sleep with makeup and try to wake up before him to fix myself up. I hated that, but men make me feel they want me to look beautiful. Now I can wear my comfy flannel pjs to sleep and pull my hair up and be comfortable. Call it freedom of sleep!

ALLYSON: No pressure to compromise, which used to mean we did it his way.

JUDY: I've been in relationships for a majority of my life. Looking back, I've always appreciated the times without a man in my life, when I didn't have to compromise all the time. That's what being on my own means to me . . . an opportunity to make decisions based purely on what I want and what's good for me. When I'm in a good relationship, I can live with compromising. But I do enjoy the time when I don't have to . . . the time I can think in terms of me instead of us.

A Few Final Words

Ah, the joys of being on your own! I've explained throughout this book how important it is to develop your autonomy, but it's hard to find enough words to express how glorious, how joyous, how POWERFUL it feels, now that I've discovered the wonders of owning my life! That's what this is all about—not giving your life away to someone else, not giving someone else the power to make or break your happiness, not losing your ability to appreciate the glory of yourself, not feeling like you have nothing when there's no man around. I've taken responsibility for creating my own happiness. No man will do that for me anymore! Being involved with a good man, which I'd love, will enhance my already wonderful life, will give my sex life more variety, and might make my life sweeter. But he'll never be my life. I already have that honor.

I used to go from one jerk to another because I had to have a boyfriend. I believed, like so many of you, that if I didn't have a man, my life was empty. In between men, I'd look back and reminisce about the last one, while trying to get a replacement. Yet most of them drove me crazy. The energy I wasted complaining about men to friends just astounds me in retrospect. While I had pieces of happiness with each of them, my life rarely felt happy in general. I'd often be worried about HIS feelings and HIS desires. The time and energy I put into making him happy was certainly much more than I ever gave to myself.

I consider myself very blessed. Having embraced my own sense of spirituality and definition of God, I've learned to turn inward for making decisions, to have total faith that what I need will be mine, that I can completely control my life and happiness, and that I have the power to create everything I need. What a change from the wimpy doormat I used to be!

I truly enjoy being on my own. Although I still *want* a partner (very much!), it's such a relief not to *need* one anymore. I've worked very hard on building my self-esteem and learning that I'm worthy of the best. While I now attract more men than ever, I'm very selective about whom I'll share my precious time with. If I think he's a jerk or will be too much work, I choose not to be with him. I can have more fun doing what I love, without someone putting a damper on things. It'll take a special man to make me compromise on how I live. I know he's out there, and when the time is right, I'll consider myself blessed to meet him. But I'd rather not waste my time with jerks. I don't have nearly as much energy to give men anymore. Today I crave time by myself.

So, you see, there are wonderful advantages to being on your own. As you make your way through life, never forget that you always have choices. My goal in writing this book wasn't to tell you how to find or keep a man. There are plenty of other books if you want to go in that direction. I've instead chosen to provide tools for finding and keeping YOURSELF by becoming as an autonomous woman. There are no rules that have to be followed, other than trying to make choices that create a satisfying life for you. The key is never to forget that you always have choices. It's your choice to settle for a jerk. It's your choice to make excuses for a man you think you need in your life. It's your choice to make your happiness hinge on having a man. It's your choice to create your own.

So, girlfriends, for the last time I'll highly recommend putting most of your energy where it counts—into yourself. Forget about the upbringing that told you that only a man can make you complete. You'll never feel complete unless you're complete by yourself. Stop worrying that you may not have the perfect looks or body. Appreciate all the beauty that is you. Don't settle for a man who you know isn't good for you. Trust that when it's meant to be, you'll meet a great man. Take control of your own life instead of giving it to HIM. Only you should own that power. Work on your self-esteem. That's the key to finding happiness. Give yourself lots of love because you deserve it! And never, never, never forget—not in the heat of passion, not under a barrage of wonderful words, not after meeting what seems like the man of your dreams—that ALL MEN ARE JERKS UNTIL PROVEN OTHERWISE! Love and respect yourself enough to make him prove otherwise over a long time with his actions, not his words.

When I meet a man who I want to spend time or even my life with, I'll be ready. Now my life is defined. He'll be able to enhance it, sweeten it, and be a special part of it, but he won't *be* it. Today is the first day of the rest of my life, and I choose to spend it being happy. What a wonderful blessing it is to own your life! I wish all of you this blessing.

Afterword

I hope that reading this book made you think about what you let men get away with, what you expect from them, and what you settle for. You probably won't change your habits immediately, but women say the reality I lay out makes it much harder to tolerate unpleasant behavior from a guy. Similar to salt on a wound, your new enlightenment will accentuate the hurt more and make it harder to put up with behavior that makes you feel bad. Becoming empowered with men takes time and patience. But it's worth it to feel in control of your responses to them!

It's harder to stay with a jerk once your eyes are open and your good sense is activated. But cut yourself slack if you don't feel strong enough to leave your current one. The need for the sweetness you get from a guy is powerful. It can be hard to walk away from one who satisfies strong needs. If you decide you deserve more than sweet crumbs from a jerk but don't have the courage and fortitude to dump him yet, work on focusing your energy on YOU. Make more plans with friends. Try getting comfortable with doing things you like solo, and most importantly—do everything in your power to build your self-love. Take baby steps until you feel comfortable enough to dump him if you still want to.

Cheryl e-mailed right after she finished reading this book, frustrated about living with a jerk, knowing she should leave but couldn't. She said, "I know I'm horrible for staying but I'm too weak to leave." I reassured her it was okay. This book doesn't magically make you strong enough to dump him on the spot or avoid jerks completely, but it does give tools to get to that place. I advised Cheryl to work on her life outside of the relationship. Have fun and nourish friendships. Be kinder and more loving to herself. She admitted to having low self-esteem but promised to use my mantra, "commit to yourself!" Four months later, she wrote:

> I have a new hairdo, a mani/pedi, five pounds less, more solid connections with friends, and I feel better about building a relationship with me. And surprise—I'm moving out on my own! It's scary, but nourishing myself for four months without worrying about Tony made me stronger and excited about taking more control of my life. As you said, it's MY life. I let Tony rule it, but no more! I'm getting the first tastes of how good it feels to live for me and enjoy making me important. Tony noticed the difference and actually tried harder to be nice but it's too late. I'm starting to believe I deserve a man who treats me well all the time. I actually smile now when I say, "I love me." Not quite there yet but I like working on it.

Many women ask what gives me strength to choose being solo over being with a jerk. I realized that self-love is a critical component of the power to keep jerks out of your life. The more you love and appreciate yourself, the less nonsense and bad behavior you'll tolerate since you're in a better place to more easily recognize you deserve better and the more you'll seek people who are consistently kind. The more self-love, the more likely you are to attract a good man. I value myself, and my time, enough to only be with a man who reflects that.

After hearing from many women who struggle to build self-love, I launched The Self-Love Movement at HowDoILoveMe.com. My agent was about to sell my book, *How Do I Love Me? Let Me Count the Ways*, when a spiritual message said to give the book away for free so more people can benefit. It's on HowDoILoveMe.com as an e-book, for free. And, there's a pledge you can sign: "I commit to do my best to do something loving for myself, however big or small, for the next thirty-one days." Doing things that make you feel good put you into a more loving mood. Every little kindness you do for yourself is a brick in the foundation of self-love. When you start to love yourself, you're better able to create a life that allows you to be happy with or without a man.

Enjoying your own company is your biggest weapon against jerks. It helps you keep the serve in what I referred to earlier as romantic Ping-Pong. Often when you get fed up, you back off and spend more time solo. Then he lures you forward with romance, some good behavior and sweet promises until he thinks you're hooked. When he returns to jerky behavior because he has the serve, you back up again. Then you go forward when he starts his sweet routines. Instead, keep the serve by NEVER going all the way back to where you were. Even if you're in a committed relationship, maintain the life that's separate from him, which I discussed in Chapter Eighteen.

Let him always feel a little insecure about whether you'll leave or won't be available when he wants you. Keep plans with friends, even if he asks to see you. Have a life outside of your relationship. Let him compete with your life instead of being it. That can be the biggest factor for whether he's a jerk or treasure. And if you don't have a special guy, keep working on making yourself healthy and happy, with faith that when you're ready, the right guy will come along.

I'm often asked if getting a life makes women intimidating to men. This is a tricky question. Independence is attractive to men, but many can't handle it. Men need to feel needed and when you have a life, they think you won't need them. They can be insecure and gravitate to the needy women they complain about. I refuse to play helpless chickie to get a guy. I used to be one, but I love how far I've come. I'm faithful that there's at least one guy who isn't scared of a powerful woman. I don't need one to take care of me but mutual support would be great!

Own your power instead of letting your need for a man suck it out of you. You DESERVE to be in control of YOURSELF. Love yourself enough to believe that! When you love yourself first, your jerk alert system will be strong and your responses to men will give you the best shot at having a great relationship. Enjoy that power!

Index

About the Author

DAYLLE DEANNA SCHWARTZ is a speaker, self-empowerment counselor, and bestselling author of fourteen books, including *Nice Girls Can Finish First*. She's also the founder of The Self-Love Movement, through which she's giving her book, *How Do I Love Me? Let Me Count the Ways*, away for free. Daylle has been on 500+ TV/radio shows, including *Oprah*, *Good Morning America*, and *Howard Stern* and quoted in dozens of publications, including the *New York Times*, *Cosmopolitan*, *Redbook*, *Men's Health*, *NY Daily News*, the *New York Post*, and *Marie Claire*. Daylle writes a column on *Huffington Post* about self-empowerment and Lessons from a Recovering DoorMat on Beliefnet. She specializes in helping people learn how empower themselves so they can increase their self-love, take charge of their own lives, and tame their people-pleasing natures.

Contact Daylle Deanna Schwartz at *daylle@daylle.com*, *www.daylle.com*, or *www.howdoiloveme.com*.